FREE LUNCH

FREE LUNCH

HOW THE WEALTHIEST AMERICANS ENRICH
THEMSELVES AT GOVERNMENT EXPENSE
(AND STICK YOU WITH THE BILL)

David Cay Johnston

PORTFOLIO

PORTFOLIO

Published by the Penguin Group

Penguin Group (USA) Inc., 375 Hudson Street, New York, New York 10014, U.S.A. • Penguin Group (Canada), 90 Eglinton Avenue East, Suite 700, Toronto, Ontario, Canada M4P 2Y3 (a division of Pearson Penguin Canada Inc.) • Penguin Books Ltd, 80 Strand, London WC2R 0RL, England • Penguin Ireland, 25 St. Stephen's Green, Dublin 2, Ireland (a division of Penguin Books Ltd) • Penguin Books Australia Ltd, 250 Camberwell Road, Camberwell, Victoria 3124, Australia (a division of Pearson Australia Group Pty Ltd) • Penguin Books India Pvt Ltd, 11 Community Centre, Panchsheel Park, New Delhi - 110 017, India • Penguin Group (NZ), 67 Apollo Drive, Rosedale, North Shore 0632, New Zealand (a division of Pearson New Zealand Ltd) • Penguin Books (South Africa) (Pty) Ltd, 24 Sturdee Avenue, Rosebank, Johannesburg 2196, South Africa

Penguin Books Ltd, Registered Offices:
80 Strand, London WC2R 0RL, England

First published in 2007 by Portfolio,
a member of Penguin Group (USA) Inc.

1 3 5 7 9 10 8 6 4 2

Copyright © David Cay Johnston, 2007
All rights reserved

LIBRARY OF CONGRESS CATALOGING IN PUBLICATION DATA
Johnston, David C.
Free lunch : how the wealthiest Americans enrich themselves at
government expense (and stick you with the bill) / David Cay Johnston.
p.   cm.
Includes bibliographical references and index.
ISBN-13: 978-1-59184-191-3
1. Subsidies—United States.   I. Title.
HC110.S9J64 2008
338.973'02—dc22   2007039164

Printed in the United States of America
Set in Bembo with Officina Sans
Designed by Daniel Lagin

For Lesli An, Kendall, Marke, Amy, Andrew, Steven, Molly, and Kate,
who have each enriched my life beyond measure

Contents

FREE LUNCH

PREFACE

A KNOT OF TRAVELERS WAITED IMPATIENTLY ON THE CURB AT RONALD Reagan Washington National Airport, the air heavy and still, trapped beneath an overturned bowl of clouds. Weary and anxious to get to their hotels, they fidgeted, but said nothing as the minutes dragged.

When the shuttle bus finally arrived, everyone hustled aboard, the last few people packing in like so many sardines. The bus lurched forward, off on a circuitous route to the rental car garage.

A thin man began talking out loud, perhaps to relieve the tension from being trapped between strangers and wobbling towers of luggage. Soon everyone knew he had retired from the Agriculture Department, moved back home to Midwest farm country, and discovered he could earn a living because of his knowledge of how Washington works. On behalf of some clients, the man droned on to no one in particular, he had endured three airplane flights this very Sunday to reach the nation's capital.

"I'm here to get money from the government for my clients," the man said.

"That's why we're all here," a voice called out. "The only reason anyone comes to Washington is to get money from the government."

Everyone laughed. Instinctively, I tapped my pants pocket to make sure my wallet was safe.

Chapter 1

WITHOUT EVEN ASKING

A T BANDON DUNES, ON OREGON'S RUGGED AND REMOTE SOUTHERN coast, men at play pretend they're in the eighteenth-century Scotland of Adam Smith.

By the tens of thousands they come from all over the world to three golf courses in the style of the Royal and Ancient Golf Club of St. Andrews, the official shrine of golf since 1754. Smith lived not far from this shrine when he developed the theory of market capitalism that guides economic policy to this day.

The Chicago entrepreneur who created Bandon Dunes, Mike Keiser, describes it as exceptionally, and unexpectedly, profitable. That he earns outsize profits is surprising. America has 16,000 courses. His lie far from the centers of commerce where his players live. When Keiser wrote a check for his first thousand-plus acres, land that had been on the market for years, his wife thought he might as well have tossed the $2.4 million into the wind. But Keiser paid only half the asking price because no one else had the vision to see what could be done to transform the land. Locals knew it as a place to hunt rabbits and occasionally poach a deer by day, while at night amorous teenagers drove down the dirt roads looking for a secluded spot beside the sea.

Gorse covered the land. Gorse is an Irish shrub that grows in impenetrable stands six feet tall or higher. If ignited during the dry season, its oily leaves burn ferociously. Three times in the past century, gorse fires reduced the neighboring town of Bandon to ashes, the last time in 1936.

By car, Bandon Dunes is a hard five-hour drive from Portland. The path goes through the rich farmlands of the table-flat Willamette Valley. It then winds west over the coastal mountains. Getting caught behind a logging truck, a rare reminder of a once vibrant industry, can slow the pace for miles.

Once the road reaches the coast, it is south for an hour to Coos Bay. It is the only urban area for miles and the only deep-water port right on the coast within a day's sail north or south.

Nature endowed the area with a temperate climate, clear water, and enough timber and salmon to last forever. But the lumber companies, eager to squeeze out ever-bigger profits, cut faster and faster. The firs and cedars matured at their own pace, however. The imbalance continued until there was little left to cut on the private lands. Then the spotted owl became a cause célèbre. That added to pressure on government to allow less logging in the area's national forests. New machinery reduced the need for mill workers, and the Japanese began buying raw logs, removing more blue-collar jobs. As the eighties began, the region's timber business collapsed.

Over the decades the government had dammed rivers and creeks for electricity and water storage. To mitigate the damage to nature, government paid for hatcheries to perform tasks that nature had done for free. Still, the runs of chinook and coho dwindled. By 2006, there were not enough salmon to sustain a commercial fishing season.

For a generation now, it has been hard times in what had been a workers' paradise. Families with children moved on. Home-cooked methamphetamine became a scourge. The one hope for a brighter future now lies in all those visitors coming to golf at Bandon Dunes, another 25 minutes down the highway from Coos Bay.

Many of the golfers avoid the long drive, traveling instead in the luxury of private jets. A few arrive in little Learjets with no restrooms. Many more come in private planes the size of junior jetliners. Before the first golf course opened in 1999 perhaps three private jets a year landed at Coos Bay. Now about 5,000 corporate jets arrive annually. Soon that is expected to grow to 7,000 or more private jets, all ferrying players eager to experience what Mike Keiser calls "dream golf."

When players reach Bandon Dunes they discover that, like the Scottish original, the fairways are broad and rough. The links sprawl among the depressions and rises in the coastal dunes. The land seems to undulate, emulating the swells that roll across the Pacific until they crash on the rocks or break on the strip of taupe sand that runs for three miles below the golf course bluffs.

The links at Bandon Dunes appear to be works of nature, so picture-perfect that they suggest Mother Nature retained Kodak as her exterior decorator. In fact, earth graders remolded the sand to create what Keiser calls "nature improved." Then gardeners planted grass and positioned silver beach weed, mock heather, and verbena along the fairway edges.

No trees border the fairways, unlike the strips of forest at country clubs that act like traffic safety barriers separating golfers commuting down narrow green lanes in opposite directions. The only trees at Bandon Dunes are random sentinels, weathered by the salt air and, in the distance, the ridgeline of a once thick forest. The Bandon greens are not the smooth and gently sloping ovals of most courses, but rippled and rolling challenges. The greens cover up to an acre, eight times larger than at a typical country club or municipal course, making it all the more exhilarating to knock the ball into a cup just four and a quarter inches across.

From the courses, two of which Zagat rates as the best in America, not a single house is visible, unlike the mini-mansions and condominiums that wall the edges of so many modern golf courses. No electric power lines mar the views, either.

Bandon Dunes is quiet; peacefully, naturally quiet, an aural oasis in the industrial world. Only rarely does the whine from battery-powered golf carts offend the ear. Except for the rare player who is legally disabled, everyone carries their bag of clubs or hires a caddy. Ocean winds, which unpredictably carry higher-flying balls, silence the burly throat-clearing of diesel rigs hauling raw logs and manufactured goods up and down the grade of Highway 101, an asphalt artery of commerce and pleasure that cuts unseen through a scraggly forest of Douglas fir a mile or so inland.

To walk Bandon Dunes is to gain a sense of how the game was played, and life lived, just before the Industrial Revolution brought us ugly factories, the inescapable noises of machinery, and riches beyond the imagining of those who lived before. Golf began six centuries ago, when life was mostly short, nasty, and boring. Men with time to idle started knocking pebbles around the sand dunes near Edinburgh Castle, aiming to drop them into natural holes. It was addictive. So many military officers missed scheduled drills so they could play *gouf* that in 1457, King James II banned the game as a threat to national security. In English the original name of the game means "strike."

What Keiser created is a veritable time machine. So thoroughly does the noise and look of the industrial world recede that one could almost expect to encounter Adam Smith, the moral philosopher, strolling along. It is easy to imagine the great Scot working out his economic insights. Perhaps he would be thinking about how pins, which had been a luxury of the rich, became cheaper than cheap once cutting wire, fashioning points, and creating heads were broken into specialized, repetitive tasks.

It was Smith who showed us that pursuit of self-interest, far more than selfless acts of charity, promotes the general welfare. In making the most of one's labors, Smith said, individual enterprise, as if guided by an invisible hand, unintentionally benefits all mankind.

Among the father of capitalism's lesser known but equally significant insights is what he wrote about the eagerness of business owners to make even more profits by thwarting the invisible hand. He warned that unchecked self-interest, especially when aided by the government, will spoil the benefits of capitalism.

"People of the same trade seldom meet together, even for merriment and diversion, but the conversation ends in a conspiracy against the public, or in some contrivance to raise prices," Smith wrote in *An Inquiry into the Nature and Causes of the Wealth of Nations.* "It is impossible indeed to prevent such meetings, by any law which either could be executed, or would be consistent with liberty and justice."

Smith followed this with an observation that is crucial to realizing the benefits of the market. His sage words are usually ignored by those who cite him as their authority for all manner of government policies:

> But though the law cannot hinder people of the same trade from sometimes assembling together, it ought to do nothing to facilitate such assemblies, much less to render them necessary.

Despite two centuries passing, those warnings seem never to have reached all the presidents, governors, senators, and cabinet secretaries who take the rostrum at the annual gatherings of the National Association of Manufacturers, the U.S. Chamber of Commerce, and the conventions of the bankers, farmers, and every other big trade group.

Throughout his writings Smith warned of the damage done when government interferes in the market by guaranteeing profits or handing out gifts. This damage can exceed that caused when government taxes unwisely or imposes rules that needlessly obstruct commerce.

It is a universal truth that it is easier to mine gold from the government treasury than the side of a mountain. Of a subsidy paid to herring fishermen, called in those days a *bounty,* Smith observed that it was all too "common for vessels to fit out for the sole purpose of catching, not the fish, but the bounty."

Today in America, Smith's "bounties" are everywhere. Whole industries outfit themselves to catch all they can. Most of these subsidies are available only to corporations and those individuals rich enough to own a substantial business. Everyone, however, is forced to finance these bounties.

Lobbyists fashion bounties tailor-made for companies they represent. State legislatures and city councils deliver them by the tens of billions of dollars each year, taking from the many to benefit the few. Even without spending money, government often confers benefits on the few. It does so by establishing arcane rules that create an advantage in the competitive market. Government also grants a lucrative favor for the few when it allows companies to shortchange workers and, especially, pensioners.

As well-paying jobs like those in the timber and salmon industries fade away, demand for subsidies grows in the belief that this will keep people working.

Some of these bounties do not even require an ask. They are just there. Mike Keiser knows that. He had to file applications for two small subsidies, one of which hardly seems worth the bother. He hired lawyers and lobbyists to seek a third. Coos Bay business leaders supported this third subsidy, believing it was a good way to create even more jobs at Bandon Dunes.

Yet Keiser benefits from four subsidies. The last is by far the biggest. He did not even have to ask for this one. It flows on automatic pilot in such a subtle way that following the trail of money under government-set rules of accounting would never reveal its true path. Yet this bounty totals more money each year than the payroll for Keiser's 325 full-time employees, including their fringe benefits and even the tips they collect from patrons. By some measures this hidden subsidy, to be examined in the pages ahead, is several times the size of his payroll.

Beneath the exquisite beauty of Bandon Dunes lurks an ugly truth. The economic development benefits at Bandon Dunes are illusory. From the perspective of one depressed community, Bandon Dunes is all win. It provides desperately needed jobs. It is making Keiser's fortune grow rapidly. But from a national perspective, those jobs are a drag on the American economy because they cost more than they are worth. So even if you never visit Bandon Dunes, never golf there, you are being forced to pay part of the cost for those who do. Many of them are far richer than you will ever be. They hardly need your help.

If subsidies that cost more than the benefits they generate were unique to Bandon Dunes, they would be of little consequence. But subsidies are not confined to one small and needy place. The harsh reality is that for the past quarter century, policies adopted in the name of Adam Smith, policies that supposedly strengthen the invisible hand guiding the market, have weighed down our economy while simultaneously stuffing the pockets of those among the rich and powerful who solicited them or, like Keiser, were just standing in the right place at a lucrative time. This is our story, not of one free lunch, but of the many banquets at which billions and billions of your dollars are being served to the richest among us.

Chapter 2

MR. REAGAN'S QUESTION

IIT'S BEEN NEARLY 30 YEARS SINCE RONALD REAGAN ASKED, "ARE you better off now than you were four years ago?" and tens of millions of American voters responded with a resounding no.

With their votes the citizenry fired not just one unpopular and unlucky president but granted the new president, and eventually his party, broad authority to reconstruct the relationship between the government of the United States and its economic system. By overwhelming numbers, middle-class, well-to-do, and wealthy voters agreed that the economic malaise of the seventies—inflation, skyrocketing energy costs, deficits, high unemployment—was the sour fruit of a half-century of government interference with the "invisible hand" of the nation's market-based, capitalist economy.

The promised solution was to get government out of the way—to let business operate largely free of public oversight in the form of government programs, rules and regulations, or at least with a lot fewer of them. The voters agreed to let the "private sector" of companies, corporations, associations, and charitable organizations take over as many of the duties of government as practical. "Government is not the solution," Reagan famously declared as the battle cry of his revolution. "Government is the problem."

So, it is only reasonable nearly three decades later to ask a new question: Are we better off than we were a generation ago?

On the surface the answer is obvious: Of course we are. Since 1980, the national economy has more than doubled in size in real terms. More than half the wealth built up since the United States began was created in just the past quarter century. Even taking into account population growth, the overall economic success is striking. For each dollar per person in 1980, the economy in 2006 generated $1.68.

At the same time the costs of many goods have fallen and their quality has improved. The real price of color televisions plummeted more than 75 percent—and for the same money you can buy bigger screens with images so fine they reveal every skin pore or errant strand of hair.

Even at $3 a gallon, gasoline in 2007 costs about the same in inflation-adjusted dollars as it did in 1980. Tires last far longer, costing less per mile. Airfares are much cheaper. Long distance telephone calls are virtually free. Useful and fun products that did not exist in 1980 can be bought cheaply, from Dell laptops playing feature-length DVD movies to stylish Razr cell phones to iPod music players, smaller and lighter than a pack of cigarettes, that hold 5,000 songs. The stock market has replaced the local bank as the place where people keep their savings. The inflow of buyers has helped drive the total real value of the stock market to five times its worth in 1980. Seventy percent of Americans own their own homes. A few million own two. All these residences are collectively worth about $20 trillion.

Yet despite all this success in hard dollars and improved product quality, for the vast majority of Americans the answer as to whether they are better off is again, almost three decades later, a resounding no.

The gross numbers and averages about economic growth obscure one overwhelming truth: The benefits of this bonanza flowed overwhelmingly to those at the apex of the economic pyramid. The base of that pyramid has weakened as average incomes have shrunk and more risks were forced upon them by government policies that favor those at the top.

For the bottom 90 percent of Americans, a group we will refer to as the vast majority, annual income has been on a long, mostly downhill slide for more than three decades. The vast majority's average income peaked at $33,000 way back in 1973. By 2005 it had fallen to a bit more than $29,000. Even with three decades of economic expansion, the vast majority has to get by on about $75 less each week than it did a generation earlier, tax return data show.

Since the economy grew and grew, where did all the money go? Part of it went to corporate profits, which have been growing much faster than wages. And the portion that flowed to individuals as wages, interest, dividends, and other forms of income generated by the market? The growth went straight to the top.

Of each dollar people earned in 2005, the top 10 percent got 48.5 cents. That was the top tenth's greatest share of the income pie since 1929, just before the Roaring Twenties collapsed into the Great Depression.

Within that top 10 percent, basically those who made more than $100,000, the gains were highly concentrated at the very top. Most of the increase went to the top half of 1 percent and most of that to the top tenth of 1 percent, who made at least $1.7 million that year.

How government encourages this concentration of incomes at the very top, resulting in worsening conditions for most Americans, will be examined in a later chapter. For now, keep in mind this one astonishing fact extracted from official government tax data: in 2005, the 300,000 men, women, and children who comprised the top tenth of 1 percent had nearly as much income as all 150 million Americans who make up the economic lower half of our population. Add the income the rich are not required to report and those 300,000 made more than the 150 million.

This growing concentration of income at the top is nothing like the distribution of income America experienced in the first three decades following World War II. Nor is it like that found in Canada, Europe, Japan, Australia, and New Zealand. Instead it resembles the distribution of income found in three other major countries: Brazil, Mexico, and Russia.

In ways that most Americans do not imagine, but that have been thoroughly documented by political scientists, sociologists, and others, these three nations and the United States are alike. They all have a rapidly growing class of billionaires. They have growing, and seemingly intractable, poverty at the bottom. And all four countries have a middle class that is under increasing stress. These four countries are also societies in which adults have the right to vote, but real political power is wielded by a relatively narrow, and rich, segment of the population.

Many Americans read about soaring incomes at the top and assume that making a lot of money is the just deserts for those who worked hard and created flourishing enterprises. Real economic growth, after all, requires a society of industrious people who labor, save, invest, and take risks in search of economic reward. Those who succeed deserve the fruits of their labors.

But the distribution of income in a society does not take place in a vacuum. It is also the product of government rules. And those rules were written by people, not handed down from some immutable power.

Government can, and does, take from some to give to others. Taxing adults so that children can be educated is an obvious example.

Without even touching money, government can cause huge transfers of wealth within the economy. For example, the Big Four commercial sports leagues are exempted from the laws of competition, allowing them to charge higher admission prices than they could get in a free market. Movie theaters and video arcades enjoy no such protection from competition for the limited amounts people can spend on entertainment.

Government can, and increasingly does, give money to businesses outright. It also funnels it in subtle ways to places like the Bandon Dunes Golf Resort. Government also gives away public assets, such as land or minerals, or sells them for far less than their value. Conversely, government can use its constitutional power of eminent domain to seize private property from one owner and give the land to someone else, as it once did for President George W. Bush, making him a wealthy man in the process.

Rewriting the economic rules that define our society in the past few decades has been done under the banner of "deregulation" and its promise that less government means more economic growth. The term itself is a misnomer. No society is free of regulation. Everything has rules, everything. Baseball's rules go right down to how many stitches are on the ball (104).

In the past quarter century or so our government has enacted new rules that have created not only free markets, but rigged ones. These rules have weakened and even destroyed consumer protections while increasing the power of the already powerful.

The distribution of incomes also reflects the tools that society provides citizens to support themselves. Children who go to schools with minimally competent teachers, outdated textbooks, and asphalt playgrounds are unlikely to have the same economic success as children who attend schools with master teachers, the latest books supplemented by music, arts, and laboratories, and expanses of lawn for play.

We do not live in a laissez-faire economy in which there is no interference from government and people are allowed to do as they please, operating the economy by making contracts with one another. We have rules. Over the past three decades the rules affecting who wins and who loses economically have been quietly and subtly rewritten.

The richest Americans and the corporations they control shaped and often wrote these new rules and regulations under which our economy now functions. The rich and their lobbyists have taken firm control of the levers of power in Washington and the state capitals while remaking the rules in their own interests. They have also imbued private organizations with the power to make rules that few outside of the process understand, but that influence the distribution of income. These same people also just happen to be the primary source of the campaign donations that put politicians in office and keep them there. Politicians, as lawmakers, enact the rules. As presidents and governors they appoint both the administrators who decide when to enforce the rules and many of the judges who interpret them.

Rules define a civilization. Without rules, there is no civilization. Over the great sweep of human history, brute force has held sway. But with the Enlightenment, the spread of literacy, and mass communication, we began to expand the sphere of rule-making beyond warlords and kings to the nobles; then to the manufacturers and traders who started the world on its long march to economic growth; and finally, in America, to the common man. Wherever the world has civilizing rules based on some moral or practical principle we see prosperity and freedom, though not always together.

In America, however, the long expansion of who plays a role in deciding the rules has ended. The base of influence has begun to contract. In part this is because of the campaign finance system, which transfers power to those who donate and who steer donations. In part it is because advances in human knowledge have made the economy so much more complex that fewer people understand, or have the time to learn about, the issues. Less than a century ago, Congress debated economic policy by reviewing the life cycle of a cow. Today hearings are filled with talk of complex abstractions such as a supposedly naturally occurring rate of unemployment, monetizing debt, and acronyms such as LIBOR (the London Interbank Offered Rate of interest).

The rules on which we founded this nation sought, imperfectly for sure, to create individual freedom with equal justice and opportunity for all. We spent two centuries refining those rules through experience, political struggle, a civil war that cost 620,000 American lives, and a civil rights movement that wrought change peacefully.

To succeed in the long run, rules must have a moral or practical basis and the support of the people. If society says that you may do one thing and not another, there must be some rationale or the rule will be flouted. There is no legitimacy in officials writing rules as they choose simply because they have the power to do so. Such is tyranny.

The Founding Fathers recognized this when they took that great leap to create our republic more than two centuries ago. They provided for checks and balances, recognizing the need to limit power and to control it. To many people, power is of little consequence, just as many people care little about beauty or riches. But to those who lust for power, of what use is acquiring power unless they can abuse it? In this, the philosophy of the power monger is no different from that of the cancer cell, which mindlessly seeks growth for the sake of growth until it overwhelms its host.

To control abuses of power, we write rules. The nature of those rules determines the shape of the society we live in. The rules we put in place during the five decades following the collapse of the Roaring Twenties economy marked a historic change in America.

Beginning with the New Deal in 1933 and, especially, with bipartisan consensus after World War II, our elected leaders worked to build and strengthen the middle class. Government invested in the nation's most valuable assets: the brains of its citizens. Government financed higher education for millions through the GI Bill and made college free or kept tuition so low that anyone with ambition and smarts could get a degree. Government invested in basic sciences, public health, and medical research; built the interstate highways; and allowed unions to negotiate for higher wages. We created consumer protections and environmental protections. We created a set of rules to make America a land with a large, growing, and stable middle class.

An unexpected by-product of this, fueled by the increased value of human minds and the economic demand this knowledge created, was the rise of a prosperous upper middle class of people who had plenty but still had to work to enjoy the fruits of their labor. These are the two-income professional couples, the working wealthy whose economic substance is far greater than their political influence.

But in the last quarter century or so, we have turned away from these policies, shifting risk onto those least able to bear it by taking away protections for consumers, workers, retirees, and investors.

For more than a quarter century now our government has been adopting rules that tilt the playing field in favor of the rich, the powerful, and the politically connected. These rules accomplish this by taking from the uninformed, handcuffing law enforcement, squelching whistle-blowers, and making it ever harder for those who were wronged to get redress. The new rules have taken special aim at those supposed economic criminals, the regulators.

The reasons for this shift go deep into the human condition.

In his most famous speech, in front of the Lincoln Memorial in 1963, Martin Luther King Jr. said he had a dream that one day his four daughters would be judged by the content of their character, not by the color of their skin. We have made great, if far from complete, progress in judging people without regard to that superficiality. But on another front we have gone backward. Today we often value people less by the content of their character than by the contents of their wallet.

In this way we are not unlike the ancients. Just as the Greeks once told tales of those who became intimate with the gods, our society is awash with television programs, magazines, and tabloid columns that celebrate the wealthy as gods and demigods of our age. Often we celebrate wealth for its own sake, without regard to whether it was obtained by means honest or corrupt, or is used for purposes noble or foul. We not only celebrate the rich for being rich, we shower gifts and praise on them for nothing more than having money, or sometimes for just the appearance of having money.

The pursuit of ever more financial zeros and commas on net worth statements has in turn produced a moral breakdown at the top of our society that has spilled onto the front pages. Most of the rich have not lost sight of everything but their own net worth. But enough have that they are twisting our culture and our values in ways that tear at the fabric of society.

In less than three decades presidents of companies have gone from apologizing when they had to lay off workers to boasting of the riches they obtained through mass firings. We sing the praises of investors who owe their wealth not to creating businesses, but to buying companies in deals that required destroying lives and careers, just so that they could squeeze out more money for themselves. Too many of us missed the irony when Gordon Gekko, rewriting the eighth and tenth commandments, looked into the camera and declared "Greed . . . is good. Greed is right. Greed works."

To the addicted, money is like cocaine: Too much is never enough. This mass addiction to money has grown in the past three decades into widespread theft of shareholder assets by executives. The well-known cases from the Wall Street bubble—Ken Lay of Enron, Bernie Ebbers of WorldCom, and Dennis Kozlowski of Tyco—were just the tip of the proverbial iceberg. Many more got away with cheating their shareholders, their workers, and the taxman than were ever considered for indictment.

One of the new rules has been to make sure that there are far too few cops on the beat on Wall Street to even write down all the legitimate complaints, much less pursue more than a handful of wrongdoers. More important, the actions of Lay and Ebbers and the others were just part of a massive shift in practices and policies that continues. The Wall Street scandals are not over; the conduct they revealed is just becoming institutionalized.

Steve Jobs, a founder of Apple computers, was awarded millions in stock options at a board of directors meeting that never took place. When given too much change by a clerk, the principled person returns the money. Jobs arranged to have his fraudulently issued options exchanged for restricted stock worth hundreds of millions of dollars. The government brought civil charges against Apple's general counsel and its chief financial officer, the latter of whom admitted wrongdoing, gave up $3.5 million, and said he had warned Jobs about the improper pay. Still, by late summer 2007 the government had taken no action against Jobs. The Apple board, which included Al Gore, portrayed Jobs as an unknowing victim of complicated rules even though they have been in effect since before Apple went public decades ago.

Jobs was hardly alone in the stock options scandals, which involved thousand of executives working for hundreds of companies. Many of these executives took money from shareholders through deliberate, calculated actions, including fabricating records. They differ from bandits only in that they wielded pens to steal with stock options instead of pointing pistols while demanding cash or jewelry. Their techniques were subtle and not overtly violent, but for society they are worse than street robbery, for their actions undermine the legitimacy of society's rules in ways that bandits cannot.

Unlike the common thief or bandit, these executives have the best and brightest lawyers to explain away misconduct or to obfuscate. In the rare instances when indictments are handed up, the cheated shareholders sometimes end up paying to defend the thieves who robbed them. Added to this are the legions of publicists who are paid to report what their bosses want us to hear, the antithesis of journalism's call to pursue the facts without fear or favor.

The ranks of these image shifters are growing, while across the country many journalists are being laid off as people pay less attention to the news, reducing further the chances that inconvenient facts will become known. Nor have other watchdogs fared better. Later we will examine the fate of the brave bureaucrat who first exposed the stock options frauds.

Best of all for the stock options thieves, they had a friend somewhere in the White House. The federal prosecutors who had dared to go after them were fired. Yet in hearing after hearing before Congress no one would say just who made the firing decisions or why, not even the attorney general of the United States. We were told only that the prosecutors performed poorly, despite sterling written evaluations to the contrary. So not only have the standards of business been corrupted by the love of money, but also one of the most powerful and sensitive centers of power in our government, the Justice Department, has been compromised in the service of greed.

The new rules also enable executive pay schemes that reward those who mismanage companies by handing them vast personal fortunes, even though they destroyed wealth for everyone else. Many of these executives make money in a world in which they face little or no risk but can reap great reward, another area in which Adam Smith, the father of capitalism, warned us about moral failure and its corrosive effects.

All of this can be traced back to how the government sets rules and enforces them. Many wasteful rules are gone. But so are many virtuous rules, replaced by ones that encourage and even reward misconduct.

At the same time that the rules have been rewritten to favor the already rich, new rules have been written that ensure harsh treatment for the poor, whether they are indolent or the victims of such misfortunes as being born not so bright or healthy as the average person.

In this era of rules for the rich we act as if poverty is a *free good,* meaning in the argot of economists that it is not scarce but readily available. In that sense poverty is indeed a free good, but it is not a cheap one. Coping with the foul effects of poverty costs us a half trillion dollars a year, a sum greater than what we spend on Social Security benefits. Poverty wastes minds and spirits, robbing all of us of opportunity. When poverty fosters crime it costs us more than the harm done to our wallets and our safety, or even the expense of a system to hunt down, prosecute, and incarcerate offenders. It makes us less trusting, less willing to see ourselves as one people in our great experiment in self-governance. How we deal with poverty as a society is a major factor in why the vast majority are worse off, for unlike the superrich, they cannot live in gated communities, fly in private planes, or hire bodyguards for themselves and private schools for their children.

For a nation whose leaders frequently invoke their belief in the Bible, curious indeed is how the political rhetoric ignores the overriding duty of the New Testament to care for the poor. "Sell all that thou hast, and distribute unto the poor" for "it is easier for a camel to go through the eye of a needle, than for a rich man to enter into the kingdom of God." Jesus said those who believe must sacrifice for the poor; we sacrifice for the rich at the expense of the poor.

The worst poverty is that of the man who does not know how to fish. Even if he has the means to obtain hook and line, of what good is a tool that one does not know how to use? People with the skills to sustain themselves and improve their lot build our society. Denying the basic skills needed to succeed, starting with a decent education so that one can comprehend more than simple instructions, is itself a form of crime.

Under what theory of morality do we grant those already in a superior economic or legal position ever more power, especially when that power derives from rules in fine print that defy normal human understanding?

Consider one example, the business of lending money. Usury laws that protected consumers against rapacious lenders existed until 1978. Now they are gone because of a Supreme Court decision. In that case the high court warned Congress that it needed to enact new laws to protect borrowers. That warning was ignored in the lucrative trade of selling access, if not votes. In place of rules that protect the vulnerable, the innumerate, and the foolish, our government has set forth onerous new rules that reward those who prey on the poor. We used to prosecute loan sharks. Today a television commercial featuring Gary Coleman urges people to borrow money at 99.25 percent interest, paying back almost $10,000 to borrow a quarter that much. These new rules help Goldman Sachs and Lehman Brothers and Citibank exploit the poor, the unsophisticated, and the foolish. These lenders, or their fronts, can now charge rates and impose penalties that were illegal, even criminal, a generation ago. These and other lenders engage in conduct that goes way beyond that of Michael Milken, the junk bond promoter who made a fortune pushing risk onto corporate balance sheets the way addicts inject heroin into their veins. Milken was vilified by many; not so the latest usurers.

The result? In the past 25 years, one American family in seven has sought refuge in federal bankruptcy court. They filed for relief from their debtors, not to immorally scam the system, but because they were forced into it. Exhaustive research by Elizabeth Warren of Harvard Law School and her associates into bankruptcy court filings has proven that the vast majority of people seek refuge from debtors after any two of three events combine: divorce, job loss, or major medical problems.

The response of our leaders to this is instructive, for it shows how much of the wisdom of our founders we have lost. Two centuries ago, a sitting justice on the Supreme Court, James Wilson, was jailed for not repaying money he had borrowed to invest with a fellow signatory to the Declaration of Independence. Back then debtors could avoid imprisonment by securing all doors and windows, conducting business by means of notes tossed in and out of the upper-floor windows. Those sent to *gaol* usually were held in a place with few locks and keys, where you brought your own furnishings and food. Imagine what would happen today if a brilliant jurist who filed bankruptcy were nominated for the Supreme Court.

Today we do not jail debtors. But under a new bankruptcy law written by credit card lenders, we deny some people the fresh start that the constitutional provisions on bankruptcy were designed to ensure. Senators and representatives, after a decade of gathering up campaign contributions from the lenders and their lobbyists, adopted rules that can leave the sick and the jobless at the mercy of corporate Javerts pursuing Jean Valjeans until they die.

In this same era we have turned what were once denounced as vices into pastimes. Witness the explosive growth of casinos and other gambling. And now we even subsidize some of the gambling halls with money that was promised to help the poor, the elderly, and the sick. In this way does Donald Trump benefit from money intended for the least among us to burnish his image as a supposed billionaire.

The checks and balances provided by oversight, inspection, investigation, and, in extreme cases, prosecution have all been gutted in pursuit of deregulation and supposedly smaller government. It has become difficult and sometimes impossible just to find someone to take a complaint that an employer refused to pay wages or locked people in to make them work or stole the retirement money. When there is no policeman on the beat the greatest beneficiary is not the taxpayer who is relieved of the cost of maintaining that police officer, but the thief. And when bridges, tunnels, and dams are not inspected and repaired we are all in danger.

Despite all the deregulation rhetoric, government grows ever bigger. The number of federal government workers shrinks, but the ranks of people who are hired on contract at much greater cost increases. In 2000 workers hired on contract cost our federal government $207 billion. By 2006 this had swelled to $400 billion—rivaling the expense of either Social Security or interest on the federal government's growing debt.

These contract workers typically cost twice as much as civil servants doing the same work, yet they are even less accountable. In Iraq we court-martial and imprison soldiers who under the stress of relentless urban combat kill innocents in a fit of anger or misjudgment. But the contract soldiers who fight alongside them, at two to ten times the pay, operate in a law-free zone, any killings they commit for foul reason unpunished and, some of our leaders assert, beyond the reach of any law.

At home, government and companies cooperate in withdrawing contracts and other documents from the public record. The profits generated by these companies are used, in part, to lobby for more contracts that drive up costs even further. Executives of these companies are also strategic donors to politicians, helping to ensure the continuing flow of tax dollars to their businesses. This is a benefit unavailable to even the most empire-building bureaucrat.

On another front, government is easing up on rules that ensure clean water to drink and fresh air to breathe. When companies dump toxics instead of cleaning up at their own expense, they force everyone to bear the costs of environmental pollution. The Cuyahoga River in Cleveland was so polluted with flammable chemicals that it caught fire at least nine times starting in 1868. But it was not until the 1969 fire brought national news coverage that national debate ensued about pollution and economic growth. Only then did government adopt rules to give us cleaner air and water—and thus save us some of the anguish and the cost of asthma, cancer, and heart disease. But under the guise of deregulation, many of those rules are being relaxed, repealed, or ignored.

Now we face a similar problem that damages lives and costs us dearly. A growing array of businesses and whole industries profit by dumping their real costs of capital, equipment, and even labor onto the taxpayers. This new problem is *economic pollution*.

We shall see the economic pollution caused by just one industry in which Tyco International, General Electric, and Honeywell are major players. This industry owes its entire profits not to unleashing the forces of competitive business, but to silently shifting its largest labor expense onto the taxpayers.

Under deregulation we have created a host of dependent companies that hold out their very large hands to take money from Washington, the state capitals, and towns and cities everywhere. Wal-Mart, Target, and a host of lesser-known retailers all count on government handouts when they open new stores. These subsidies serve not only to enhance their profits, but also to undermine locally owned businesses that are crucial to the social fabric of communities. These retailers are not, by far, the worst offenders, however. Examples abound of companies and industries that foul the national ledgers, degrading the income and wealth of us all through economic pollution.

Sometimes the banner of deregulation can make people rich at the cost of others' lives. We will follow the career of an economics professor who embraced the idea of getting government out of the way of business, yet made his business career cultivating government, leaving behind a trail of deaths and costs that were shifted onto the taxpayers. His name is John W. Snow and he rose to become our government's Treasury secretary.

The benefits of the nation's overall growth in incomes and wealth flow like a mighty river of greenbacks to the powerful, wealthy men and women who have twisted Mr. Reagan's revolutionary creed. They want more government, just so long as it makes them richer. They have captured for themselves and their class the benefits and rewards of a government that is today as intricately involved with the private sector as it ever has been. They have found the proverbial free lunch, enjoying a sumptuous feast and leaving their bill for the rest of us.

There is, of course, no such thing as a free lunch. Every cost must somehow be accounted for and paid. When bars offered a free lunch in the 1800s, the cost was built into the nickel charge for beer. For our purposes, a "free lunch" refers to an economic benefit received by one party that is paid for by another by government action or inaction.

For example, when a developer receives a plot of land free or at a discount, your taxes may have paid to buy it, the original owner may have been cheated out of its market value, or someone else not at all obvious got stuck with the real cost. When an executive shortchanges the pension plan, making his company appear to be more profitable, he inflates the value of the company stock and therefore his stock options. When the pension later fails and the workers get less than what they were due, or the taxpayers have to make up the part of the shortfall guaranteed by the government's Pension Benefit Guarantee Corporation (PBGC), the executive gets a free lunch. Our economy is riddled with these subsidies, many of which are intentionally subtle and hard to detect.

Executives' free lunch is a major factor in America's growing inequality and why our economy is closest to those of Brazil, Mexico, and Russia in how it distributes resources.

The evidence of a growing divide between the superrich and everyone else in America is so overwhelming that all but the few lightweight ideologues among economists acknowledge this harsh truth. When George W. Bush was running for president in 2000 he famously referred to a white-tie audience at a Waldorf-Astoria dinner as the "haves and the have mores." He said that "some people call you the elite. I call you my base." By 2007 even the Bush White House had publicly acknowledged that the divide between the superrich and everyone else was a real concern.

Since that talk about the "have mores," a national debate has arisen over just what is going on. Why are the rich getting so much richer, while the middle class struggles and the poor fall behind? Why are the richest of the rich—billionaires—pulling away even from those whose net worth is in the many millions? The cable and broadcast television networks, national news magazines, and scholarly conferences have all examined the question of why inequality is growing and what it means.

Is education behind increasing inequality, as the White House says? Or could it be globalization, with cheap labor in China and India combining with free trade to create new world-scale fortunes? Or is it technology, from ever-faster silicon chips to drugs that soothe what ails you? Or maybe it is just a proper reward for talent, with corporate executives getting their fair share of the wealth they create for shareholders.

All of those answers are right—and wrong. What they all have in common is that they are just superstructures arising from the same foundation. The real answer, like the focal point of Edgar Allan Poe's "The Purloined Letter," is right in front of our eyes. We just have to discern it amid the clutter of daily living.

Since 1980 it has become official policy to ensure that the rich receive the benefits of government. This is a shift from government policy in the years after World War II to grow the middle class, remaking America into a land of better-educated and healthier people, a land of suburbs and single-family homes where opportunity was based less on status and wealth than on hard work and merit.

So who is better off today than they were 30 years ago? The middle-aged factory worker whose plant closed even though it earned a healthy profit or the Wall Street investment banker who brokered the deal to ship the machine tools overseas, where pay is three or four dollars per day? The billionaire CEO or the middle manager whose company health insurance has been cut yet again? The war contractor or the brain-injured veteran?

Nearly three decades after Mr. Reagan's revolution, the single biggest piece of our economy, a third of it, is still government. From raking leaves in city parks to buying stealth bombers that cost $2 billion a copy, government takes the same share. But money for the basics that make society work is growing scarce. From those leaves in the park to textbooks to highway bridge maintenance to food safety inspections, money is dwindling because so much has been diverted to the already rich through giveaways, tax breaks, and a host of subsidies that range from the explicit to the deeply hidden.

Evidence that the elites have captured the government and are milking it for their own benefit is so overwhelming that, on one level, you can find it as an unstated assumption in everyday news reports. With this idea in mind, the degree to which it has become part of the background to our national political, economic, and social discussions will leap out at you from the pages of the newspapers and the observations of the pundits. It has become the basis for advertisements about how buying a luxury home or a share of a corporate jet may be within your reach, thanks to an assist from the government.

In the pages ahead we will examine just how thoroughly government has become the servant of the rich, showing how:

☐ Warren Buffett's company has a two-thirds-billion-dollar, interest-free loan from our government for more than 28 years, just one of many ways that the government has boosted the investment returns for which he is so renowned.

☐ President George W. Bush owes his fortune not to the oil business, at which he failed, but to a sales tax increase that was funneled into his pocket, a fortune further enhanced by his paying millions less in income taxes than he should have.

☐ George Steinbrenner not only gets lavish subsidies for his baseball team, he also made a fortune from a scheme that damaged national security.

☐ Paris Hilton has resources to cavort shamelessly because her grandfather, thanks to government, snatched a fortune away from poor children.

☐ Donald Trump benefits from a tax that was enacted to help the elderly and the poor, but part of which is now diverted to his casinos.

And beyond these brand-name Americans are legions of the superrich of whom few have heard, who owe their fortunes less to their enterprise than to the generosity of our Uncle Sam and his nieces and nephews in state and local government.

There is a reason that 35,000 people are registered as lobbyists in Washington, double the number of lobbyists employed there in 2000. They are there to seek favors, from outright gifts of your tax dollars to subtle changes in rules that funnel money to their clients, thwart competition, hold you back, and buoy others. Among the ironies is that many of the most damaging policies have been created in the name of Adam Smith, the original modern economist. Indeed, if that eighteenth-century Scotsman could come back today, he might smite the plutocrats setting the government's bill of fare and cast out the rule-changers. No doubt he would remind us of his eighteenth-century insight that subsidy economics are inherently inefficient and wasteful, often costing several dollars to give away one.

Back in 1964 Ronald Reagan started telling a story he repeated many times on the long road to the White House. It was about how the masses ruin democracy by sucking dry the nation. Reagan attributed his tale to an eighteenth-century British historian whose name he consistently mangled, Lord Woodhouselee, Alexander Fraser Tytler. Professor Tytler never wrote the words attributed to him, but they have become central to the argument used by those who came to power with Mr. Reagan, and those who followed, to justify their policies. In one tape-recorded speech in 1965, Reagan said:

> A democracy cannot exist as a permanent form of government. It can only exist until the voters discover they can vote themselves largesse out of the public treasury. From that moment on the majority . . . always vote[s] for the candidate promising the most benefits from the treasury with the result that democracy always collapses over a loose fiscal policy, always to be followed by a dictatorship.

Whoever wrote those words got it partly right. But just as Karl Marx never envisioned commercial sports as the opiate of the masses, neither did most of those who agreed with Mr. Reagan consider the prospect that the elites would be the ones to vote themselves the public's treasure.

Let's begin by examining two free lunches. The first case examines the moral hazard in a government policy that rewards reckless corporate behavior. The second explores the reasons so many jobs are headed offshore, and who benefits.

Chapter 3

TRUST AND CONSEQUENCES

HALF AN HOUR BEFORE DAYBREAK ABOARD THE AMTRAK SILVER Star heading to New York from Florida, the South Carolina skies were fair. The thermometer hovered comfortably in the low seventies. It was the start of the glorious final day of July 1991.

The clickety-clack rhythm of the rails rocked the 407 passengers as they dozed. Among them was Paul Palank, a Miami police sergeant on his way to meet his wife and children for a family reunion near the nation's capital. Palank loved trains as much as he feared flying.

At a minute past five, the train approached the town of Lugoff, a farming community that the DuPont Company transformed into an industrial center when it built a chemical plant there in 1948. The same tracks that supported Palank and his fellow passengers on their journey north often carried CSX railroad hopper cars filled with chemicals to make Orlon, a synthetic "miracle fiber" that came out of World War II research. On a siding parallel to the Silver Star stood a string of empty hopper cars waiting for a CSX train to haul them away to be refilled. Freight traffic was so much more important, and more common, than passenger trains that railroad companies didn't name the switch Lugoff after the town, or even after the DuPont factory. Railroad engineers called the train switch the Orlon Crossing.

The Amtrak train was traveling two miles an hour below the posted speed limit when the twin locomotives and the first twelve cars passed over the Orlon Crossing. Then the switch broke.

Six passenger cars hurtled off the tracks. The impact flipped over the first hopper car, whose hardened steel wheels cut like a knife through the metal skin of the passenger cars. By the time everything came to a halt,

77 people were injured and 8 were dead, including Sergeant Palank. He was 35 years old.

More than eight hours later, Angelica Palank arrived at the train station in Alexandria, Virginia, to greet her husband. Eager to see him, Angelica pushed her youngest son Taylor's stroller just as fast as five-year-old Josef could move his little legs to keep up. As the family waited on the platform, a woman told Angelica that there had been an accident. Angelica did not believe her. A northbound train approached and she felt relieved. When it blew by the station, Angelica turned anxious. She and the children hurried downstairs, hunting for the arrivals-and-departures board. Train 82, the Silver Star, was not listed. She asked a ticket clerk, who gave her an 800 number to call. The clerk pointed the frantic young mother to a pay telephone. A stranger's voice at the other end delivered the horrible news.

In the weeks ahead the families of the injured and dead settled their claims, discovering in the process how remarkably modest payments are to the survivors of transportation crashes and to the heirs of those less fortunate. Only Angelica Palank refused to go along. She did not believe the crash was an accident. She did not believe her Paul died because of some random bit of misfortune that no one could have seen coming. Determined to learn all she could about how Paul was killed, Angelica sued.

To get the truth Angelica Palank would have to put herself through law school. She could never flinch as she took on one of the richest corporations in America, a personal trial that extracted a heavy toll on her and her children. Ten relatives died in one year, but still she stuck to her cause. Friends and neighbors cut the grass and brought meals. At one point, she nearly lost her home to unpaid property taxes. It was scary and nasty, as is all litigation about real wrongs. When she found lawyers willing to take her case—Christian D. Searcy and F. Gregory Barnhart in West Palm Beach—their work began to peel back layer upon layer upon layer of corporate denials and superficial government inquiries. In time they uncovered a trail pointing not to bad luck, but to policies with a blatant disregard for safety.

The compulsion to increase profits can blind men to risk, especially when those at risk are strangers. Society imposes rules on corporate behavior to protect public safety in the face of baser impulses. These rules require enforcement, though. They also require a corporate culture that appreciates the importance of safety. As Adam Smith wrote, "The object of justice is the security from injury, and it is the foundation of civil government."

For more than two decades, the ideology of blind faith in markets, combined with the view that government is inherently inferior to self-regulation, has caused politicians to trim enforcement funds. Trim long enough and the little cuts sever muscle. Ultimately they slash to the bone. Such was the case in the derailment of the Silver Star. But it took one diligent woman and her lawyers more than a decade to demonstrate how harmful these ideas about trusting all companies to do right can be.

Before Angelica Palank's lawsuit got going in earnest, the National Transportation Safety Board examined the crash. The investigators quickly deduced that the accident was not a chance happening. Rather, it resulted from improperly done repairs. Railroads—like airlines, meat-packing plants, and other businesses where hidden dangers lurk—employ inspectors to double-check what safety workers do. This saves lives and avoids lawsuits. Yet the safety board found that the CSX inspectors somehow failed to notice the Orlon Crossing was in a dangerous state of disrepair.

CSX maintenance crews had used shims to level the crossing, even though the switch "is not designed for adjustment." Granite rock, known as ballast, covered the wobbly switch mechanism. Once the investigators cleared the ballast away, they found this vital switch was without a proper pin to hold the pieces in place. The switch was held together with nothing but a rusty nail. The safety board concluded that CSX inspectors "could have and should have seen the switch deficiencies during a normal inspection and, with appropriate action, could have prevented the accident."

Although businesses complain frequently about excessive government paperwork, neither the railroad nor the Federal Railroad Administration, the agency that is supposed to set and enforce safety standards, required much recordkeeping. CSX's inspection process, the safety board concluded, "lacked an adequate documentation procedure."

The roadmaster and some of the work crew used the jury-rigged shims because their employer never allowed them enough time or money to do their jobs properly. CSX cut corners to inflate its profits, which in turn meant riches for its executives, whose pay packages were tied to reported profits and the price of CSX shares.

John W. Snow, a lawyer and college economics professor who rose to become the CSX chief executive, was an early champion of markets as the most efficient regulator of transportation industries. It was an idea he promoted as an assistant secretary in President Ford's Transportation Department before he joined the railroad. Under his leadership, the railroad aggressively cut costs.

CSX publicists encouraged articles about Snow's drive for efficient capital investment. Typical of the stories was one praising the company's change from four engines to three on some hauls. These trains arrived later, but still on time, while saving the cost and fuel of an entire locomotive. His handlers did not make him available for stories about the bridges that became eyesores after years, and then decades, without painting. And in polishing Snow's image as a champion of efficiency, they certainly did not encourage anyone to look at the systematic shortcuts in safety.

Palank and her lawyers dug deep into the cutbacks in safety, deeper than the National Transportation Safety Board. They looked for systemic changes, for a pattern. Eventually they found CSX workers who would talk: Allen Clamp and Robert Griffith.

For three years, Clamp was an apprentice foreman under Buster Bowers, the roadmaster on the section of track in South Carolina where Paul Palank died. Clamp testified that it should have been obvious to CSX that there were too few men to perform the required safety inspections and maintenance. In the crew's race to cover track as quickly as possible, Clamp testified that Bowers never "performed a disassembly inspection, never walked a switch, and conducted no inspection, or inadequate inspections." Clamp said under oath that Bowers even directed him to fill out false inspection reports.

CSX tried to get this testimony thrown out. Five years had passed between the time Clamp last worked under Bowers and the Lugoff crash. CSX said that made the testimony ancient and unreliable. A Florida state appeals court let the testimony stand, noting that the other rail worker, Robert Griffith, confirmed that Bowers also had instructed him to falsify inspection reports.

At trial, CSX urged jurors to not believe the former employees. One Palank lawyer, Greg Barnhart had a counterargument: "CSX said, 'Why would we do that?' We said it was to save $2.4 billion," the money CSX had saved on maintenance.

In his own way, Barnhart was showing the jury the deadly effects of economic pollution. He explained how CSX benefited because it shifted the cost of maintaining safe tracks off its owners and onto the unsuspecting public, which unknowingly assumed a risk of injury or death.

The first jury that heard the Palank case awarded the family $6.1 million as compensation for their loss. Then came the second trial before a new jury, its purpose to determine whether CSX should be punished on the theory that the Lugoff crash was the result of greed encouraging a corporation to turn a blind eye to danger.

The second jury heard all about the $2.4 billion not spent between 1981 and 1993, most of those the years when Snow was fully in charge of CSX. The jury heard how in 1987 the Federal Railroad Administration had told CSX that its practices were unsafe. They heard how the company stuck to its cost-cutting policies anyway.

Testimony showed that the National Transportation Safety Board findings, alarming as they were, had missed much more damning facts. A panel of three Florida judges later wrote that the Orlon switch was defective and the cross pin

> had been broken for at least seven months prior to the derailment. The Orlon switch had been installed backwards ten years earlier, and part of the broken cross pin was buried under several inches of [granite] ballast placed between the ties more than seven months prior to the derailment. The evidence further shows that a proper inspection would have revealed the broken cross pin. In addition, there is evidence that CSX had actual knowledge that the cross pin was defective because the record shows that CSX periodically greased a plate installed on the switch with graphite to make the switch operate.

What that meant was that for a full decade CSX had escaped paying the cost of repairing the Orlon switch. Every day CSX trains loaded with freight, including toxic chemicals, crossed the Orlon switch. So did Amtrak passengers, unaware they were riding over the equivalent of a bomb waiting to go off.

The jurors were incensed. They awarded the widow and her children $50 million in damages, taking 1 percent of CSX's net worth. The jurors also wrote a note on the verdict form: "It is hoped that CSX trainers will emphasize [the] need to inspect both ends of cross pins."

Judge Arthur J. Franza upheld the punitive damages award. He delivered a stinging rebuke of CSX. "The clear and convincing evidence shows that Silver Star No. 82's tragic derailment was caused by willful, wanton negligence," Judge Franza wrote, adding that he considered the railroad's conduct to be "borderline criminal."

"Clearly," the judge wrote, CSX "knew of the peril created by its reductions and the company chose to proceed on its own course."

Then the appeals began. Three Florida judges who took up CSX's pleas for relief ruled against the railroad. The judges said that testimony by former employees showed that "CSX knowingly endangered public safety."

The judges called CSX's conduct a "flagrant violation of the public trust . . . Keeping with the policy that punitive damages should punish and deter, a jury of six reasonable persons concluded that $50 million would adequately communicate to this defendant that this type of reprehensible conduct should not and would not be tolerated."

The appeals court approvingly quoted Judge Franza, who ruled that while CSX saved more than $2 billion, "society paid with eight human lives. . . . The clear and convincing evidence showed that the price of cost-cutting safety to turn over larger profits is too great of a price."

CSX then appealed to the Florida Supreme Court, saying that its conduct was reasonable. Further, any damage should be based only on the value of the section of track near the crash site, not the company's entire net worth. The Florida Supreme Court rejected CSX's claims.

Finally the litigation came to an end in early 2002, more than a decade after Paul Palank's death, when the United States Supreme Court said that it would not hear CSX's appeal.

Angelica Palank said she felt that she had accomplished her goals. She had proven that the crash on July 31, 1991, was not bad luck but the predictable result of deliberate misconduct that flowed from the top of the company. After paying her lawyers and income taxes on the punitive damages, she donated the rest of the money to a foundation in her husband's memory. Today a few million dollars remain to finance grants for a cause her husband cared about deeply, abused and neglected children in and around Miami.

CSX said it was disappointed that the Supreme Court would not give it a chance to show that the jury and the Florida judges were wrong. CSX even suggested the proper punitive damage was zero. Kathy Burns, one of the CSX publicists, called the punitive damage award "unwarranted and excessive."

Lobbyists from CSX and other companies had, in the meantime, descended on Tallahassee to persuade the state legislature that big puni- tive damage awards were bad for business. Today Angelica Palank could not get $50 million in punitive damages because of a law signed by Gov- ernor Jeb Bush. It severely limited any future damage awards no matter how awful the misconduct.

Even with the award that the courts left standing, the cold calculus that cutting safety is immensely profitable remains in place. The total damages to the Palank family, both to compensate them and to punish the company, came to a bit more than $56 million. The money paid to all of the others, who settled without litigation, was a fraction of this. Viewed in the context of what CSX saved, however, even the total dam- ages were not punishment at all, just a minor cost of doing business. For every dollar CSX saved by cutting corners on safety it only had to give back four cents.

We teach children that crime does not pay, but the grown-up truth is that "borderline criminal" behavior can pay handsomely.

From the perspective of CSX, or any railroad, the economics of shortchanging safety continue to make sense. Two years after the Palank case ended, James E. Hall, a former chairman of the National Transpor- tation Safety Board, told *The New York Times* that the loss of lives in rail accidents reveals "a systemic failure . . . It's been something that has just not grabbed the attention, unfortunately, of the public." He was speak- ing of deaths at rail crossings, but his point is equally valid across the board.

Although many travelers worry more, as Sergeant Palank did, about dying in a plane crash or being hit by an 18-wheel rig on the highway, since the year 2000 Americans have been dying at the rate of about one per day at railroad crossings. A few of these deaths are suicides by train or the bloody product of fools driving around signal arms. Some are also the result of crossing arms that fail to activate. Others occur because signal arms sometimes bob back up after coming down, endangering even care- ful drivers and their passengers. At crossings with no signals, foliage that the railroads have not trimmed in accordance with the rules add to the death toll as people drive unaware onto tracks just as millions of pounds of steel bear down on them.

In Britain only about 18 people per year die at rail crossings. Major crossings have fencelike barriers that cars cannot flit around. Even after taking into account that America has five times as many people as the

United Kingdom, the death rate at crossings in America is four times that of Britain.

Between 1995 and 2000 derailments increased 28 percent, nearly triple the 10 percent increase in freight hauled. Yet even with more accidents and more deaths, the economics of cutting spending on safety are compelling from the railroad's perspective. The fines imposed for safety violations in the United States are minor, more like parking tickets than deterrents. The maximum fine is $20,000. The average fine is about $1,600. So the railroads play the percentages, weighing risk versus cost. Risk wins easily.

Most switches are safe. And not every unsafe switch will fail. Keeping every one of the thousands of switches around the country in proper repair is very costly, especially as a competitive market drives transportation prices down. After all, the jury-rigged repair of the backward Orlon switch held for years. Those switches that do fail will probably damage cargo, not kill people. Even killing people doesn't cost the railroads very much. As the CSX case demonstrated, all the injured and the families of the dead except Angelica Palank accepted their modest settlements quickly. So long as insurance costs less than repairs, this dangerous trade-off will continue no matter what the railroad industry says about its commitment to safety.

Since the imperfect rules of the marketplace actually reward dangerous risk taking, the only thing that could prevent this lethal gamble is effective government regulation. In this century just 4 of the first 3,000 rail-crossing accidents were fully investigated because of ever-tighter budgets for government safety offices. One railroad, Union Pacific, even said that federal regulators were so overworked they told the railroad to "stop calling" after every crash, which explained a big drop in minor accidents it reported.

The industry, since 2001, has steadily tried to assure the public that all is fine with the railroads because accident rates are falling. Then came eight CSX derailments in seven weeks as 2006 turned into 2007. That prompted the Federal Railroad Administration to send inspectors out across 23 states. Their inspections of CSX found more than 3,500 violations, 199 of them rated serious cases of failure to comply with the law.

What no one reported at the time is that railroads are by far the most deadly form of commercial transportation in the country, the exact opposite of the industry's carefully orchestrated campaign to deceive with statistics. "Freight rail is by far the safest way to move goods and products across the country," the Association of American Railroads tells the public.

Few people realize how deadly trains are because crashes usually involve one or two deaths and thus get little attention in the news. They also lack the emotional appeal of plane crashes, which fill us with a sense of dread because flying through the air at nearly the speed of sound seems to defy common sense.

Still, airliners are America's safest form of transportation by far. Some 600 million passengers board planes each year, yet often a year and sometimes several years pass between fatal crashes. Big trucks kill about 5,100 people per year, trains about 930, and airliners about 140.

Measure deaths by the distance traveled, however, and trains are 52 times more deadly than trucks. Trains kill 130 people per 100 million miles traveled, compared with 2.5 deaths in big-rig truck accidents and 1.9 deaths in plane crashes, Transportation Department statistics show. It is easy to miss that because the official government statistics use a measure of only a million miles per accident for trains, but 100 million miles for trucks and airliners.

Bad as those official figures are, they severely understate how dangerous trains are. Truckers drive on highways surrounded by cars. Trains run long stretches through rural areas where there are no crossings. In such places a crash would hurt only the engineers on board and perhaps some jackrabbits. If we had a measure of people killed per 100 million miles of travel in populated areas, where roads cross tracks and homes are almost as close by as freight cars parked on sidings, the death rate would be many times greater than the official figures.

Just as the CSX workers found ways to deal with demands that they inspect more track in a shorter amount of time, government agencies also adjust to unrealistic budgets. Some workers in private businesses fake reports and make slipshod repairs. The more noble of them work off the clock if necessary in an attempt to set things right. Some CSX workers testified that they worked extra hours for no pay, but that even these efforts were not enough to overcome the callousness of the railroad's management and its dogmatic belief in market ideology.

The government agencies, without anywhere near enough money to oversee safety, play similar games. They tell Union Pacific to not call, they write superficial reports, and when it comes to accidents at rail crossings, they thoroughly investigate only 4 out of 3,000 cases.

These responses are human nature at work, as predictable as eating when hungry. Give managers more than they can possibly do and they will find a way to redefine their workload to what can be done. When cuts in budget and personnel increase gradually, the public unwittingly accepts unsafe conditions, just as the clickety-clack of the rails lulled passengers into sleep until the Orlon Crossing's deadly repairs gave way.

Even a reliable system of safety rules means nothing, however, if there are no consequences for misconduct. At the end of the day, after litigation that went all the way to the United States Supreme Court, for CSX there were no consequences. CSX paid nothing for its recklessness.

CSX simply sent a bill to Amtrak seeking reimbursement. It sought, and got, the full amount it had paid to the injured and the families of the dead. Amtrak even paid the $50 million that the jury ordered to punish CSX. Since the government owns Amtrak, what CSX did, in effect, was to stick the taxpayers with its bill.

The jurors, though, had no idea. Reporter Walt Bogdanich, who won a Pulitzer Prize for exposing unsafe rail conditions, grows animated when he describes "this sham trial, an absolute sham in which everyone on the jury thought CSX was being punished and CSX knew that no matter what happened it would not cost them one cent."

When Amtrak was formed in 1971, the freight railroads persuaded Congress to let them stop carrying passengers. But they wanted more than to shed that obligation. The freight railroads wanted to be insulated from any claims arising from Amtrak using their rails. The railroads reasonably sought not to be responsible for claims arising out of misconduct by Amtrak. A crash caused by a drunken Amtrak engineer or a badly repaired axle on a passenger train should be paid for by Amtrak.

Congress looked out for the freight railroads, which unlike Amtrak were a vibrant source of campaign support. A federal law shields the freight railroads from claims by Amtrak passengers and anyone hurt by an Amtrak train. Under federal law all claims arising from Amtrak passengers, even in cases where Amtrak was not at fault, must be paid by Amtrak.

Under these rules it does not matter that Amtrak did nothing wrong, its trains traveling below the speed limit, its crew alert and sober, its rolling stock in sound condition. It does not matter that the courts found the cause of Paul Palank's death was CSX's reckless disregard for human life. Under the contract, all that matters is, at the moment the rails or a switch or a shoddy repair job gives way, does the train passing overhead belong to Amtrak? Only if a freight train is overhead when the failure occurs is the freight railroad on the hook for the damages.

What this means is that CSX and John Snow got a free lunch. You got stuck with their bill.

Economists have a term for situations in which someone gets rewards but has little or no incentive to avoid risk: a *moral hazard*. The term is usually applied in insurance cases. A policy that covers every cent with no deductible may cause people to be less vigilant about husbanding their lives or property. A policy may even encourage the unscrupulous to burn down a failing store to collect the insurance money and avoid bankruptcy. We are reminded of this most often by those exposés on local television in which a hidden camera captures a firefighter or construction worker building a brick wall in his backyard at a time when he was collecting workers' compensation. What we seldom see exposed are the roofing contractors whose disability insurance forms list 35 low-risk secretaries and 1 high-risk roofer, allowing them to cheat on their premiums.

Those who occupy the executive suite and gamble millions of dollars on the lives of others are rarely seen as engaged in morally hazardous conduct. Yet reward without risk is a form of moral hazard that blinds us to the consequences of our acts. The trade-off between safety and stock price is an important part of the story of how the ideology of blind faith in markets is remaking America. But the moral hazards of this blind faith are not limited to cutting corners on safety. We also have rules that encourage a new way to make the rich richer at the expense of working people. It is a strategy called *labor arbitrage*.

Chapter 4

CHINESE MAGNETISM

CHINA IS A MAGNET FOR CAPITAL. THE LOW COST OF ITS LABOR force and its nimble entrepreneurial class—aided by a government focused on creating wealth, jobs, and industrial capacity—draw investment at an astonishing rate. The Chinese communist government has created an economy that grows at 8 percent or more a year, more than twice the rate in the United States in good years.

So much capital flows from America to China that in a single year, 2005, Shanghai built more high-rise space than exists in New York City. A few years from now, Shanghai is expected to have 5,000 skyscrapers, more than twice the number built in New York City since Elisha Otis invented the modern elevator in 1853. The Chinese economy is a modern-day miracle, its growing prosperity celebrated worldwide as a victory for the forces of global free trade.

Yet free trade is hardly free. Like everything else, rules govern trade. Our rules encourage and protect trade. Every economist knows that major shifts in trade cause economic disruption. The costs of this disruption are being paid by the millions of Americans whose jobs are disappearing and whose hopes for the future are diminishing. How our government's rules help the rich grow vastly richer at the expense of almost everyone else in America, sometimes in ways that threaten our national security, is illustrated by the story of how one entire American industry, albeit small, succumbed to China's magnetic pull.

In 1982, competing groups of scientists around the world found a way to combine iron and boron with a somewhat rare earth called neodymium to make extremely powerful and lightweight magnets. These magnets quickly found a market in computer hard drives, high-quality microphones and speakers, automobile starter motors, and the guidance systems of smart bombs.

General Motors created a division to manufacture these magnets, calling it Magnequench. The automaker used the powerful new magnets in starter motors for cars and trucks, cutting their weight by as much as half. It even used the new magnets in the 11-pound electric motor of its Sunraycer, which won the first solar-powered vehicle race, its skin of photovoltaic cells converting Australian sunshine into electricity. GM also made 80 percent of the magnets used in smart bombs, the kind that can be guided to a target to maximize damage and, hopefully, minimize deaths of innocent bystanders.

About 260 people worked at the profitable Magnequench factory. Then in 1995 the automaker decided to sell the division. Because the deal was for only $70 million it attracted little attention. The buyer was a consortium of three firms led by the Sextant Group, an investment company whose principal was Archibald Cox Jr., the son of the Watergate special prosecutor whom President Richard M. Nixon famously fired.

In the few press reports Sextant got most of the notice, but the real parties behind the purchase were a pair of Chinese companies—San Huan New Material High-Tech Inc. and China National Nonferrous Metals. Both firms were partly owned by the Chinese government. The heads of these two Chinese companies are the husbands of the first and second daughters of Deng Xiaoping, then the paramount leader of China.

At the time of the sale, GM was trying to win permission to become a player in the burgeoning automobile and truck markets in China. Many companies made accommodation deals with China to get approval to enter the market there (though none dare call it commercial bribery). This was no ordinary concession for commercial reasons, but part of a policy by Beijing to acquire high-technology industries with military significance. One of those daughters, Deng Nan, was at the time vice minister of China's State Science and Technology Commission, whose responsibilities included acquiring military technologies by whatever means necessary.

Complaints about the sale of Magnequench were made to the U.S. government because of the military applications for the magnets. Still, the Clinton administration, an ardent proponent of globalization, approved the sale. It did impose one condition: that the new owners keep magnet production and technology in the United States.

Soon the new owners of Magnequench were busy buying up other magnet factories in the United States, including GA Powders, an Idaho firm that had used taxpayer money to develop the powerful new magnets. Once the new owners had a monopoly on production of these powerful magnets in the United States, they began shutting down facilities and moving manufacturing to China. By 2003, the original GM factory in Indiana was the last American production line for the powerful magnets. Once it closed and its equipment was hauled off, the United States became dependent on China for these magnets, including the ones needed for smart bombs.

Clearly, the promise to the Clinton administration had become hollow. Senator Evan Bayh of Indiana wrote to President Bush in 2002 expressing concern that shutting down magnet production and moving it to China was not improving national security. How could this sale possibly be good for America? Bayh asked. The senator, a Democrat, later told colleagues that "it's not very smart to rely on China for a critical component of an important weapons system for our country."

The significance of this became clear when the Chinese launched a missile in early 2007 that shot down one of their own satellites. In a war with the United States, the ability to knock out American eyes in the sky would give China a huge advantage. Few Americans got the point, however, after only one day of short articles and brief newscast reports, hardly any of which connected the dots.

That production of magnets made with neodymium is now a Chinese monopoly is not the end of the story. America cannot just resume making these magnets at any time. Not only is the technical knowledge largely gone, but America's only neodymium mine shut down in 1996. And 85 percent of our planet's known stores of neodymium are in one country: China.

The Bush administration has never answered Senator Bayh's questions about why it allowed this specialized form of magnet manufacturing to move to China. It has instead issued blanket statements asserting it has taken all appropriate steps to safeguard Americans from foreign threats. However, the Government Accountability Office, the investigative arm of Congress, does not share the administration's sanguine view of magnet production moving to China.

When foreign governments or firms want to acquire American companies whose business affects national security, the deals are supposed to be examined in advance by an official government review panel known as the Committee on Foreign Investment in the United States. Studies by the Government Accountability Office show the committee does little to secure the national interest. More than 1,500 such deals have been approved since the committee was created in 1988, only a dozen of which were sent to the White House for review. Only one of these was denied. That occurred in 1990 when the first President Bush killed the sale of a Seattle aerospace-parts maker to China.

The accountability office found that, in many of these deals, the committee examination took place only after the sale to foreign interests was completed, an exercise not in locking the barn door after the horse ran off, but in merely affirming that the latch had been left open.

Lax oversight has particular ramifications for national security, but broader and equally dire economic consequences arise from the unique way that the United States subsidizes offshoring through our tax system. This important story begins with a most curious Chinese law.

After President Nixon's visit to China in 1972, American oil companies sought to explore there. Right off, they asked the Chinese to enact a corporate income tax. The Chinese were bewildered. To a Communist Party official, taught that the state should own the means of production, a corporate income tax was a bizarre idea. Besides, who ever asks to be taxed?

All became clear when the Americans explained their intent. The American oil companies did not want to actually pay taxes, but to reduce their obligations to the United States government. The American businessmen and their tax lawyers explained that Congress taxes corporations (and individuals) on their worldwide income. With a Chinese corporate income tax, however, the taxes they owed to the United States would go down for two reasons. The first reason is that American business profits earned overseas are not taxed so long as the money stays offshore. The second reason is that the United States allows American companies to reduce taxes on their profits by the amount they pay to foreign governments. This is not the usual deduction worth 35 cents on the dollar, but a dollar-for-dollar credit. Thus a dollar of tax paid by Exxon Mobil to Beijing is a dollar not paid to Washington.

Like the Chinese income tax, this U.S. tax credit originated with the oil industry. Back in the 1920s, when drilling for oil was a risky game with many dry holes, the oil industry paid a uniform 12.5 percent royalty to the owners of oil taken from the ground. The House of Saud, having emerged victorious over the competing Arabian Peninsula warlords and in need of cash to maintain its newly consolidated power, wanted to raise the royalty rate. The Treasury secretary at the time, Andrew Mellon of the Pittsburgh banking and oil family, suggested a different approach. He recommended that the Saudis just tax the oil companies to raise money. Mellon then persuaded Congress to adjust the corporate income tax to give the oil companies—and any other companies earning profits over-seas—the dollar-for-dollar credit against taxes due to Washington.

Mellon's change in the government's rules was brilliant from the point of view of an oilman. The Saud family would get more money, the oil companies would be indifferent because American taxpayers would be picking up the cost of enriching the Saudis and, most important of all, there would be no competition over royalty rates, no risk that royalty rates would increase. Adam Smith would not have approved. He had warned of government fixing the market to benefit those with power and property. But then, who wants to compete when the government will fix the market for you?

The Chinese communists agreed to the request that they enact a cor-porate income tax, having experienced one confirming example of Len-in's dictum that "the capitalists will sell us the rope with which we will hang them."

The corporate income taxes paid in China are not like those in the United States. Instead of going for the general support of the govern-ment, money paid to Beijing is often used to benefit the company that pays. Taxes may finance a new road or railroad spur or police presence and other services the company requires.

The lesson in all this is that the top Chinese communist officials may have learned more from Adam Smith than the American capitalists who so often invoke his name. What the Chinese took from Smith is a deeper understanding of how government policy can guide, and misdirect, the invisible hand of the market. And, from their perspective, they fully grasped the idea of acting in your own self-interest.

But wait, there's more.

A company with operations in the United States and another coun-try can borrow money at home, deducting the interest and thus lowering its American taxes. At the same time it can earn interest on untaxed cash it keeps overseas. So when an American company closes a factory here and moves it to China, provided it meets some technical rules, it can deduct the interest charges on its United States tax return while building up profits offshore that may never be taxed.

On top of all of this, a company that moves its factory to China will not have to worry about pesky union organizers seeking more pay or even reasonable work rules, like toilet breaks and job safety committees. Mao said that political power grows out of the barrel of a gun, a cruel reality known to every grassroots union organizer in China.

During the Reagan years, China grudgingly agreed to play by a set of civilized rules in return for receiving most favored nation status with the United States, a huge benefit for countries trading with America. Later China joined the worldwide trade movement. China was supposed to impose basic environmental controls, treat unions fairly, and respect human rights.

For their part, China and other poor countries complain that such requirements were not imposed on America and Europe when they developed.

These demands by first-world trading partners were an attempt to level the playing field with workers in other parts of the globe while bringing rudimentary workplace advances to Chinese laborers. No one was under the illusion that China would follow the highest American or European standards for pollution controls or welcome organized labor demands, but by forging agreement on these issues, the humane aspects of modern life might get a toehold in China's developing economy. At least that was the plan. There is one significant group fighting proposals to give Chinese workers the right to organize—American businesses that want to pay as little as possible in China.

With near total impunity, China ignores rules it finds inconvenient. Counterfeit copies of American software turn up in the offices of the Chinese government. Pirated movies and music are openly sold on the streets of major Chinese cities. Reports of forced labor abound. Only government-controlled unions are allowed—and independent organizers sometimes are shot. Toxins pour into China's rivers and foul not just its air, but the air everyone in the Northern Hemisphere breathes. Dangerous additives designed to create the appearance of high protein content have been found in animal food, killing some American pets by destroying their kidneys. Later, toxic ingredients were discovered in some human food, toys, and toothpaste that China had exported to the United

States in 2007. Beijing did act to stem this particular scandal, by executing a former senior government official.

As recently as 1985 trade between the United States and China was balanced, with exports to China equal in value to imports from China. Since then exports to China have grown enormously, but imports from China have grown five times faster, government data show. In 2006 the trade deficit with China reached $232 billion. That equals more than $60 per month for every man, woman, and child in America.

To get a feel for how large this trade deficit is, think about how much you have in income taxes deducted from your paycheck. In 2004, when the trade deficit with China was $161 billion, it was significantly more than the $126 billion of income taxes paid by the bottom 75 percent of Americans. Politicians rile people up about the burden of taxes. But few of them take on the government rules that encourage ever-larger trade deficits that drain our wealth and put American factory hands out of work to help China prosper.

China suppresses many American imports. It imposes all sorts of barriers to trade that do not qualify as tariffs, but which still tend to suppress American imports. Japan has done this for years, coming up with safety rules, for example, to effectively block competition by American-made cars and many other products. Korea does this, too. Hyundai and Kia have learned to build reliable cars and now have 1,300 dealerships in the United States. There is just one Ford dealer in Korea. Ford sales are smaller than they were a decade ago. Korea exported 700,000 cars to the United States in 2006, but imported fewer than 5,000 American cars. That imbalance accounted for the vast majority of America's $13.3 billion trade deficit with Korea that year. Like Japan, Korea uses unique safety, tax, and other rules to make sure that so-called free trade creates an inflow at the expense of Americans, especially auto workers. Our government policy enables what would be better called unfair trade.

Trade with our two neighbors is also imbalanced. In 2006 we imported $136 billion more from Canada and Mexico than we sold to them, partly because we buy almost a third of our oil from them.

Census Bureau trade data show that in 2006 just four countries— China, Japan, Canada, and Mexico—accounted for 60 percent of our worldwide trade deficit of almost $764 billion.

The results of this tilted playing field have been disastrous for American factory workers and communities that relied on factories. Tens of thousands have lost their jobs to the rigged game the politicians, and their donors, call "free trade." Autoworkers have begun working under new contracts in 2007 that cut the wages by as much as $13 per hour. That is a pay cut of more than $26,000 annually. Compounding the pain are cuts in retirement benefits and health care. Together these throw workers who had reached the middle rungs of the income ladder back down into the lower half, while adding uncertainty about their incomes in old age. At the same time their counterparts in China are moving up the income ladder, though not nearly as far because China still has far more people than jobs and real unions are still ruthlessly suppressed. For the financiers who arranged these deals, and for the factory owners, however, the rules on trade set by our government have proven enormously lucrative.

To further understand how government policy is enriching the few and impoverishing many in America, it is important to understand the economics of trade and the new circumstances of globalization.

A basic principle of economic theory is *absolute advantage*. For centuries different regions of the world have prospered making goods that exploited the natural resources and native skills of that area, something that gave its citizens unique advantages in the marketplace. For example, it makes no sense to build a steel plant in Bora Bora, but a lot of sense to build one in Ohio, which is near iron ore, coal, and cheap barge and rail transportation.

A related principle is called *comparative advantage*. England and Portugal both make textiles and wines. However, the relative cost of making wine is higher in England while the cost of making textiles is higher in Portugal. Each country gains if it makes more of the product it is best at and trades for the other, which is why the British drink Portuguese wines and the Portuguese wear British cloth.

None of the comparative advantages are fixed to the ground, however. With capital flowing freely across borders, so do skills, flattening comparative advantage. Fine wines are now produced in California, Chile, and Australia. The cobblers of Italy cannot meet the global demand for shoes, even if they worked day and night. Most people can't pay Italian prices, either, so mass scale manufacturing of shoes and many other goods has shifted to China, where labor is steadily increasing in skill level. The Chinese now make seven billion pairs of shoes per year, a pair for everyone on the planet each year and then some. In theory, and in the long run, free trade should make the world richer because production will reach maximum efficiency as each country returns to the idea of comparative advantage, specializing in what it does best. But while waiting for this economic paradise to arrive by and by, people have to eat.

Thanks to the new rules governing global trade, the owners of capital dine very well. Free trade really means that capital flows freely across borders, and so do the products and services financed with that capital. Push a button and in a fraction of a second a billion dollars goes from Wall Street to Shanghai. Hire a ship and the products made with that capital come back to the United States. People cannot move as easily, however. Not only are there issues of language and culture, but governments impose rules on who can immigrate and what work they can do. The difference between rules governing the flows of capital and labor has created a powerful new force in the global economy: *labor arbitrage.*

On Wall Street there are billionaire capitalists who built their fortunes a penny, a nickel, and a dime at a time. Their business is called arbitrage, from a French word meaning decisive judgment. Arbitrage traders follow a company's stock on global stock exchanges. If the price of a company's shares is slightly lower in London than, say, New York, that difference can be captured as profit. The arbitrageur executes simultaneous trades to buy shares in the cheap market while selling the same number of shares in the higher-priced market. There are apartments in Manhattan filled with Renoirs and Monets bought from arbitrage profits.

Computer technology boosted arbitrage returns by making trades faster. Today trades are done by computers that spot price differences and execute trades faster than any human can.

Dave Cummings specializes in such turbocharged trading through his firm Tradebot Systems. His company employed about twenty people in a Kansas City storefront until 2003 when it moved to New York because Cummings had a problem with the speed of light. It takes 20/1,000 of a second for a signal from a computer in the Midwest to reach Manhattan. After careful study, Cummings concluded that cutting the time delay to just 1/1,000 of a second increased his firm's profits, even after taking into account the higher costs of running his business in New York City.

Exploiting differences in the price of labor between two markets produces profits, too. Indeed, the potential profit in global labor arbitrage makes stock arbitrage look like chump change.

Consider a factory paying $27 an hour to 1,000 workers in Indiana.

From the company's point of view, the total cost of employing these workers, including fringe benefits and taxes, is about $40 per hour. The company shuts the factory, packs the machinery in grease, and puts it on a boat to China, where the equipment is reassembled in a new plant. Unskilled workers can be hired in China for as little as a quarter an hour.

Manufacturing in China means some costs are higher. The company will need to send executives and managers to China regularly. It will have to maintain a few there full-time. Paying for American-style housing and private schools for an executive's children is costly, as is paying for the family's periodic home leave. Product quality may suffer, especially at first, which will also cut into profits.

Then there is the cost of shipping the manufactured product halfway around the world. However, sending a television set by sea from China to California costs less than shipping it by rail from California to Chattanooga, which in turn costs less than shipping it by truck to a suburban retail store.

Let's generously assume that all those added costs of doing business in China raise the effective cost of labor to the equivalent of $4 an hour. That means the owner of that Indiana factory can save $36 per man-hour worked by moving production to China.

Moving those 1,000 jobs to China adds $72 million to the company's annual profits if prices are unchanged—the $80 million not spent in the United States less the $8 million spent hiring Chinese labor and covering increased costs for shipping and executive travel.

In a competitive market there is simply no way that a company with 1,000 workers producing a widely available product can raise prices enough for the same volume of production to increase profits by $72 million if it stays in America. Even by moving to China it cannot capture all of that $72 million because competition means prices should come down as other manufacturers cut their labor costs by moving their production offshore. But so long as prices fall by less than the savings on wages, then profits are bigger when American companies move their factories to China. Even if prices fall so much that $70 million less revenue is collected, the company still makes a $2 million profit increase by going to China.

Politicians who favor more such trade frequently assert that free trade brings new investment to the United States from distant lands. But this foreign investment in the United States, known as *insourcing,* is not helping create jobs, government data show.

In 1990, foreign-owned companies employed 3.8 million Americans. By 2003 they had bought companies that employed another 4.5 million workers, as well as starting new companies that created 290,000 jobs. That suggests that by 2003 foreign-owned companies had more than 8.6 million employees in America before taking growth into account. They didn't.

Foreign-owned companies employed just 5.2 million workers, analysis of the official data by Robert E. Scott of the Economic Policy Institute shows. So, even foreign-owned companies are shedding jobs in America, not adding to them. The net effect of insourcing by foreign-owned companies was the elimination of 3.4 million American jobs. While insourcing creates some jobs, the constant pressure to move even those jobs offshore is the inevitable result of how our current government rules encourage this labor arbitrage.

Let's return to that fundamental economic principle of comparative advantage and what it means in this radically changed global context. In the global economy, a comparative advantage remains only as long as governments and companies protect it. In the case of the neodymium magnets, the United States developed and adopted a new technology that China now controls. So what happened? Three issues coalesced— tax rules that subsidize offshoring, a lack of political interest in holding on to a manufacturing resource that enhances national security, and the labor arbitrage rules that encourage moving jobs to China.

As a result of our government's policies and actions, the Chinese government was saved the risk and expense of developing a new technology with military as well as commercial significance. Further, Beijing acquired this technology at a bargain price because it used its leverage— controlling which American companies are allowed to invest there—to pay less than full value.

All of this leads to a hard truth. Under current government rules, destroying American jobs and creating jobs overseas is the single most effective way for manufacturing companies to increase profits. From the point of view of shareholders and executives, any policy other than moving equipment and jobs offshore as fast as possible is a waste of corporate assets. Executives have a duty under law to husband assets and earn the maximum profit. They have no duty to stop economic pollution. Given our current rules, any CEO who is not moving as fast as possible to move equipment and jobs offshore should be fired. Are those the rules we want? Are those the rules that will make our society prosper and endure?

Every economist is taught that while international trade results in overall gains to the planet, it also creates winners and losers. For the losers the results are grim. The losses they suffer are not temporary effects, like closing a factory for retooling, but permanent losses. The factory jobs that have gone to China, India, Bangladesh and other very low-wage countries are not coming back.

Another bedrock principle of economics is a tendency toward what economists call *equilibrium*. Most of us know this as simple supply and demand. When a frost damages the orange crop, or war in the Middle East reduces the flow of oil, then prices rise. People buy fewer oranges when they cost more, but they need gasoline to get to work so when prices rise they must cut spending on something else. How much price influences demand is called *elasticity*. Demand for oranges is elastic, for gasoline inelastic.

From the perspective of a company, people who do factory and most office work are so many oranges and tankers of gasoline; their labor is just another commodity purchased in the market. Minimally skilled labor is far more common in China than it is in the United States. This means that until the vast supply of Chinese labor is fully employed, the forces of supply and demand, combined with our government's current rules, will relentlessly force more and more jobs to move to China, depressing wages in the United States. The process will continue in other countries with vast labor pools and enough stability to attract capital. By the time a global equilibrium is reached and the downward pressure on American wages eases we will all be dead—and so may our great grandchildren's great grandchildren.

Traditional manufacturing work is not the only labor that is going offshore, either. Any work done on a computer can be moved overseas. Banks, software firms, and airlines now have people in India answering calls, eliminating a major source of modestly paid work in America. The big accounting firms now hire Indian firms to prepare tax returns. Ads in the *Los Angeles Times* are laid out by a company in India that promises 100 percent perfect copy every time. Computer-assisted design and engineering work is often sent to India and China. Reuters, the British news agency, fired 20 American and European journalists in 2004 and replaced them with 60 new hires in India, saying it was to save money.

White-collar jobs moving offshore may well be the next great economic issue confronting America. It is a problem that even the most ardent advocates of free trade are beginning to acknowledge has a huge potential to disrupt our society.

An emerging concern can be found in official statistics on advanced technology. China is selling ever more advanced technology to the United States, running a trade surplus in this high-value segment that tripled in just five years.

In the next decade or two, as many as 40 million American jobs will be at risk of moving overseas, according to an analysis by a leading supporter of free trade. That means that more than one in four jobs in America may evaporate. To put this in perspective, in 2007 there were about 147 million civilian jobs in America, fewer than 7 million people were unemployed, and another 4 million or so wanted work but had been without a job for so long that they were no longer counted in the labor force. The loss of 40 million jobs would be an economic catastrophe worse than the Great Depression.

This estimate was made by Alan Blinder, who was a vice chairman of the Federal Reserve under Alan Greenspan. Blinder, a respected economist at Princeton University, once wrote that he is "a free trader down to my toes." But his detailed analysis of how many Americans hold various types of jobs shows that almost every kind of work done at a computer or with a telephone is vulnerable.

Losing those jobs would mean wasting a vast investment in education, not to mention the toll such disruption is likely to take on individuals, families, our sense of the future and ourselves, and perhaps even the domestic tranquillity we have taken for granted for so many decades.

"The balance is shifting against us," Blinder asserted about jobs moving overseas. "If you look backward you see low-skill, drudgery work like call centers. If you look forward you see a lot of professional work like accountancy" going overseas.

Trade, he concluded, is no longer confined to products you can ship in a box, from automobiles to zithers. It now extends to any service that can be performed electronically. We are, Blinder wrote in *Foreign Affairs* magazine, at the beginning of the third industrial revolution. It might better be called the Triumph of Global Capital over Jobs Revolution.

The first industrial revolution was the great movement from farm to factory that began right after Adam Smith's time, as industrialization and the ability to manufacture identical products on a mass scale created both vast new wealth and a lot of the misery that Charles Dickens chronicled. Back in 1810, more than 80 percent of Americans lived and worked on farms, a figure that has dwindled to little more than 1 percent today, Blinder noted.

The second industrial revolution began in the middle of the twentieth century as services began to supplant the making of things. Today less than a sixth of jobs are in manufacturing, while services provides roughly the same share of jobs that farming did in 1810, as Blinder wrote.

Blinder says we are in the early stages of the third revolution, one he calls the information age. "The cheap and easy flow of information around the globe has vastly expanded the scope of tradable services, and there is much more to come," Blinder wrote. "Industrial revolutions are big deals. And just like the previous two, the third industrial revolution will require vast and unsettling adjustments in the way Americans and residents of other developed countries work, live, and educate their children."

Blinder believes that direct service jobs, such as making beds in hotels, must by their nature stay in America. But even some jobs we may think of as direct service are already at risk or may become so as technology advances. At the Hilton, you can get your room key from a kiosk, reducing the need for front desk clerks. Radiologists have already begun to see the reading of X-rays move offshore. Blinder said he thinks most physicians' jobs are safe, but a look at technology journals reveals that doctors have done surgeries with remote robotics, so one day residents of Boston may be operated on by doctors in Beijing.

There are reputable economists who say Blinder is dead wrong about tens of millions of existing jobs being at risk. Blinder himself says that fewer than half of the jobs at risk will actually migrate offshore. And even those who agree with him expect new economic demands to create new jobs. After all, in the sixties, there was a fear that computers would automate so many functions that by today many millions would be out of work. Instead, computers created new, and often interesting, work opportunities. And the digital economy has had the curious effect of increasing demand for paper, ink, and file cabinets. Still, just 15 million jobs going offshore would mean 10 percent of the jobs now in America would migrate.

The first two jobs revolutions had in common one trait—people of average or even below-average intelligence could do many of the jobs with no more than a high school education. Will that be true in the digital, high tech third wave? And if it is not, what will be the consequences of living in a society where the brightest and hardest working are rewarded and almost everyone else is reduced to servant-level jobs and wages?

Among leading economists, the belief is nearly universal that this third revolutionary wave rolling across the globe is so powerful that nothing can stop it or even alter its course. There are, Blinder says, no cures, just palliatives. He suggests spending more on job retraining, changing the education system for the future, making health care available to all whether they have a job or not, and improved protections for pensions. Training and education and health care must be financed, whether by government or private means. In a future in which tens of millions of high-paying jobs migrate offshore this raises an obvious question—who would pay for these economic Band-Aids?

To just assert that globalization will have its way with our future and that a jobs revolution is unstoppable and uncontrollable is both irresponsible and dangerous. Yet that is just what many of our political leaders and their economic advisers say on television every day. On the television programs that tout stocks, anyone who questions free trade is ridiculed by the hosts, who brook no serious discussion.

Overall, the net result of our government policies is that America is selling its wealth to China and other countries, not unlike the widow of a profligate husband who must part with the art, the furniture, and eventually the house to sustain herself. At the end of 2006, the United States was spending more for what it bought overseas than it sold, resulting in a record trade deficit of $902 billion. That meant that for every dollar generated by the American economy about seven cents was leaving the country, worsening America's status as the world's most indebted nation. Just a generation ago we were the world's leading creditor nation.

As Warren Buffett calculates it, America is selling close to 2 percent of its wealth each year to sustain our appetite for imported oil and cheap manufactured goods, many of them mere trinkets. Once we get down to selling the house, how will the children and the grandchildren live? And what of generations yet unborn?

Revolutions, unchecked, bring violent change that destroys the good and the innocent. Karl Polanyi, one of the most influential anthropologists, wrote in his 1944 book *The Great Transformation* that the rise of fascism in the thirties and World War II resulted from masses of scared people, with no sense of control over their economic destiny, acting in ways small and great from economic fear and the panic it induced. In America today, out among the people who are not major campaign donors, there is economic anxiety aplenty, a rational response to the loss of so many well-paying jobs to China and other countries with more workers than work. It would not take much to turn that anxiety into irrational fear. Yet our leaders have little time to truly understand the concerns of people who do not pay to be heard with their campaign contributions, so we get policies skewed toward the interests of the rich and powerful.

The whole premise of America is that we are free to choose our destiny. It is only through constant critical evaluation of our circumstances that we can identify new problems and address them. We can react to the forces of change and shape them, or at least adapt to them, so that we maximize the benefit and minimize the harm. Or we can just let a narrow but powerful segment of our society continue to have the rules written to suit their desires. Better to elect leaders with the judgment to explore what can be done than to risk an economic disaster that brings forth leaders who will exploit our misfortune and, as happened in the thirties, scare us into relinquishing our liberty.

Of course, life is not all work. But even when it comes to play, the culture of taking from the many to enrich the few infects our society, as we will see next.

Chapter 5

SEIZING THE COMMONS

THE DOOR TO APARTMENT 24C OPENS ON A HALLWAY KITCHEN THAT flows into a central room crowded with furniture as plain as it is solid. Everywhere there are books. A few rest atop the wrought-iron skeletons of three treadle sewing machines, forced into retirement by the advent of electricity until given new employment as end tables.

Ed Hogi found Apartment 24C in a nearly new building in the South Bronx in 1976. When he showed it to his wife, Joyce, she knew instantly that this was the best place to raise Jana, Marc, and Francesca. It came with the luxury of three bedrooms. It was also just steps from a subway stop, where people living in the poorest congressional district in America are seamlessly transported beneath the neighboring congressional district, the richest in America, on their way to the vast job market in midtown and lower Manhattan.

What captivated Joyce was what she saw from the big windows along one wall of the central room. To the far left, she saw Yankee Stadium. Its noise and bright lights would be an annoyance, but mercifully for only 81 home games each year. What delighted her was a green ribbon of urban parks that seemed to flow from the House that Ruth Built. One block featured tennis courts, another a swimming pool, others fields of grass for running and playing catch. Hundreds of oak trees ensured cooling shade in summer. There was even a cement rink where the Hogi children would learn to ice skate in winter and to roller skate in summer.

The parks that nurtured the Hogi children and countless thousands more were the dream come true of an Irish immigrant named John Mullaly. He laid an early stone in the foundation on which America's vast and prosperous middle class was built, a foundation to whose condition few people give much thought.

Mullaly was a reporter for the old *New York Herald* in the years after the Civil War. He wrote about the squalid conditions of the immigrant class. He reported on cramped tenements where disease flourished. And he noticed that poor children had no place to play except the streets, which before cars and buses were littered with horse apples. In 1881, approaching the age of 40, Mullaly quit newspapering. He persuaded some men of means to finance a campaign to provide New York City with parks, not just for the nearly 2 million who then lived there, but the millions more that he was sure would come.

At the time, Paris had an acre of park for every 13 residents, Chicago and Boston an acre for every 100. In New York the politicians had also promised an acre of park for every 100 people, but reality was closer to one acre for every 1,500. Mullaly argued that for $8 million, a vast park system could be built that would make the city more attractive. Delay, he warned, would drive up costs as the tide of immigrants made cheap land on the fringe of the urban core expensive.

Mayor William Grace fought the plan, saying it would cost $20 million. That failed to staunch public desire for places to play, relax, and escape urban drudgery, so the mayor mounted a disinformation campaign. Squads of men spread through the tenements warning that the parks would cost $50 million. They said it would force big rent increases, a scary prospect in an era when hunger was common. And they said the whole thing was a scheme to enrich a few by gouging the poor.

The charges resonated. Poverty was a common experience for both native born and newcomer in nineteenth-century Manhattan. People saw government as intimately connected with their own fortunes. They paid attention to who was getting rich off their taxes, especially when they received little or nothing in return. More than a century later, the mayor's false charges would have unexpected significance.

Mullaly spent the rest of his life fighting for the park system. In the end it cost what he said. Today the Bronx has the only extensive park system among New York's five boroughs. Greensward today links Van Cortlandt, Bronx, and Pelham Bay Parks as well as Crotona, St. Mary's and Claremont Parks.

One bitter cold winter day in 1915, John Mullaly, about age 72, was found dead in his tenement bedroom. He had 15 cents in his pocket, the equivalent of about $3 today. The official lies about soaking the poor so that the few could grow rich were just that, lies. While today sitting officeholders sometimes arrange to have buildings named for them, 14 years passed before the city government honored this selfless man, renaming part of Macombs Dam Park after Mullaly.

Joyce Hogi knew none of this when she looked down from the narrow balcony of Apartment 24C. Like everyone else, Hogi took the parks for granted and assumed they would always be there. She never imagined that someone might covet this commons until one July day in 2005. Hogi, by then a widow and a grandmother with a swimmer's cap of white hair, spotted a flyer on the windshield of a car parked along the Grand Concourse in the Bronx near her home. The flyer announced that Mullaly Park, and part of Macombs Dam Park, would be demolished.

Soon Hogi learned that a month earlier, in just eight days and with no public notice, the two parks had been taken away from the people and given to a billionaire. Quickly usurping the commons required careful coordination at every level of government from city council members in the Bronx and the mayor in Manhattan to the statehouse in Albany and federal officials.

The beneficiary of this exercise in seizing the commonwealth to promote the *narrowwealth* was George Steinbrenner, principal owner of the New York Yankees. The parkland was seized for a new stadium with 60 luxury skyboxes, larger and more lavish than the 18 that had been grafted onto the girders at the original stadium. Luxury boxes allow the corporate rich to enjoy commercial sports without having to mingle with the masses, which is to say with their customers and employees. The skyboxes at stadiums, both commercial and collegiate, connect to private passageways that permit the box owners and their guests to avoid the jostling crowds when the game ends and everyone rushes for the exits. The corporate rich pay a great deal for the privilege of being separated from the crowds, virtually all of it tax deductible—meaning, in turn, that the hoi polloi bear part of the cost of being segregated from their economic betters.

Just as the public financed Mullaly Park, so too are tax dollars financing the new Yankee Stadium. Estimates of the public share started out at $229 million, then jumped past $300 million and then $600 million. The ultimate cost will almost certainly be more. Refurbishing the old Yankee

Stadium in the early seventies, budgeted at $25 million, actually cost $119 million. For the new stadium, all cost overruns are supposed to be paid by the Yankees, but more subsidies can be layered on later, too.

How did Steinbrenner get such solid support from elected officials that they would all work in secret to help him steal the parks like a thief in the night? He hired people with influence and flattered others, notably former mayor Rudy Giuliani, who could be seen grinning under his Yankees cap at many home games. The local council and state legislature members were bought off, legally, with free tickets they could give away to home games and small grants they could direct to community groups.

Federal officials came to inspect the parks. Because tax dollars had been used to improve the parks, the land could not be seized unless parks of equal value replaced them. The officials were told that the stadium project had the backing of every important political official. The federal officials were also told that there were no public protests, which was true, but only because the public had no idea what was going on. While the Joyce Hogis were kept in the dark, Steinbrenner was not. On many of the e-mails tossed back and forth among government officials at all levels, the Yankees were copied, as Patrick Arden of the *Metro New York* newspaper discovered.

The Yankee Stadium subsidy was, in an odd way, a vindication for the concerns voiced by Mayor Grace more than a century before. This time there really was a scheme to use parks as cover to take from the many to benefit the few. The difference was that the twenty-first-century mayors, Rudy Giuliani and Michael Bloomberg, were eager to open the public purse for Steinbrenner, to take from the many to benefit the few.

Today, all over America, state and local governments lavish funds on commercial ballparks while holding public parks to a starvation diet and allowing buildings to deteriorate, grounds to go to weeds, and activities to grind to a halt. The number of full-time recreation professionals fell during the eighties and nineties. Adjusted for population growth, park staffing by full-time professionals is below the levels of the sixties.

Cities switched to part-time workers, whose numbers nearly doubled during those years. The part-timers work for low pay, with few or no benefits. They also tend to have little training.

Starving parks comes at a price much higher than rundown buildings and absent flowers. It also means idle young hands do not have opportunities to play games, learn skills, and interact with others in healthy ways, but instead turn to what opportunities are available, often in the "devil's workshop."

A few years after the Hogis moved into their apartment in the South Bronx and began enjoying the nearby parks, something quite different was taking place across the nation in Los Angeles. In 1978 California voters passed Proposition 13, which promised relief from rapidly rising property taxes. Howard Jarvis and other promoters of the initiative talked incessantly about how good it was for homeowners. The truth was that two-thirds of the savings went to industry, business, and landlords like Jarvis.

With passage of Proposition 13, local governments in California felt an immediate and sharp drop in property tax revenues. Spending on street maintenance, libraries, and parks, among the more visible areas, were all slashed. Within eight years the Los Angeles city parks staff was cut in half. These cuts would have been even deeper but for a plan developed by James E. Hadaway, the city parks director. He devised a fix that has become increasingly widespread at all levels of government: charging fees.

These private funds, Hadaway said, would only be supplements to enhance the parks budget, to provide extras for those who paid for extra services. But within a few years this policy produced two systems of parks, separate and unequal.

In the prosperous areas, on the Westside and the hillsides of the San Fernando Valley, the fees flowed and the parks flourished. Flowers blossomed on the edges of lush lawns while air-conditioned community centers with clean carpets offered an array of programs, even ski trips.

In places where people of lesser means lived, like Pacoima on the northern side of the San Fernando Valley and the flats south of downtown, the parks withered. Not enough people had money to pay fees for recreation "extras" so many recreation programs for children just ended. Many of these parks, 75 of which the city officially labeled troubled, operated with one staffer, few balls, and dry water fountains. They became dead parks.

Hadaway's agency sent canvassers out to public places to ask people directly about the parks. Most people reported being afraid to use their neighborhood park, with the level of fear highest in working-class neighborhoods, especially those on the edge of public housing projects where joblessness was endemic. "They feel the parks are unsafe," Hadaway said of the city as a whole, adding ominously, "I believe them." His director of security called them "terrorized parks."

The parks with yellowed lawns, hot and dirty recreation buildings, and too little money for qualified leaders to plan and organize activities quickly evolved. They developed a new social ecology, ruthless and damaging to young lives. Gangs filled the vacuum. In interview after interview those gang members willing to talk to me expressed remarkably similar views of the world. The police, they said, were just another gang, no better than their own, but officially sanctioned. Some said it did not matter whether they committed a crime or not, because the cops would find a way to frame them and send them off to prison. In this, without knowing it, they had intuitively grasped the reason for William Blackstone's famous observation that it is better that some who are guilty go free than even one person who is innocent be wrongly imprisoned—so that people have reason to obey the law because it is just.

In the dead parks, crime was rampant. A careful observer could see folded greenbacks furtively exchanged for packets of folded paper filled with drugs. Turf wars over perceived slights brought young men brandishing guns while, for reasons we shall see later, frantic calls to the police by park directors often went unanswered for hours, if at all. The cruel reality of this separate and unequal funding forced many parents in Los Angeles and other cities to keep their children home, denying them part of the foundation for successful lives as adults, denying them what Joyce Hogi so treasured in New York for her own three children.

In the elbow of the downtown Harbor Freeway ramp that heads west into the Santa Monica Freeway sits Toberman Park, one of the deadest of the dead. Herb Price, the Toberman recreation director, sat in one of two decrepit office chairs that wobbled constantly and seemed about to collapse, their quality on a par with his dark and unpainted office, the sunlight obstructed by layers of dirt and the shadows from heavy metal screens. Would-be thieves had pried back the screen corners in several places before they gave up, perhaps realizing there was nothing inside worth taking.

"What's different today from the sixties is the drug problems and the gang members," Price said. Back then the city had money to keep kids busy. Gangs were a much smaller problem, their pool of recruits kept out of trouble by an almost limitless supply of organized activities from softball games to making sculptures with Popsicle sticks and glue. The city also provided jobs to college students, who enforced, however inexpertly and unevenly, boundaries on behavior. But as the budgets were cut, healthy activity faded away, gangs rose to deadly prominence, and drugs became freely available until, Price said, "about once a month, I have to call the paramedics because someone OD'd."

Price and other recreation workers, including part-timers, were told their job duties included maintaining order, which often meant telling drug users and gang members to leave. Few were courageous, or foolish, enough to confront gang members. But when they called the police for help the cops often failed to show. When they did, the cops usually came in several cars, each with two officers carrying guns and wearing Kevlar vests. "It's dangerous here and the city won't even talk about hazard pay," Price observed dryly.

At two dozen parks, groups of children gave interviews to a stranger in which they articulated the boundaries of various gangs. There were few differences of opinion about which streets were safe to cross. Some boys and girls said they wished they could go swimming on hot days, but they almost never did because between their homes and the public pools lay territory too risky to cross, even with a grown-up holding their hand. All of these youngsters were familiar with a chilly entry into the lexicon of urban life—the drive-by gang shooting.

Wise as they were to nuances of gang culture and geography, few of these children, who were mostly between 7 and 11, had been to Disneyland. Most had seen images of the Magic Kingdom on television, yet had no idea it was within an hour's drive. In the parks where fee money was abundant, however, everyone seemed to have a story about one of their visits to Disneyland, some from trips organized at their neighborhood park recreation center.

Among the youngsters at the dead parks, hardly any had actually seen the Pacific Ocean beaches, even though they lived within a few miles of the shore. Not one child asked how he or she might get to the beach or pursued the stranger's suggestion that, since the beaches were free, they could play on the sand and in the waves all day if their parents took them. Many said they had seen the beaches on television, but that was their only connection to what most Southern California youths treat as a birthright, the beach culture of sun, surf, and fun music. In park after park, their answers were a depressing indication of the tight boundaries that life had already imposed on their expectations for their futures.

The proponents of markets as the solution to all problems want to eliminate public parks. Some of them attack parks on moral grounds, while others say they are economically inefficient or demonstrate how socialism pervades American society, threatening freedom.

The Cato Institute, the nation's leading promoter of libertarian ideals, laid out the case for eliminating public parks in 1981. The second issue of the *Cato Journal* called for "the outright abolition of public ownership and the transfer of the parks to private parties" because financing parks through tax dollars means "coercion." Instead, Cato argued, "existing public parks could either be given away or sold to the highest bidder."

A key assertion was that because visitors are not charged, parks are overused. That is the exact reverse of what happened in Los Angeles. Park use was heaviest where people were affluent enough to pay fees. In poor and working-class neighborhoods, cuts in government spending and a lack of private resources to replace public funding resulted in woefully underused parks.

Milton Friedman, the intellectual godfather of market-solution prophets, urged the elimination of national parks when he was Barry Goldwater's economic adviser in the 1964 presidential election. As for city parks, Friedman wrote that putting up tollbooths to charge everyone entering would be too complicated given the small size and multiple entry points of most parks. This was presented as a matter of reluctant practicality, not principle.

Ranking not far below Friedman in the pantheon of market-solution prophets are F. A. Hayek, and Ludwig von Mises, who was Hayek's mentor. Hayek won a Nobel in economics and his book *The Road to Serfdom* is a key part of the free market economic gospel.

The Ludwig von Mises Institute denounced public parks in 2007 as "nature socialism." The institute declared that "the formation of state and national parks must, at some point, use aggression" because even when parkland is donated to government "from that point on its maintenance and management would require victimization through further taxation." Any land owned by the government involves "the violation of rights," the von Mises Institute concluded.

Such arguments may seem extreme because they have received little news coverage. The nutty idea that parks pose a danger to freedom is widely discussed, however, among those who have been making government economic policy for much of the past three decades. And these ideas, and the journals in which they are presented, are basic source documents for the influential editorial page of *The Wall Street Journal*, which champions policies that make the rich richer.

Under even sharper assault are special-purpose public parks, notably municipal golf courses. In North Carolina, the San Francisco Bay Area, and other places municipal golf courses are denounced as subsidy schemes because their fees typically do not cover their full costs, at least not the way the money is accounted for in city budgets.

Whether these golf courses may save money by, for example, keeping people active and thus holding down Medicare costs is not measured in city budgets or contemplated by market ideologues. Nor is the aesthetic benefit of greenery in tightly packed cities. What is most curious, though, is that these attacks ignore using the market to measure the value of parks. Land near urban parks typically sells for significantly more than land without such amenities. The extra property taxes thus generated have been shown in some places to more than make up for the untaxed value of parks even when they generate no fees.

Suggestions that municipal golf courses serve a public purpose, that they add a thread to social cohesion and stability, are rejected out of hand. The market ideologues see only a subsidy for those affluent enough to afford golf clubs—or children allowed on a swing without paying a fee. People who buy tickets to a movie theater, the argument goes, get no such subsidy.

Besides, the Friedmanites say, government should not be competing with private golf courses. The land should be sold to developers, at least in San Francisco, the money used to relieve the burden of taxes. Thomas Sowell, the economist who holds the Friedman chair at Stanford's Hoover Institution, and the John Locke Society barely give a nod to the idea of parks as amenities that help sustain a healthy society, the idea of parks championed by John Mullaly.

At the same time that public parks have atrophied in many cities for lack of public funds to maintain them, the market for commercial ballparks is flourishing, as we shall see in the next chapter.

Chapter 6

PRIDE AND PROFITS

ROM ST. PETERSBURG TO ST. LOUIS AND BEYOND, CITIES THAT DID
not have a big-league baseball, football, hockey, or basketball team
have built stadiums and arenas in the hope that they would come.
Smaller cities, like Rochester, New York, built stadiums for less popular
sports like professional soccer, even when there was no hope the facilities
could pay for themselves. Often there was no sign that team owners had
put their own money at risk.

The beneficiaries of this spending pepper the Forbes 400 list of the
wealthiest Americans. At least 27 of these billionaires own major sports
teams. Nearly all of them have their hands out.

Arthur Blank, a founder of the Home Depot, owns the Atlanta Fal-
cons football team. Mark Cuban, the Internet entrepreneur, owns the
Dallas Mavericks basketball team. H. Wayne Huizenga, who made a fortune in trash hauling and another with Blockbuster, owns the Miami
Dolphins football team. Mickey Arison, whose Carnival line carries half
of all cruise passengers, owns the Miami Heat basketball team. They are
just a few of the billionaire owners of commercial sports teams who have
stuffed gifts from the taxpayers into their already deep pockets.

The billionaire team owners seek these payments because commercial sports is not a viable business, at least not as it is operated in America.
Although baseball, basketball, football, and hockey teams are all privately
held, they disclose limited information about their finances. From that
data, one crucial fact can be distilled: while some teams are profitable,
overall the sports-team industry does not earn any profit from the market. Industry profits all come from the taxpayers.

In a market economy, the team owners would have to adjust or cover the losses out of their own deep pockets. Instead they rely on the kindness of taxpayers to enrich themselves at the expense of the vast majority who never attend these sporting events.

Subsidies for sports teams have grown steadily. From 1995 through 2006, local, state, and federal governments spent more than $10 billion subsidizing more than 50 new Major League stadiums and countless minor league facilities. "This trend is only accelerating: Government spending on sports facilities now soaks up more than $2 billion a year," Neil deMause, author of the book and Web site *Field of Schemes* told Congress in 2007.

According to *Forbes* magazine, the Big Four sports had revenues in 2006 of $16.7 billion. They counted a tenth of that, slightly less than $1.7 billion, as operating income, which is one way to measure profits.

Putting together the estimates by *Forbes* and deMause shows that the entire operating profit of the commercial sports industry comes from the taxpayers. The subsidies, in fact, cover a third of a billion dollars in operating losses before this boost from the taxpayers pushes the industry into the black.

Another way to look at these figures is to consider the subsidy a discount on the prices fans pay for tickets. There are about 135 million tickets sold by the Big Four commercial sports each year, so the subsidy

COMMERCIAL SPORTS

SPORT	OPERATING PROFIT* (IN MILLIONS)
Baseball	$ 496
Basketball	$ 207
Football	$ 832
Ice Hockey	$ 125
Total	$ 1,660
Subsidy	$ (2,000)
Net Loss before Subsidy	**$ (340)**

* Before interest, taxes, depreciation, and debt repayment

Sources: *Forbes; Field of Schemes*

equals about $15 per ticket. As we shall see, however, the subsidies do not actually flow to the ticket buyers, who instead pay above-market prices.

Also, the figures from *Forbes* cover only operating profits and losses, not all costs. No business or industry can continue in the long run without covering all of its costs. Not taken into account by *Forbes* were interest paid on borrowed money, taxes, and paying down debt. Add in those costs and the actual losses for the commercial sports industry, absent subsidies, are far greater than $340 million a year.

Subsidy economics tends to drive prices up, not down, as recipients chase subsidies more than customers. Adam Smith figured this out in 1776. He examined the subsidies in his day for commercial fishing. In his era the word *bounty* referred to gifts the government bestowed on the owners of herring ships. He concluded that to collect subsidies, people will appear to engage in a commercial activity. Smith wrote:

> The bounty [subsidy] to the white-herring fishery is a tonnage bounty; and is proportioned to the burden [size] of the ship, not to her diligence or success in the fishery; and it has, I am afraid, been too common for vessels to fit out for the sole purpose of catching, not the fish, but the bounty.

To see how that observation applies to commercial sports, consider the failing Montreal Expos baseball team. Major League Baseball, which is a corporation jointly controlled by the team owners, bought the Expos in 2002. They kept the team in Canada for three more years, sustaining losses equal to what they paid for the team. Then Major League Baseball moved the franchise to the District of Columbia, renaming the team the Washington Nationals. The next year the league sold the team to a group of politically connected investors led by Theodore N. Lerner, a billionaire Maryland real estate developer. The Lerner group paid $450 million. Selling to the Lerner group allowed the other owners to recover what they had spent and make a profit of about $210 million. That is an extraordinary return on investment, nearly doubling the league's money in four years.

What caused the value of the team to more than double in four years? Did the market for baseball suddenly turn red-hot with fans eager to attend? Not at all. Major League Baseball attendance in 2005 was virtually the same as in 2000, the league's statistics show. Instead, the billionaires who own Major League Baseball went fishing for a subsidy.

Even before they moved the team, Major League Baseball sought taxpayer money for a new stadium in Washington. Eventually the city government agreed to spend $611 million on a new stadium. More than anything else, it was that subsidy that made the value of the team rise. In effect, the billionaire owners of the 30 Major League Baseball teams received a transfer of wealth from the taxpayers just by moving a failing team to a city willing to lavish more than a half billion taxpayer dollars on a new stadium.

Lerner's group appeared to pay a lot of money for the team. In reality, they got the team for free and may even turn out to have been paid to buy the team. How? The purchase price was $450 million while the subsidy is worth $611 million, or $161 million more than the purchase price.

If Lerner's group can capture just three-fourths of the subsidy, they will have effectively acquired the team for free. As we shall see in the next chapter, even a badly managed team was able to capture 80 percent of its subsidy, more than the Lerner group needs to make its effective purchase price zero. If the Lerner group captures more of the subsidy, then they will in effect have been paid to acquire the team.

Further, the Lerner group gets to sell the naming rights for the new stadium, a gift from the taxpayers worth many tens of millions of dollars. Citigroup, the bank and insurance company, is paying $20 million a year for two decades to have its name on the new Mets stadium in New York. A British bank, Barclays, agreed to pay the same amount once a new arena is built in Brooklyn for the New Jersey Nets basketball team, which plans to change its name to the Brooklyn Nets. (While that basketball arena benefits from free land and all sorts of tax breaks, it is mostly privately funded.)

But even that is not the end of it. The Washington Nationals have announced that when they move into their new stadium in 2008 they will raise ticket prices to almost the highest among the 30 Major League teams. The average price for season tickets will rise 42 percent, from $21 a game to $30. The most expensive seats will nearly triple to $400 from $140. Baseball teams moving into subsidized new stadiums and arenas on average raise ticket prices by 41 percent and some have doubled their average admission price, deMause calculated.

These increases will mean less spending by consumers on other recreational activities, from nightclubs and movie theaters to video arcades. One proof of this was observed by economists who study commercial sports subsidies. During the long baseball strike of 1994, business at bars and nightclubs in league cities boomed, cash registers filling with dollars not spent on expensive baseball tickets and stadium hot dogs.

What is truly perverse in the case of the Nationals is the reason that this particular team can charge so much for its best seats. These seats are not, as one might imagine, those closest to the action on the field. Instead, they are the seats that are in the sight lines of television cameras. Getting on television is valuable to politicians trying to implant a memory of their faces in the same way that shampoo bottles come in distinctive shapes, as visual clues to encourage purchases without thinking. Also, being seen with powerful officials has value for the rich and their lobbyists. A leading sports marketing consultant, Marc S. Ganis, noted that any sports franchise around the nation's capital can command sky's-the-limit prices for seats that enhance this symbiotic relationship between elected and corporate powers. "There is always a market for those great seats, especially those that are in the television camera angles," Ganis said. "With a new stadium in the nation's capital, where visibility and proximity to power is most important, these seats should sell very easily."

Less visible are commercial sports-team finances. In 1997 Paul Allen, cofounder of Microsoft and at the time the fourth-richest man in America, with a net worth of at least $21 billion, put 18 lobbyists to work engineering $300 million of Washington State taxpayer money for a new football stadium. The total cost to taxpayers for this gift is far larger than the advertised figure. By some estimates it totals close to three times the amount advertised. Once this public gift was assured, Allen bought the Seattle Seahawks football team.

This gift came with a condition, however. The law authorizing the subsidy requires that "a professional football team that will use the stadium" must disclose its revenues and profits as a condition of its lease to use the stadium. But Allen makes public only the finances of the shell company that signed the lease, First & Goal, not the team itself. Christine Gregoire, when she was state attorney general, promised that she would enforce the disclosure clause. But after the Democrat was elected governor in 2004, she had other priorities. (The Seattle Mariners baseball team, which is subject to a similar requirement, discloses team profits.)

The huge gifts of money that wealthy owners of sports teams wheedle out of taxpayers are a free lunch that someone must fund. Often that burden falls on poor children and the ambitious among the poor. Sports-team subsidies undermine a century of effort to build up the nation's intellectual capacity and, thus, its wealth. Andrew Carnegie poured money from his nineteenth-century steel fortune into local libraries across America because he was certain it would build a better and more prosperous nation, which indeed it did. These libraries imposed costs on taxpayers, but they also returned benefits as the nation's store of knowledge grew. That is, library spending is a prime example of a subsidy adding value.

Many people born into modest circumstances have risen to great heights because they could educate themselves for free, and stay out of trouble, at the public library. To cite one example, Tom Bradley, the son of a sharecropper, learned enough at the local library as a boy to join the Los Angeles Police Department. He rose to become its highest ranking black officer in 1958 when he made lieutenant. Bradley went on to be mayor for two decades. But today library hours, as well as budgets to buy books, have been slashed in Los Angeles, Detroit, Baltimore, and other cities, yet there is plenty of money to give away to sports-team owners.

Art Modell, who pitted Cleveland and Baltimore against each other in a bidding war for his football team, was asked in 1996 about tax money going into his pocket at a time when libraries were being closed. It was a well-framed question. His Baltimore Ravens is the only major sports team whose name is a literary allusion, to the haunting poem by Edgar Allan Poe for his lost love Lenore.

"The pride and the presence of a professional football team is far more important than 30 libraries," Modell said. He spoke without a hint of irony or any indication that he had ever upon a midnight dreary, pondered weak and weary the effect of his greed on the human condition. How many Baltimore children who might have become Mayor Bradleys will instead end up on the other side of the law? That may not be measurable, but that some will because of Modell's greed is as certain as the sun rising in the east.

We starve libraries—and parks, bridge safety, and schools—to enrich sports-team owners. Yet that industry does not produce a profit from the market, although some teams may. This would not surprise Adam Smith. Likewise, he would not be shocked to learn that instead of adjusting the pay of the employees who labor in the field to reflect market realities, player wages have soared. The average baseball salary is more than $2 million annually, and a few make 12 times that much. Subsidies, Smith wrote, embolden the imprudent and encourage waste:

> When the undertakers of fisheries, after such liberal bounties [subsidies] have been bestowed upon them, continue to sell their commodity at

the same, or even at a higher price than they were accustomed to do before, it might be expected that their profits should be very great; and it is not improbable that those of some individuals may have been so. In general, however, I have every reason to believe they have been quite otherwise. The usual effect of such bounties is to encourage rash undertakers to adventure in a business which they do not understand, and what they lose by their own negligence and ignorance more than compensates all that they can gain by the utmost liberality of government.

A few team owners have, however unintentionally, acknowledged that building new stadiums and arenas is not a viable investment.

In Seattle, Howard Schultz, the billionaire chairman of the Starbucks chain of coffee bars, wanted taxpayers to spend $202 million to expand Key Arena, where his Seattle Sonics basketball team played mediocre games. Schultz was not a pure beggar, unwilling to risk any of his own money like so many other team owners. He offered to put up $18 million of the estimated $220 million cost. In effect, he was seeking a 12-to-1 return on his money. But at least he had some of his money in the game. Sonics president Wally Walker explained that the team needed the taxpayers to pick up 92 percent of the cost because the team simply could not afford it. "I wish there was a way for it to work privately," Walker said.

Schultz threatened that his Sonics would fly off to Oklahoma City if he did not get this bounty. The tactic, which had worked so well for Modell and others, failed Schultz. Local voters overwhelmingly rejected his demands in 2006, a sign that at least some citizens have grown weary of making gifts to billionaires whose sports teams cannot turn a market profit. Schultz then sold the team to a group of Oklahoma investors.

Threatening to move a team unless the public pays up has become a finely developed enterprise. Arranging to collect this legal loot employs lobbyists, economists, and marketing firms, all charging hefty fees for their help in digging into the pockets of taxpayers. When Modell was playing Cleveland off against Baltimore, Betty Montgomery, then the Ohio attorney general, came up with a one-word description of this tactic: blackmail.

Such tactics work only because of one of the great economic ironies of our time. Commercial sports games are about competition, but the leagues themselves are exempt from the laws of competition.

The baseball, football, basketball, and hockey leagues control entry into the market, including who can buy a team and where it can play. The leagues deny membership to any team taken over by local government, effectively nullifying the constitutional power of eminent domain for any city that wants to buy its team to make sure it stays put. The power of eminent domain to force the sale of property is, however, used to acquire land cheaply for new stadiums, as we shall see in the next chapter.

Normally these restraints on trade would be a crime under the antitrust laws. But the Supreme Court in 1922 and again in 1953 exempted Major League Baseball from the laws of competition. The other three leagues—basketball, football, and hockey—are effectively exempted from most of the laws of business competition, as well. This exemption from the laws of competition is crucial to their power to extract subsidies. Without their power to control who can own a team and where it plays, the ability of team owners to extract subsidies would weaken and perhaps even evaporate.

The sports leagues are also exempt from the tax laws, although the individual teams are not.

In a free market anyone with the necessary capital could start a team and compete. That is just how soccer works in Britain. It also explains why Britain has so many more teams, 13 in greater London alone at last count. Their admission prices are much lower than American commercial sports teams. Even in the mega-market that is New York, commercial sports consists of just two teams each for baseball, basketball, and football, and three ice hockey teams. In a free market there would be many more.

The value of the leagues' exemption from the laws of competition is illustrated by the odd fact that Los Angeles, the nation's second-largest city, has no football team. So long as that city remains teamless, the owners of football franchises use the threat of moving to the nation's second-largest market to extract money through public financing of new stadiums, rent rebates, and other official favors. Surely this would seem incongruous to the settlers who called their community El Pueblo de Nuestra Señora de los Angeles de la Porciuncula.

The Town of Our Lady the Queen of the Angels of Porciuncula is named for a small chapel run by Francesco di Bernardone, the son of a rich twelfth-century textiles merchant. As a young man sporting about with the sons of noblemen he came upon a beggar. The others refused alms, but young di Bernardone emptied his pockets and gave all that he had, following the admonition of Jesus in Luke 18 to "go and sell that thou hast, and distribute unto the poor." This generous man came to be known as St. Francis of Assisi, the founder of the Franciscan order devoted to serving the poor, which began in his little chapel, called Porciuncula, or "little piece of land."

In New York City, the new economic order of taxing the many to give to the richest few drew sustained support from Rudy Giuliani, who likes being called America's mayor. Giuliani cut and trimmed the budget for parks and libraries. Over the years he slashed the very amenities and tools that enabled people to enjoy urban life and rise above their circumstances. Giuliani showed no such need for restraint when it came to funneling taxpayer money to George Steinbrenner, who made sure the mayor always had the most visible seats in the house. Giuliani, a self-described Yankee superfan, pressed for a new Yankee stadium in Manhattan, despite the economic reality that land in midtown is so valuable that all new buildings there are skyscrapers.

While high-rise office buildings create economic activity year-round, sports stadiums drain public resources while creating economic dead zones around their edges. Stadiums are to urban economies what surge tanks are to rivers.

Surge tanks are a byproduct of nuclear power plants, which generate electricity at a steady rate 24 hours a day. In the dead of night and morning, when demand for power is low, surplus electrical power is used to power gigantic pumps that lift vast amounts of water from rivers to storage reservoirs and tanks, like those on the Hudson River Palisades upstream from New York City. On hot afternoons and evenings, when demand for power peaks, the water is released, spinning turbines to generate electricity as the water flushes back into the river. Sucking water up and then flushing it back creates dead zones because fish and fowl cannot survive the fierce artificial currents. In the same way, having 50,000 or so people flow into a ballpark and then rush back out again 81 times a year kills economic activity in the immediate surrounding area. The logical place for a ballpark is where the foreseeable uses for the land are very low in value, like the edge of a city or a spit of land off the beaten track. Proposals for a ballpark in midtown Manhattan, or the downtown of almost any major city, are best filed away under "economic idiocy."

Teams seeking subsidies come up with reports purporting to show huge economic gains if a new stadium is built. Often the claims are uncritically accepted. The crucial issue when a subsidy is proposed is the impact on the finances of the local government, known as *fiscal impact*. Unless the annual flows of tax revenues more than pay for the bonds being issued, then some other part of the municipal budget will suffer. Even then it will probably suffer because people's budgets for recreation are limited. A dollar spent at the ballpark is a dollar not spent at a restaurant, bar, or other place of leisure time activity, thus transferring the jobs and economic effects from many businesses to a single sports team.

Joyce Hogi laughed when she read the reports claiming that the city would be tens of millions of dollars ahead, and her neighborhood would experience big economic gains. *You don't have to be an economist to figure out that this is nonsense,* she thought. "The Yankees have been here for almost a century. Look around at how they have made the South Bronx prosper," she chuckled. Hogi grinned at the thought that anyone would believe Steinbrenner. Besides, she noted, the new stadium would have fewer seats than the old one. And while the luxury boxes, fancy restaurants, and sports memorabilia shops might create more jobs, they were low-wage and seasonal, with no benefits or future.

New York City's Independent Budget Office, which analyzes city spending, did review the Yankee numbers. The experts could not find any hard underlying facts to support some of the Yankee figures, which grew larger in each new report. Ronnie Lowenstein, who ran the office, concluded that any gains from a new stadium were minor, if not imaginary.

Most of the news about Giuliani savaging the budgets for public parks while working to lavish money on commercial ballparks came as discrete events in separate stories. But a few writers started connecting the dots, like Charles V. Bagli in *The New York Observer* and later in *The New York Times*, and the team of Neil deMause and Joanna Cagan writing for an irregularly published Brooklyn zine. Soon deMause made commercial sports subsidies his specialty and began tracking stadium deals for the *Village Voice*, eventually pulling the public record together in *Field of Schemes*. Much of that record is cleverly obscured so that few have an appreciation of how thoroughly market principles have been trounced by this form of socialist redistribution to the richest.

One of the most interesting tidbits deMause dug up involved an unannounced gift of $25 million of public funds that Giuliani gave the Yankees during his last days in office. The mayor gave the Mets baseball team the same gift. What the mayor did was to let each team hold back $5 million a year on their rent for Yankee and Shea Stadiums, which the city owns, and use the money to plan new stadiums. The economic effect was the same as if Giuliani had ordered the New York police to stop every city resident at gunpoint and demand six bucks.

What Giuliani kept secret, and deMause uncovered, was that the Yankees used some of this money to hire lobbyists to arrange a further taxpayer subsidy for their new stadium. The team even billed taxpayers part of the salary paid to Randy Levine, the Yankees president. During Giuliani's term in office Levine was his economic development deputy, in effect the city official whose job was to arrange gifts from the taxpayers to rich investors who had curried favor with the mayor. Whether the Mets did the same is unknown because the city has spurned requests for records detailing how the Mets spent their $25 million.

The chutzpah required to bill taxpayers for lobbying against their interests was just one sign of how giveaways for the rich erode moral values. While our cultural myths include imaginary welfare queens driving Cadillacs, the reality is that many of our nation's richest take from those who have much less without losing a wink of sleep.

Levine, the mayoral aide turned Yankees president, revealed one aspect of this truth in 2006, as the city council prepared to formally approve the new Yankee stadium subsidy. Levine asserted in an interview that there was no subsidy. Reminded that the Independent Budget Office for the city had concluded that public gifts were the equivalent of immediately writing the Yankees a check for $275.8 million, Levine smoothly shifted gears. He said the budget office was not competent to measure the subsidy, which he valued at "only $229 million."

I asked Levine about the morality of this gift, whatever its size, and its coercive nature. Levine said he agreed that taxes are taken by threat of force, that they are not voluntary. So how did Steinbrenner the billionaire justify taking tax money from people with so much less? Levine, not missing a beat, replied that gifts from taxpayers to those who invest in big projects "are the way government works today."

There it is, plain as day, what subsidies for the richest are doing to America. Levine said he did not see any other dimension to the question. The government rules say that the rich can take from the poor and the middle class, so some among the rich do, and without qualms. To those doing the taking, that's that. Since the rules allow it, what's the beef?

Left out of Levine's cold calculus is how we arrived at these rules and who arranged for them. Left out is the role of campaign contributions in gaining the hearts and minds of politicians who make the rules and who know, if they want the money to keep flowing, that they must demonstrate fidelity, if not fealty, to their donors. Also left out of this calculus is any question about whether the rules we have are right, moral, or even practical.

For the recipients of money taken from others for private benefit, the rules act as a moral salve, allowing them to feel justified without examining their conduct. After all, they are just following the rules.

Remember, rules define a civilization. Rules tell us what kind of conduct is acceptable and what kind of people we choose to be. Policies that work against the general welfare undermine a society.

That Steinbrenner would eagerly stuff hundreds of millions of dollars from taxpayers into his own pockets with no qualms is not surprising. Steinbrenner has spent a lifetime soliciting subsidies with such gusto that even weakening national security has not tempered his lust for tax dollars.

During President Reagan's term a major national security goal, aimed at intimidating the Soviets, was building the Navy up to 600 ships. Projecting more American military power across the seas required new vessels to refuel other ships at sea. The Navy awarded a contract for two refueling ships at a cost of almost $100 million each to a Louisiana shipyard. It built them on time and within budget.

Two other oilers were to be built in Philadelphia, but the contractor went broke. Steinbrenner lobbied to get the hulls towed to his Tampa shipyard to be completed. Capt. Karl M. Klein, the Navy officer overseeing the contract, flew down to Tampa to check out Steinbrenner's shipyard. "I was shocked," Klein recalled. "I knew it wouldn't work.

"This shipyard was full of debris," he said. "It was literally littered with excess and unusable materials, some of which didn't even belong in a shipyard. There was no indication of any attempt to keep the shipyard clean." To qualify for the contract, Steinbrenner was required to own software that scheduled the complex tasks of building a ship to ensure an orderly flow of work and payments to suppliers. But the captain said, "They had no usable scheduling software." More amazing was that Steinbrenner was no newcomer to shipbuilding. He had spent his entire adult life pocketing subsidies under a federal law designed to make sure that the nation had the infrastructure and skills to build ships, even if it was cheaper to build them overseas.

Captain Klein started documenting all the violations and failures in Tampa. But his diligence was nothing compared to what Steinbrenner

had—friends in high places. Steinbrenner met with Senator Daniel Inouye of Hawaii, a Democrat. Another Democrat, Representative John
Murtha, a former Marine officer and a power on military spending, came
down to Tampa. "Where's the Navy, why are they doing this and causing all these problems" for Steinbrenner? Murtha demanded. Congress
ordered the Navy to keep feeding money to Steinbrenner. Soon a special
appropriation, a classic congressional earmark, sent millions of extra tax
dollars to Steinbrenner, despite the fact that the ships were not being
completed and Steinbrenner was not even paying his vendors.

Steinbrenner had his own version of events, one that goes to Adam
Smith's observations about outfitting for the subsidy, not the fish. "When
you buy a shipyard," he observed repeatedly, "you hire one welder, one
fitter, one painter, and 12 lawyers."

Klein thought, *That's true because you're not building or fixing ships;
you're getting contracts and fighting not to finish them.*

Before long the Navy had paid out more than $450 million. All it
had to show were two useless hulls, which to this day sit rusting in the
James River. The Senate Permanent Subcommittee on Investigations
held a hearing in 1995. On a claim of ill health, Steinbrenner escaped appearing. Captain Klein did show up, eager to tell the truth about Steinbrenner. Just as Klein eased into the witness chair, Steinbrenner's lobbyist
called a press conference outside the Senate hearing room. The reporters
hustled out into the hallway to get that story, not Klein's.

Three weeks later Steinbrenner was healthy enough to travel to
Washington. The billionaire was allowed to testify in private, out of the
glare of lights, cameras, and microphones. Harold Damelin, the chief in-
vestigator, asked Steinbrenner, "Did you ask Senator Inouye to assist you
in connection with the problem you were having with the Navy?"

How Steinbrenner interpreted the question goes to the way that superrich subsidy seekers rationalize reaching into your pocket. "When I
went in, no," Steinbrenner said. "I said to every single person I went
to—all I would like to have is fair treatment. I would like to be playing
on a level field. I never asked them specifically, 'Do this, get me the
money, do that.'"

Of course Steinbrenner did not directly ask, any more than the ser-
pent told Eve what would follow if she tasted the apple. Steinbrenner's
denial is on a par with the chairman of Exxon Mobil saying he does not
pump gasoline and mob boss Joseph Bonanno saying he had never seen
heroin. But then, could even George Steinbrenner live with himself if he

had to admit that he took from the poor so that he could have even more?

In building the new Yankee Stadium, Steinbrenner yet again exploited the taxpayers, this time by getting around a law written to protect them. In 1986, Senator Daniel Patrick Moynihan sponsored a law banning the use of tax-free bonds to finance stadiums, exactly the financing being used by the Yankees and the Mets. So how did Steinbrenner and the Mets owners get around that law? How did they manage to benefit from triple tax-free municipal bonds that add to the burdens of federal, state, and city taxpayers?

First, the Yankees and the Mets will not pay rent on their new stadiums, which the city will own. If they paid rent, the Moynihan law would prohibit the sale of tax-exempt bonds to finance the stadiums. But since the stadium bonds must be paid for, where will the money come from?

"These bonds depend upon an unusual arrangement for repayment," New York City's Independent Budget Office explained in a report. They sure do. Instead of paying rent, the Yankees and Mets bond interest and principal will come from PILOTs. That is an acronym for *payments in lieu of taxes*. Just as businesses that move to China have figured out how to make their tax dollars benefit themselves, so is the concept of private gain from taxes being applied with growing success within the United States by some of the richest Americans.

What happened next illustrates how thoroughly our government has been captured by the rich and powerful, how the assumption that favors must be granted to the rich permeates government today. The Yankees and the Mets went to the Internal Revenue Service for a special dispensation known as a *private letter ruling*. Anyone who is given such a letter can proceed knowing his or her tax breaks will be honored. This is true even if the letter is bad policy and even if it contradicts the law. These letters are issued by the IRS office of chief counsel.

IRS chief counsel Donald Korb, a lawyer as brilliant as he is contentious, gave the team owners what they wanted. Representative Dennis Kucinich, Democrat of Ohio, who wanted an explanation, summoned Korb to Capitol Hill.

Prickly as a cactus pear, Korb said that the law against municipal bond financing of commercial sports arenas was quite clear. It was not allowed. However, during the Clinton administration, someone had written regulations that created an unintended loophole. Korb adamantly insisted that the IRS did the right thing, giving the Yankees and the

Mets approval under the flawed regulations. He said that once the teams got what they asked for, he did the right thing by ordering up new regulations to close the loophole.

There was just one problem with Korb's reasoning—the IRS is under no obligation to issue a private letter ruling. Indeed, just days before Korb had complained that he did not have enough lawyers to issue all of the private letter rulings and other guidance sought by taxpayers. His solution was to ask private interests to draft new tax regulations and rulings, which government lawyers would then review and amend before making them official. Paul C. Light, a New York University scholar who studies the federal workforce, succinctly described Korb's proposal: "It's not the fox guarding the henhouse; it's the fox designing the henhouse."

Korb could have turned the fox away. He could have just deferred the Yankee and Mets requests, especially given the shortage of lawyers to issue such rulings. Then he could have sought to fix what he believed was an error in the regulations. Instead, Korb allowed the richest among us to get what they wanted, even though he had concluded that the law itself did not allow this result.

When it comes to finding ways to mine the Treasury, Steinbrenner is a master. But he has never pulled off the trick of one Texas man who championed a tax increase that flowed into his own pocket and then promoted himself as the champion of tax cuts.

Chapter 7

YOUR LAND IS MY LAND

MANY COMMERCIAL SPORTS FRANCHISES IN AMERICA HAVE NEVER earned a profit from the market. The only increases in value that the teams reported came from the taxpayers. Among them was the Texas Rangers baseball team during the nine years it was owned by a partnership put together by George W. Bush, a tax-shelter salesman who went on to become governor of Texas and president of the United States.

When the Rangers opportunity came along, Bush was a man of modest wealth, though he had a valuable asset in his father, then serving as president of the United States, as well as a gold-plated Rolodex. Young Bush got on the telephone and raised money from truly wealthy investors to buy the team. He bought a 2-percent stake for $600,000 using borrowed money.

On the surface the Rangers were not an attractive investment. Their owner had pulled them out of Washington in 1972 and moved them into an aging minor league stadium that guaranteed they would lose money. A subsequent owner, oilman Eddie Chiles, tired of his expensive hobby. Chiles was looking to sell the team before his time on Earth ran out. Bush told potential investors that buying the Rangers was a sweet deal because all the team needed to become valuable was a new stadium. He brimmed with confidence about solving that problem even though he had no experience in baseball, construction, or stadiums, and a track record of not paying close attention to the details that make or break oil-and-gas tax-shelter investments.

What followed was an early indicator of Bush's extraordinary success at marketing. Bush is arguably the greatest salesman of our time, having sold not just friends but political opponents on a war costing more than a trillion dollars and thousands of lives with the kind of pay-no-attention-to-that-pool-of-oil-under-the-engine polish that used car salesmen only dream about.

The Rangers investors had pockets plenty deep enough to build a new stadium, but that was not what Bush had in mind. Bush planned to have taxpayers pick up the tab. That would seem to be a hard sell in Texas, where root canals are more popular than taxes. But he succeeded.

One of his first moves was to threaten to move the Rangers out of Arlington, a prosperous suburb midway between Dallas and Ft. Worth. It was the same tactic Modell has used, the one that the Ohio attorney general described as a kind of blackmail.

The tactic worked. Bush and his allies arranged for a special referendum, held in January. Arlington voters were asked to approve a half-cent increase in the sales tax. The proposal emphasized how much of the money spent at Arlington's amusements parks, car dealerships, and shopping malls came from people who lived outside the city. That also meant that many of those who would be taxed would not have a vote. The Bush investor group hired professional campaign consultants—Democrats—to manage the election. The opposition, predictably, objected to higher taxes. More than that, they protested that it was just not right for people rich enough to finance their own stadium to force others to buy it for them. The campaign pros, with $130,000 to spend, easily rolled over the barely organized local opposition in the special referendum, in which few people voted.

The new stadium required about 17 acres of land. The Bush partners wanted more than 200 acres to develop a whole entertainment zone including hotels and restaurants. Not everyone wanted to sell their land. In a free-enterprise economy, the Bush partners would have had to bid up the price of land until willing owners decided to sell or, if that failed, move on to another location.

A free market, the kind Adam Smith wrote about and that Milton Friedman canonized, gives great power to reluctant sellers, especially the last owner, provided the project cannot succeed without his parcel. By holding on while others sell, the last person can command a premium price, sometimes an extraordinary price. That high price is also a reward for taking the risk that the proposed project will collapse, leaving the landowner waiting until another opportunity to cash in comes along.

Bush and his partners decided to ignore market principles. They were practical businessmen. They simply had the city of Arlington seize all the land they needed and more, using government's power of eminent domain to get the land they coveted, but were unwilling to buy in the market.

The Bill of Rights sets the standard for payment of seized property as "just compensation." Invoking eminent domain inherently lowers market values. It does this by putting a cloud over continued ownership, making *just* a synonym for discounted. Eminent domain also creates an incentive for governments to offer the lowest price they can get away with. Landowners who do not like the price offered by government can go to court. Such a challenge requires deep pockets to finance litigation, itself a risky enterprise. Most people, faced with a government determined to seize their property, just take what they can and get out.

When government uses its power of eminent domain for a public purpose—a new military base or a highway or to preserve a swamp that is nature's nursery for fish and fowl—the compelling question is whether an alternative piece of real estate could be used, perhaps land whose owners want to sell.

When government uses this power to take one man's land to enrich another man, a moral hazard arises. The hazard was well known to America's founders. Alexander Hamilton, at the Constitutional Convention in 1787, said that protecting "the security of property" was one of the two "great objects of government."

The moral hazard is that the powerful and connected will manipulate the levers of government to redistribute wealth, forcibly taking from someone else so they can grow richer still. The Texas Republican Party repeatedly recognized this moral hazard in its platform. One year it said, "Public money (including taxes or bond guarantees) or public powers (such as eminent domain) should not be used to fund or implement so-called private enterprise projects." The platform did not mention sports stadiums back then, but they were specifically cited in later years.

The Mathes family, rich but not so well connected as Bush, fought to save their Arlington horse ranch from condemnation for the new

stadium. They were certain that the value of their 13 acres would continue to rise as Dallas and Ft. Worth grew into a megalopolis. And they
liked their horse ranch. The city's best offer of $800,000 was, in their
view, beneath contempt. Because of a fortune made in manufacturing
early television sets under the Curtis Mathes brand, the family had the
resources to hire one of the best eminent domain lawyers in the state, a
Corsicana attorney fittingly named Glenn Sodd.

Sodd said the case was about "welfare for billionaires," the abuse of
the system by the politically connected and the morally suspect taking of
land, not for a vital public project, but to add to the fortunes of a few
rich men. The trial in Ft. Worth lasted two weeks. It took the jury just
90 minutes to award the Mathes family $5 million. Interest increased that
figure by half. A free market would have resulted in an even higher price,
had the Mathes family held out until late in the game and then sold without government interference. But they did not want to sell at any price.
They were forced out.

The sports authority that the city created had already leveled the
land. It sold stadium bonds to build a beautiful old-style brick and granite
stadium. It planted cooling trees throughout the extensive parking areas
that occupied what had been the Mathes family horse ranch. The Rangers negotiated a rent-to-own deal. It was nothing like what happens
when the poor rent-to-own appliances. The poor pay exorbitant interest
rates, so only a little of their money goes to paying for the purchase. The
Rangers, however, got their deal interest free. Every dollar they paid in
rent was counted toward the purchase price. So was the money they
spent maintaining the stadium. On top of this, they had the right to buy
the stadium for $60 million, even though the cost of building it was
more than three times that much. What Bush told the investors was right.
This was one sweet deal.

The lawyer who represented the city's sports authority in the financing was Ray Hutchison, a Republican insider, husband of Senator Kay
Bailey Hutchison and, by all accounts, the leading authority on Texas
municipal bond finance. Hutchison said the total value of the subsidy
was $202.5 million.

That figure illustrates how subsidy economics concentrates money in
the hands of a few while destroying broader wealth, which is at the core
of the economic malaise felt for so long by a majority of Americans.

The investors Bush assembled paid $86 million for the Rangers.

They sold nine years later for $250 million. The $164 million profit was $38.5 million less than the subsidy.

This shortfall goes to the core issue in subsidy economics: whether the subsidy produces a greater overall gain than it costs.

Martin Feldstein, a Harvard University economics professor and former adviser to President Bush, pointed out that some government subsidies benefit society. "A subsidy for flu vaccines is good because if you are vaccinated I am less likely to get flu by contagion." But job subsidies are a drag on the economy, he noted, "unless the local gain exceeds the loss in the rest of the nation."

Respected economists have intensively studied subsidies for commercial sports teams. Three decades of published research all points to one conclusion: subsidies for commercial sports teams never produce a net gain for society. They are just a government-sponsored transfer of wealth from the many to the few.

In Texas, the numbers reveal that the Bush partnership failed to add any economic value to the Rangers, either. Every dollar that Bush and the other investors pocketed when they sold the team came from the taxpayers, from that subsidy. And even their $164 million profit is illusory because it does not take into account inflation. Adjust the purchase price upward for inflation and the profit drops to $134 million. This means that the Bush investors captured less than two-thirds of the money they took from the pockets of taxpayers.

An alternative way to look at this is that the Bush group captured the whole subsidy when they sold the team for $250 million. That would mean that the value of the team itself plummeted to less than half what the investors paid Eddie Chiles. By trading away top players for minor talents and other mismanagement, this argument goes, the team itself was worth less money.

Either way the result is the same. Bush and his investors made no economic profit from the market when they sold the team. The only money they received came from the increased sales taxes that flowed into the stadium deal.

Hutchison told me that the fact that the investors captured only a portion of the subsidy should surprise no one. Subsidies, he said, are inherently inefficient. Hutchison said that in his experience no one ever captures the full value of the subsidy, much less adds value to it.

Bush has always portrayed the Rangers deal as a successful investment.

"It has been a win-win for everyone involved," Bush said in 1998. That is a curious argument since those taxpayers who never attended a baseball game lost some of their money to higher taxes and received nothing in return.

When Bush spoke about the Rangers deal he never called it a subsidy. He last talked about it when he was starting his run for the presidency. His advisers wanted to get the question of hypocrisy out of the way as early as possible. They did not want nagging questions comparing the candidate's public statements about limited government and his personal conduct in enriching himself at the public trough. Bush stuck to a few practiced lines. He said simply that the whole Rangers affair "was a successful business venture for me and my partners."

From the point of view of those at the receiving end, subsidies are a successful investment. Just as the lenses and mirrors of telescopes concentrate light from distant galaxies and funnel it to a single point, so did the Rangers subsidies gather pennies and dollars from children buying crayons and adults buying new cars. These taxes were then funneled into the pockets of Bush and his partners. Bush has always maintained that, since voters approved the tax hike, there is no issue worth discussing.

On his 1998 income tax return, which he made public, Bush reported a long-term capital gain of almost $17 million from the Rangers sale. Based on the stake he bought he would have earned a bit more than $2 million. Bush got far more because his partners gave him a 10 percent stake as compensation for putting the deal together and being one of two general partners. That is a common arrangement, with the general partner often getting 20 percent. The other general partner, who actually ran the organization, got only five percent.

That Bush and the other general partner together received only 15 percent shows, in economic terms, how risky the venture was. The Rangers investors got a better deal than the usual 80/20 split; they got 85/15. One risk was that the taxpayers would not pay for a new stadium or allow the use of government's power to condemn land for it. Another risk was whether Bush could pull off the tax subsidy deal, even with his father in the White House and many people eager to curry favor with the son. Up until this time, in 1989, he had never held public office, had a history of collapsing business ventures that had been rescued by friends of his father, and was known as a hard-drinking party animal, though he said he had given up booze cold turkey in 1986 and has admitted in a backhanded way that he had given up cocaine by 1974.

Bush did pull off the Rangers deal, though. He went on to be elected governor of Texas in 1994. He used part of the profits to buy a 1,583-acre nonworking ranch near Waco.

His financial disclosures show that proceeds from the sale of the team accounted for most of his net worth and possibly all of it. A precise number is not possible for two reasons. Disclosure reports allow officials to list a range of values for investments, and 1998 was the first time Bush had to file a detailed report, not like the minimal disclosure required of state politicians in Texas. However, analysis of his income from the investments suggests at least three-fourths of his net worth came from the Rangers deal.

Having grown rich off a sales tax, Bush was not done profiting off the tax system, his 1998 tax return shows.

The IRS issued a directive in 1993 that is relevant to Bush's tax return. "A partnership capital interest for services provided to, or for the benefit of, the partnership is taxable as compensation." The 10 percent share the partners gave Bush is just what the IRS procedural guide described. It should have been taxed as compensation, not as a long-term capital gain on an investment. The top tax rate for compensation in 1998 was 39.6 percent, plus another 2.9 percentage points for the Medicare tax.

In spite of this clear directive, Bush treated the entire $16.9 million from the Rangers deal as a long-term capital gain. He paid only the 20 percent rate on such gains. The result was that after paying taxes Bush pocketed $3.7 million more than the law, and the IRS directive, seem to allow. Treating such compensation as capital gains is, however, widespread and not often challenged by the IRS.

Under government rules, tax returns are accepted as filed unless the IRS audits and then challenges a return. The two years that Bush's return would have been most likely to be selected for audit, 2000 and 2001, were the record low years for audits of high-income Americans. The richest taxpayers benefited mightily those years because, at the insistence of the most right-wing Republicans in Congress, the IRS focused on tax returns filed by the working poor. In 1999, for the first time, those who made less than $25,000 were more likely to be audited than those who made more than $100,000. The next year the overall audit rate, already at a record low, fell almost 50 percent. In the following year the audit rate for high-income Americans fell even more. Bush's chances of getting audited: about one in 370. So, like the vast majority of people who fudged on their taxes, or flat-out cheated, Bush got away with it.

Next, let's look at the other side of the story—eminent domain from the point of view of the person whose property is taken.

Chapter 8

BOUNTY HUNTERS

THE GUARDS REPEATED THEIR STERN ORDERS A FINAL TIME: *NO movement, no sounds, and no displays of emotion or we will march you right out of here. Do you understand?* After metal detectors and security screenings, surrounded every moment by guards who seemed hired for their power to cast a mean look, Kim Blankenship was thoroughly intimidated. Even if she did not recall their precise words, she felt the message. She felt as if she was wearing inmate coveralls, not her business suit. *Does the Supreme Court humiliate everyone this way?* Blankenship thought as she silently took her front row seat in the somber, dark chamber and sat frozen, waiting for her case to be called.

Is there an American, feeling the sting of injustice, who has not vowed to fight all the way to the Supreme Court? Kim Blankenship and a few other aggrieved residents of Toledo actually did. They wanted to address an issue so fundamental that it caused the first American government to collapse more than two centuries ago. Blankenship's case raised the question of whether the problem that destroyed government under the Articles of Confederation had returned, posing a new threat to the pockets, and ultimately the liberties, of the people.

Blankenship was not alone in grasping the significance of the issue that brought her to the highest court in the land. The Supreme Court accepted briefs from 38 states; New York City; Grand Rapids, Michigan; and Wayne County, which encompasses Detroit. A host of industrial groups weighed in, too, and so did the nonprofit research organization known as the Tax Foundation. They all opposed Blankenship.

What happened when these forces collided should give everyone pause, both for the safety of their wallets and for how the surreal

environment that pervades Capitol Hill has reached into the highest
court in the land.

As Kim Blankenship saw it, big corporations were using the coercive
power of government to take away what little bit of money and substance she and her neighbors had built up through hard work. What justice is there, she thought, when your mere presence becomes an
inconvenience to someone, or some corporation, with the political
power to have you removed, crushed like a bug? *How can they force me to
pay taxes that they give away to a rich corporation?* she thought.

Kim Blankenship is a welder by trade, her husband Herman an auto
mechanic. In 1991, when they were in their thirties with two boys to
raise, they decided to open their own business. Kim owned, free and clear,
a piece of land suitable for a repair garage. Kim's Auto and Truck Service
stood on the edge of a mostly Polish neighborhood, sturdy working-class
homes, some of them brick, all with neatly kept yards, many with kitch-
ens so clean you could eat breakfast off the floor.

Each month the garage receipts grew as word spread that the Blankenships did honest work at good prices. Some of their customers worked
at the Jeep plant, leaving their keys for a tune-up or a new water pump
and then walking to their shift at the oldest vehicle factory in the country. By 1997, Kim and Herman had six, sometimes seven other people
on the payroll. Then the news appeared on the front page of the Toledo
Blade—Chrysler was going to rebuild its Jeep plant, the biggest employer
in town. The 90-year-old complex, 61 buildings with leaky roofs, would
give way to a gleaming modern factory, taking advantage of experienced
autoworkers and the site's easy access to shipping by rail, highway, or
Great Lakes barge. Chrysler said it would invest $1.2 billion.

Mayor Carty Finkbeiner called it a great day because losing Jeep
would have been "like the Browns leaving Cleveland" to play football in
Baltimore. The mayor and other officials campaigned for the new plant,
not to create more jobs, but just to retain many of the 5,600 jobs which,
with overtime and fringe benefits, he said paid $60,000 a year each. The
campaign included parades, billboards, and even a little song:

> *It's more than four-wheelers*
> *We're fighting to keep.*
> *It's the people who make them.*
> *Why Toledo loves Jeep*

What Chrysler cared about was not ditties, but money. In the intensifying competition between the states to attract new investment, or to just retain existing jobs, state and local government giveaways flourish like weeds on Miracle-Gro. Corporations have become masterful at playing one city, county, or state against another. No one knows just how many consultants earn their fees playing the subsidy card, but state economic development officials in North Carolina say they have a mailing list of more than 250 such consultants seeking handouts for their clients.

Chrysler, soon to become a subsidiary of the German company that makes Mercedes-Benz luxury cars, extracted at least $280 million in tax breaks. The state gave an investment tax credit. The city of Toledo and its schools gave up property taxes from the new factory. That reduced Chrysler's cost for the new plant by a fourth. Chrysler also got the city to seize land it said was needed, which is where Kim Blankenship and the Articles of Confederation come in.

The city took 82 homes and 16 small businesses. The way the city did it made a mockery of the Fifth Amendment protection against taking private property without "just compensation." First the city went to older people, some of whom had grown up hearing their elders tell in their native tongue about the awful things government had done in the old country to people who did not know their place. Many sold fast for a fraction of what their homes were worth and moved on. When the city had acquired half the homes, it invoked its power under the city charter to declare the area blighted, a slum in need of clearance. That lowered the price for anyone remaining in the neighborhood who might have the temerity to fight for more money.

Business at Kim's garage plummeted. The Blankenships would come to work and find trucks blocking the entrance, trucks whose drivers were nowhere to be found or who said they could not move them. The electricity would abruptly go off. The street was ripped up, making it hard and at times impossible for anyone to reach their garage. The couple felt they were being pressured to give up and get out.

Blankenship and others sued. They said it was unfair that the burden of supporting the state, the city, and the schools was being shifted off Chrysler and onto them. Charlotte Cuno, whose name was listed first on the lawsuit although she did not lose her home or business, was angry that Toledo teachers had gone seven years without a raise and that there were only two computers per school. How were her three grandchildren supposed to get a decent education and make their way in the world? When her property tax bill doubled she blamed Chrysler for the bulk of it.

Blankenship was even more upset because her taxes rose and her business collapsed. "Our business has gone from $25,000 a month to $1,500, maybe $2,000, but we are still paying taxes to support Chrysler," she fumed. Blankenship also started thinking about how the state could tax her to subsidize not just Chrysler, but a direct competitor, like a new garage down the street. The unfairness of it all made her apoplectic.

At the same time, Ralph Nader was looking for a case to attack corporate welfare. He read an article by Peter D. Enrich, a professor at Northeastern University School of Law in Boston, and called him out of the blue. Nader urged the professor to find a good case to challenge giveaways to firms like Chrysler. Enrich is not a litigator, but a scholar who specializes in state government finances. In one of his articles, Enrich wrote:

> The proliferation of state and local tax incentives designed to attract or retain business investment . . . has proven troublingly resistant to reform. Despite a growing recognition . . . that the competition over business incentives is at best a zero-sum game . . . the size of the incentive packages offered for large corporate facilities reaches ever-new heights. . . . The only consistent winners are the large businesses that can pit one jurisdiction against another for reduced tax burdens, while other taxpayers and citizens pay the costs in constrained government services and higher taxes.
>
> Yet, it is futile to look to state and local policymakers to call a halt to the competition. Even a legislator who fully understands that her jurisdiction is playing a game that the states and cities cannot collectively win still cannot ignore the political imperative to try to bring home jobs and investment. . . . The states and localities face a classic collective action problem: when they each pursue their individual self-interest, they all end up worse off.

After talking to people around the country, Enrich decided that the Toledo residents had a good case under Ohio law that the Chrysler deal was so unfair that it could be struck down. He agreed to represent them for free.

The suit was filed in state court, but the state of Ohio and Chrysler got it removed to federal court to get a broader test of the subsidy issue. The federal judge assigned to hear the matter dismissed it. The Toledo residents took their case to the Sixth Circuit Court of Appeals.

The issue of whether Chrysler's tax breaks were unfair to competing businesses and individuals is how the Articles of Confederation come into play. Under the first American government, from 1781 to 1788, the states regulated commerce. They used this power to enact tariffs to protect their own businesses. Anyone trying to import, say, furniture into New York from Connecticut faced a heavy tariff by New York, and Connecticut retaliated with its own tariffs. This economic warfare was destroying the whole experiment in self-governance. Efforts to find a solution transformed into the Constitutional Convention.

The Constitution grants Congress the power to regulate commerce "among the several states." Implied, but not explicitly stated, is the power of the federal government to block protectionist tariffs and similar devices that discriminate. This legal theory is known as the *negative Commerce Clause* or the *dormant Commerce Clause*. Under this theory the Supreme Court has repeatedly struck down state taxes, and regulations that have the effect of taxes, when it found that they favor businesses within a state and thus discourage national commerce.

Enrich argued that the Chrysler tax breaks "distort the free flow of investment in an open national economy" and "impose high costs" in lost tax revenue. "The inevitable result" of such subsidies "is a significant shift of the costs of state and local government to other classes of taxpayers" like his clients, as well as "a substantial reduction in states' and localities' ability to deliver important public services" like education.

Among the evidence submitted to the court was a study by Kenneth P. Thomas, a political scientist at the University of Missouri in St. Louis. He examined state subsidies to corporations. The value of many of these subsidies is never disclosed. The states and local governments that make these gifts, and the corporations that receive them, routinely fight disclosure of the precise terms. Once the deal is done, there is virtually no monitoring after the fact to see if the companies uphold their part of the bargain, investing as much money as they promised or creating, or even retaining, as many jobs as were required for the giveaways.

Professor Thomas concluded that these gifts amounted to at least $48.8 billion in 1996. What was telling was his observation that these giveaways were worth far more than the $29.3 billion that the states collected in corporate income taxes that year. A system that appeared to tax business was in fact a scheme to give away $1.65 for every dollar that came in. Since the recipients of corporate welfare were paying little or nothing, while other businesses paid in full, this was clearly a redistribution scheme favoring the politically connected, like Chrysler, who hired the most astute negotiators.

Toledo and the state said the case was baseless. "The negative Commerce Clause prohibits barriers, not welcome mats," making an argument that evokes images not of red carpets, but of ones woven from greenbacks. "Far from 'economic protectionism,' the tax credit is freely available to all who invest in Ohio," the city and state argued.

Toledo and the state of Ohio even asserted that the Jeep plant giveaways complied with a 1991 Supreme Court finding that "it is a laudatory goal in the design of a tax system to promote investment that will provide jobs and prosperity." That glib line went to the very point Enrich was trying to get across—giveaways are a less-than-zero-sum game that from the most parochial of perspectives may appear to generate benefits, but that to society overall actually destroys jobs and undermines prosperity.

The company, by then renamed DaimlerChrysler, said simply that it was entitled to the money. It adopted the welcome-mat theory, asserting that the tax credit "is not the type of anticompetitive protectionist measure the Commerce Clause was meant to prohibit."

The appeals court ruled in October 2004 that the Chrysler tax credit was indeed a discriminatory tax that coerced companies in Ohio to not invest elsewhere. That put the tax break in violation of the federal Constitution.

The court cited the hypothetical example of two similar Ohio businesses planning to expand, one of which chooses to build in Ohio while the other keeps its existing facilities but expands in another state. "The business that chooses to expand its local presence will enjoy a reduced tax burden" just as Chrysler did. However, "a competitor that invests out of state will face a comparatively higher tax burden" because its continuing operations in Ohio will be fully taxed.

And so one chilly March morning in 2006 Kim Blankenship found herself sitting absolutely motionless waiting for John Glover Roberts Jr., the chief justice of the United States, and the rest of the court to hear her case. Chief Justice Roberts was not interested in the merits of the case, however, which were hardly mentioned in the oral arguments. This illustrates another aspect of how the markets-as-the-only-solution radicals have captured the government.

Roberts is the second chief justice appointed since Ronald Reagan's election with his promise to remake the federal judiciary. Roberts, like William Rehnquist, whom he succeeded, claims to possess a deep respect for the original intent of the Framers as his guiding principle. As a young lawyer, Roberts was a clerk to Rehnquist. He was also a special assistant to William French Smith, who before becoming attorney general was Reagan's personal lawyer. And Roberts worked in the Reagan White House. As such he proved his political reliability to an administration focused on increasing power and reducing accountability for corporations and the richest among us.

A major goal of the ideologues who nurtured Roberts is cutting off access to the courts, arguing that many grievances should be handled by legislation or not heard at all. The "original intent" theory, legal scholars have shown, relies at times on fanciful versions of history as well as third, fourth, and even fifth definitions of words to justify its decisions to deny relief or even access to the courts. In the most extreme example, the court has listened, with seeming favor, though no formal ruling, to an argument that it would be appropriate to execute a Texas man convicted of murder even if, after the trial, a videotape of the crime turned up showing he was absolutely innocent. The finality of jury decisions needs respect, the court has held over and over again, despite the flood of evidence showing that our prisons are strewn with the innocent (while the actually guilty are presumably roaming free).

In its most extreme example of disregard for decency, the court held in a 2007 case, Justice Roberts in the majority, that an Ohio inmate must rot in jail until he dies without any review of his case. Why? Because although the inmate beat the deadline he was given to file an appeal, the judge made a mistake. The deadline was three days earlier than the judge said. Justice David Souter, in his dissent, wrote that "it is intolerable for the judicial system to treat people this way, and there is not even a technical justification for condoning this bait and switch."

In line with these attitudes, turning a deaf ear to issues involving mere money and property comes easily.

Chief Justice Roberts focused the court on whether Kim Blankenship had a right to even be in court. It was an issue never raised until the case got to the Supreme Court. Taking his cue from the chief justice, Theodore B. Olson, another architect of the theories to limit access to the courts, argued on behalf of DaimlerChrysler that Blankenship and the others "cannot demonstrate any actual, concrete, and direct injury."

Douglas R. Cole, the state of Ohio's lawyer, joined in. "They haven't shown any harm to themselves," Cole said, then adding a modifier to make his statement technically accurate, "any judicially cognizable harm." The only harm they could show, Cole told the justices, was that the state would collect less money from Chrysler.

Hearing these words, Kim Blankenship had to muster all the strength she had to keep her emotions in check. *How can they lie like that?* she thought. She rolled her eyes, and then noticed a guard glaring at her as if to warn that even that subtle move would be grounds for her removal.

Cole and Olson were not lying; they were just making lawyerly arguments on what to them was a technical legal issue. Just because you pay taxes gives you no right to challenge the government. The reasoning for this standard, which is not written into any statute, is that the courts would be clogged with cases brought by malcontents, tax protesters, and anybody with a grievance and either money to hire a lawyer or time to file their own case. Of course, there is a way to address this, which would be for the courts to use their discretion to accept cases that address issues of great public significance and to toss out frivolous cases. And there was no doubt that in this case, all sides agreed the matter was of great import. Even the Tax Foundation, which usually sides with those seeking to reduce the burden of government, said in its brief that the Chrysler tax credit was bad policy. The Tax Foundation just felt that Kim Blankenship and her fellow taxpayers should take their case to the legislature.

Blankenship and Mary Ebright, who had lost her home and who was seated next to her in the front row, dug their fingernails into each other's hands to relieve the tension as the lawyers said again and again that there was no harm.

No harm. No harm! Have they seen what happened to our income? Do they care what the city did to ruin our business? No harm! I suffered plenty of harm and not just because I am paying taxes to support Chrysler instead of the schools, Blankenship thought.

Kim's Auto was mentioned five times, only once in a full sentence, and only to say that it had no right, no standing, to press the case. Olson even argued that it would be wrong to return the case to state court, where the case was originally brought.

When the Supreme Court ruled, two months later, Chief Justice Roberts made his views clear. Until this case, the Supreme Court had indicated that subsidies were acceptable, but it never explicitly made a ruling on this. Instead it implied this in the explanatory language of court opinions that lawyers call *dicta*. Chief Justice Roberts sent a message to Kim Blankenship and the other residents of Toledo who were forced to suffer so that Chrysler might prosper. It was a message directed at anyone thinking about challenging corporate welfare. So how will such challengers fare in court? Their pleas for relief simply will not be heard. Blankenship and the others had no standing, no right, to challenge the giveaway. Case dismissed.

And for what did the Blankenships lose their business? Did they lose it for the greater good of high-paying jobs at the Jeep plant? No. Lost in the legal case was this simple fact never considered by the Supreme Court: The site of what was once Kim's Auto and Truck Service is now a lawn at the factory's edge.

Now that the Supreme Court has erected a formidable legal barrier to protect corporate welfare, it should not surprise anyone how this has affected those who seek subsidies. The practice of forcing people to pay taxes that are then given away to the rich and politically connected is spreading. Even places known for their antipathy to taxes, like Arizona and New Hampshire and Texas, are eager to conduct giveaways. The high court has sent a clear signal that the policy of the United States is that government can take from the many to give to the few—and those who object will not have their grievances heard by the courts. In a way, Kim Blankenship is one with the inmate who met the deadline given by a judge, only to be turned away because of the judge's mistake. They had their cases heard by men who smugly insist that what they say and do is only what the Framers intended.

The Chrysler giveaway at least had the merit of being a subsidy for an industry which, in the words of Adam Smith, adds value. Making Jeeps and other vehicles means turning rocks, sand, and petroleum into engines, glass windows, and all the rubber seals needed to make a vehicle work. In that way Smith, though not modern economists, regarded manufacturing as adding to the wealth of a nation. But subsidies are not limited to manufacturing. Sometimes, the less significant the enterprise, the greater the subsidy.

Sometimes cities and towns will even borrow money to help create jobs that pay about ten bucks an hour plus health care benefits they can buy with a portion of those wages. Next, the story of two wealthy families whose business is fishing for subsidies—and the competitor that refuses to take them. Everywhere they go, the two families keep reeling in big ones, really big ones.

Chapter 9

GOIN' FISHIN'

OR MORE THAN TWO DECADES JIM WEAKNECHT SOLD GUNS, HUNT-
ing bows, tackle, and outdoor clothing from the little sporting goods
store bearing his name in Hamburg, Pennsylvania, population 4,100.
Hamburg lies an hour and a half northwest of Philadelphia in Berks
County, one of those countless small towns in drive-by country—off to
the sides of the interstate freeways. Most of them offer interesting store-
fronts from a time gone by, charming salespeople who know their stuff,
and just enough customers to keep the doors open.

Weaknecht served local hunters and anglers heading into the lush
glens of the Poconos, his nearest competitor 15 miles away in Reading.
He counted on a surge of customers every fall when deer hunting season
began and then again at Christmas. His best year, the register rang up a
mere $1.3 million in sales. He kept enough as profit, however, that his
wife, Julie, could stay home taking care of their three children, which to
Weaknecht meant he enjoyed a very good life.

Jim Weaknecht attributed much of his modest success to a catalog he
always kept at the front counter. It came from Cabela's, which is to hunters and anglers what the Sears, Roebuck catalog was to farm families a
century ago, a cornucopia of everything you needed and a lot more stuff
that made you marvel at what was available by mail order.

"Hunters coming in to get a bow always want to know if they are
getting a good price," Weaknecht said. "My main draw was always
price." While the prices of guns and hunting jackets have fallen over the
years, prices for bows have turned up, sharply. When a potential buyer
seemed uncertain, Weaknecht would reach for the Cabela's catalog at
the front counter, turning to the page offering the same hunting bow. "I

would show them Cabela's price," Weaknecht said. "Mine was always cheaper."

Cabela's began in 1961 when Dick Cabela returned from a Chicago furniture show to the wheat farming and cattle ranching town of Chappell, which lies on the far western Nebraska plains. It is even smaller than Hamburg. At the furniture show, Cabela paid next to nothing for a giant nest of hand-tied trout flies from Japan. He took out a classified ad in the local newspaper offering them at a dozen for a dollar. He got just one order. Then he hit on a new idea. Cabela bought ads in the back of outdoor magazines. He offered five free flies for 25 cents to cover postage and handling. Back then a first-class stamp cost four cents. Even after paying for the envelope, and recovering the mite spent on each fly, Cabela and his wife made 11 cents on each order they filled from their kitchen table.

The Cabelas built a mailing list from those who accepted their offer. They sent them mimeographed offerings of sporting goods items. In time, from this bit of postal arbitrage, Cabela's grew into a $2 billion-a-year enterprise. The lesson of how government could give a boost to business was not forgotten.

One day in 2001, Weaknecht heard that Cabela's might be coming to town. The first Cabela's retail store had opened in 1987. A second opened four years later. Both were in Nebraska. In 1998, Cabela's began an aggressive nationwide expansion drive. Hamburg was to be its eighth store. It was also to be the largest sporting goods store in the world, more than 250,000 square feet, roughly six acres. It was to have more guns and reels and hunting jackets than Weaknecht could sell in a lifetime. It would also have what the company called a "museum quality" display of stuffed deer, geese, and hedgehogs that came to Cabela's by way of the taxidermist. Alongside the dioramas of stuffed and mounted creatures, the Cabela's store would also feature a huge cold-water aquarium filled with bass, trout, and other native game fish.

The American Association of Museums would find laughable the idea that these in-store displays were anything but commercial come-ons of little educational value. Still, the pseudomuseum conferred a benefit on Cabela's. It helped sell the idea that a Cabela's was a destination, not just another store. By organizing the faux museum as a nonprofit, it also guaranteed that part of the building would forever be exempt from property taxes.

This giant sporting goods emporium was not going to be built on historic Fourth Street, with its varied architecture built over more than a century. Cabela's favored a site of flat ground catty-corner from historic Hamburg, perfect for acres of asphalt surrounding a concrete slab foundation. The land was more than a mile from the historic area. It was across both the Schuylkill River and Interstate 78, which starts in Harrisburg, the state capital, and skirts Hamburg on its way to Manhattan. Cabela's said its megastore would become the biggest tourist attraction in all of Pennsylvania, drawing six million people a year down the interstate and through its doors. It would put Hamburg on the map.

Weaknecht never believed it. Even if it was the first Cabela's in the northeast, and even if it was nearly 100 times larger than Weaknecht's Sporting Goods, it made no sense that six million people would take a day or even two to travel to out-of-the-way Berks County to visit Cabela's. *Why would people drive all day to buy a gun or a fishing pole? Why not just order out of a Cabela's catalog? Or just go to their neighborhood sporting goods store?* Weaknecht thought. The state of New York sold fewer than a million fishing licenses a year, a figure that had been dwindling slowly, while the other nearby states sold far fewer. Deer hunting licenses were also in decline, down about a fifth since 1980. And besides, Weaknecht figured, in time Cabela's would open a store somewhere else in the northeast, perhaps in New Jersey or Connecticut, or in West Virginia near the Pennsylvania border, and that would dilute any interest in the Hamburg store.

Even if Cabela's did not build another store, surely its two big competitors, Bass Pro or Gander Mountain, would open stores in the region, maybe in Harrisburg, less than an hour away and at the confluence of much busier interstate highways. Bass Pro was privately held, while Cabela's was about to go public, like Gander Mountain.

Between them the three largest sporting goods operations had less than a tenth of the fin-feather-and-fur outfitters market, which was dominated by mom-and-pop operators like Jim Weaknecht. So surely the big three would be building plenty of new stores as they tried to consolidate the industry by running little operations like Weaknecht's out of business. Cabela's and Bass Pro, and to a lesser extent Gander Mountain, were like Holiday Inn and Ramada in the early days of the interstate freeways. That one was being built generated local excitement at first, but they soon became as ubiquitous as a freeway cloverleaf. And nobody drives to a Holiday Inn to experience that brand; they just stay at the ones located most conveniently on the way to their destination.

To believe that Cabela's would draw six million visitors each year meant believing that a sporting goods store could be as big a draw as Universal Studios in Orlando, whose commercials ran regularly on television, and which was really two theme parks with enough rides and shows to keep a family occupied for several days. Why, it would mean that more than twice as many people would come every year to Cabela's as visited Hersheypark, less than an hour down the highway from Hamburg, with its roller coasters, water rides, and faux boardwalk. Weaknecht did not believe.

But what struck Weaknecht even more than the fantastic visitor prediction was the tribute Cabela's demanded. Cabela's was not so much interested in free enterprise and competition as in using the promise of economic development following in its wake to exact tribute.

"They played it up that they were not certain where they would go, it could be Delaware or Pennsylvania or New Jersey," Weaknecht recalled. "They said they could end up in Berks County or in Lebanon County, so they had the local politicians all competing for Cabela's." The winner would be the community willing to pay the most in tribute to the sporting goods chain.

The tribute Cabela's wanted totaled at least $32 million. That was more than the borough of Hamburg spent on the entire city government, from paving streets to having police patrol them, in a decade. But it was Cabela's price. Hamburg could pay up, the company made them believe, or they could watch the prosperity they could have had go to another town in the Northeast.

Cabela's isn't saying how much it cost to build that store, or any of the others. Its disclosure statements to shareholders are opaque on this point. But construction and retailing experts estimated a cost of $220 to $230 a square foot. For the Hamburg store, that meant subsidies would cover more than half the cost of construction.

The way Cabela's talked up the store, that $32 million gift to itself sounded like a free lunch for the people of Hamburg. The company characterized it as money that would come from all those hunting and fishing enthusiasts who would be driving to Hamburg. It was not supposed to cost the locals a dime.

First, Cabela's wanted an exemption from paying property taxes for the value of its building for years to come. The so-called museum part of the building would be tax-exempt forever as a not-for-profit entity. Of course, if Cabela's picked some other place for the store, it still would not be paying property taxes to the township. Thus the locals really would not lose a thing if they let Cabela's skip paying property taxes, or so the argument went.

Then there was the other big part of the subsidy. Cabela's wanted to apply this same reasoning to sales taxes. Cabela's wanted to pocket the sales taxes, using them to help pay for its building. What if the town fathers said no? Then Cabela's would go somewhere else—and those sales taxes would never materialize anyway.

On the other hand, if Cabela's did come, and did get to keep the sales taxes and not pay property taxes, there would be plenty of spillover business. Surely almost everyone driving in from New York, or the Pittsburgh suburbs, or from down near the nation's capital would want a meal. A lot of them would want hotel rooms, too. And even if only a small fraction of them decided to go shopping in the historic part of town, well, you could almost hear the coins jingling in the pockets of the Hamburg burghers. It all seemed so easy and lucrative. Restaurant meals, hotel stays, gassing up the family SUV, all of it would mean greenbacks and Visa cards coming down the interstate to little Hamburg. That the Cabela's store would be across both a river and a highway from Hamburg was not much of a concern to the town fathers. They planned a free trolley to bring those Cabela's customers over to shop in the historic downtown.

Weaknecht thought the town fathers had all lost their senses. "Cabela's got $30 million something in tax breaks," Weaknecht said. "They don't pay any kind of school taxes. They got all the breaks in the world. If I would have gotten just a million dollars in tax breaks, let me tell you, I would have run a very, very successful business."

In seeking these subsidies, Cabela's was not inventing a new scheme. It was simply improving on a technique pioneered by an icon of retailing success, Sam Walton. The Walton story was not about the brave capitalist taking on risk and proving his mettle by being smarter than the other guy, no matter how carefully the Wal-Mart company has polished and sold that corporate fairy tale.

Sam Walton practiced corporate socialism. As much as he could, he put the public's money to work for his benefit. Free land, long-term leases at below-market rates, pocketing sales taxes, even getting workers trained at government expense were among the ways Wal-Mart took every dollar of welfare it could get. Walton had a particular fondness for government-sponsored industrial revenue bonds, which cost him less in interest charges than the corporate bonds the market economy uses to raise money.

Back when Wal-Mart started grabbing every subsidy it could get, hardly anyone was paying attention to the issue. Formal records and news accounts are both scant, so the full scope of its taking probably will never be known. Phil Mattera of Good Jobs First, a group backed by labor unions that tracks corporate subsidies, plowed through old securities records and news accounts, trying to find out how much welfare Wal-Mart received. Mattera's research was paid for partly by a union for grocery store workers, the United Food and Commercial Workers International Union, which had fought Wal-Mart, which has no unions and once closed the part of a store whose workers voted for one. Mattera and his team found proof of subsidies at just 91 of the more than 4,000 Wal-Mart stores in the United States, mostly those built more recently. It also found evidence of subsidies at 84 of 91 distribution centers. The subsidies Mattera could pin down totaled $1 billion and change.

That $1 billion figure is surely far less than the actual amount of money Wal-Mart took. One indication of this comes from an interview that a Wal-Mart spokesman, B. John Bisio, gave to the *Telegraph Herald* newspaper of Dubuque, Iowa. Bisio let slip that "it is common" for Wal-Mart to seek subsidies for its new stores and that it does so "in about one-third of all projects." That suggests that 14 times more Wal-Marts received subsidies than the Good Jobs First study uncovered.

Even more revealing was the response Wal-Mart gave to the report, which was ignored by many news organizations and relegated to the back pages of many newspapers that did mention it. Mona Williams, a Wal-Mart spokesperson, told *The New York Times* that if the estimate of a billion in subsidies was correct, "it looks like offering tax incentives to Wal-Mart is a jackpot investment for local governments."

Her reasoning was pure corporate socialism and haughty to boot. And her analysis collapses under the mildest scrutiny as self-serving nonsense.

Williams said that in the previous decade Wal-Mart had collected more than $52 billion in sales taxes from customers. That cost Wal-Mart nothing; it just acted as the collection agent. Wal-Mart was even paid a tiny sliver of that sales tax money to cover its costs in processing the money. But since Wal-Mart customers would have bought the same merchandise from some other business, then government gained nothing from having Wal-Mart collect these sales taxes. In fact, if Wal-Mart really does charge lower prices, then it collected less in sales tax revenues than if people had shopped at other, more expensive stores.

Williams said the next biggest piece of this "jackpot" for local government was that Wal-Mart paid $4 billion in local property taxes in the past decade. That, too, seems like a lot of money. But in the context of Wal-Mart's size, the fact that the money was paid out over 10 years, and the burdens of other property owners, Wal-Mart paid very little in property taxes.

The $4 billion in property taxes amounts to less than 25 cents out of each $100 Wal-Mart rang up at the cash register in that decade. It is the equivalent of a homeowner with a $50,000 job paying a property tax of just $10 per month. That's $120 a year. In reality, the homeowner at that income level is likely to pay at least that much per month in property taxes. That the Wal-Mart property tax bill is so low indicates just how much it benefited from demanding tribute in the form of paying reduced property taxes or not having to pay any at all on some of its stores and other properties.

There is yet another way in which Williams's reasoning was specious. Wal-Mart builds cheap, windowless boxes, not fancy stores. The very design of Wal-Marts means their property taxes are low because the buildings are not all that valuable. Most retail stores are more expensive to build than a Wal-Mart, what with display windows, iconic designs, and various amenities. Some even add to the physical beauty of a place, landmarks instead of Wal-Mart's huge white pimples. A proper measure of Wal-Mart's property taxes would take into account any reduction in the value of these other buildings, especially any that fell vacant because Wal-Mart came to town. The fiscal jackpot from Wal-Mart property taxes? There is none.

Making sure Wal-Mart got credit for every possible part of this imaginary jackpot, Williams also revealed that the company had even paid $192 million in income and unemployment taxes to "local governments." Presumably Williams meant to say state governments, since they are the ones usually that impose such levies. At first blush $192 million seems like a big number, but in the context of Wal-Mart revenues it is smaller than the interest on the interest on a widow's mite. Wal-Mart's revenues in those ten years totaled more than $1.6 trillion. That means that the "local" income and jobless taxes she referred to amounted to about a penny out of each $100 of revenue.

Said Williams of the Good Jobs First report on Wal-Mart subsidies:

> We think the report in fact shows that the subsidies are a great thing for us. Do the math and you will see that every dollar invested with Wal-Mart has returned more than $30 for the community. We expect to see lots of other local governments will be asking for that $30 deal.

Beyond doubt, subsidies "are a great thing" for Wal-Mart. Williams made it clear that Wal-Mart plans to continue collecting all the subsidies it can. But if local governments follow her advice and do the math they will see that giving subsidies to Wal-Mart makes America worse off than if Wal-Mart did not exist.

If there were no Wal-Mart, people would still buy the disposable diapers, lightbulbs, and everything else Wal-Mart sells. The businesses that would have sold those goods would still have collected sales taxes, paid property taxes, and even paid those "local" taxes Williams mentioned.

If it is true that Wal-Mart's prices are lower, then local governments would have collected more in sales taxes from those merchants because higher prices means more sales tax. And because those merchants built nicer buildings than the windowless concrete slabs that Wal-Mart erects, they would have paid more in property taxes than Wal-Mart does. And if those businesses did not seek subsidies, but instead competed in the market, then state and local governments would not be taking from the many to give to the few who own Wal-Mart. That would mean taxes could be reduced or that there would be money for modern textbooks so that no child in the twenty-first century would read about how someday the human genome would be decoded.

That $30 would be there whether Wal-Mart existed or not. It would likely be $31 or more, assuming Wal-Mart really does charge lower prices. And without having to pay tribute to Wal-Mart, state and local governments would have more money to carry out the functions of government.

Government handouts convey clear benefits to the recipient. For Wal-Mart, eager to expand and take market share away from other retailers, government handouts reduce the costs of competing in the market. They also reduce risks. Subsidies add a layer of financial insulation to buffer the company from the inevitable unexpected developments in the market, from management errors to changes in consumer tastes. By soliciting subsidies, Wal-Mart shifted some of the risks of its expansion onto the majority of Americans who are not regular Wal-Mart shoppers.

Ignored in Williams's remarks is the fact that Wal-Mart relied on the power of government to force people to give up some of their substance for its benefit. People choose to shop at Wal-Mart; when Wal-Mart takes subsidies it forces them to pay it tribute. In forcing people to give to Wal-Mart, the company placed a burden on them, increasing its power by oppressing those with less political power and less money. That the burden on each individual was mild does not invalidate the principle. Wal-Mart and other subsidy seekers exercise unrighteous dominion and oppress those with less. This is a moral evil denounced relentlessly throughout Old Testament and New. Do we excuse a thief because the sum he took was from a holder of such great wealth that the victim did not suffer privation?

Wal-Mart earned greater profits than it could produce on its own thanks to these forced payments. The tribute people were forced to pay Wal-Mart, even if they never set foot in one of its stores, also meant they gave up some of their tax dollars that could have gone to schools and roads and parks. They had fewer tools to advance themselves and fewer amenities to enjoy life just so that the Walton family, which controls the company, could add to its enormous riches.

The Waltons are among the least generous of the wealthy families in America, the annual surveys of giving by the rich show. Relative to the size of their fortunes, and the giving of people with far less, they can be reasonably described as parsimonious. Clearly they fail to meet the biblical test of charity, which requires sacrifice. That they force others to pay them tribute and then give so little relative to their riches is conduct reproved in every great book of religious and philosophical insight. The Book of Proverbs, at 22:16, is instructive in understanding how forcing the many to give to the few hardens hearts while tearing at the social fabric, impoverishing all of society. The King James version reads:

> He that oppresseth the poor to increase his riches, and he that giveth to the rich, shall surely come to want.

The twisted genius of this strain of corporate socialism promoted by the Walton family, and embraced by the Cabela family and Johnny Morris, the owner of Bass Pro, is that it forces their competitors to pay for the demise of their enterprises. Subsidies help Wal-Mart to charge lower prices. So the existing department store that sells the same television set or towel, but gets no tribute, is taxed to benefit Wal-Mart. In this way do retail subsidies steal from the honest to benefit the greedy who manipulate the powers of government, thwarting the market. Corporate socialism made it possible for Wal-Mart to grab market share by under-cutting the competition that did not get subsidies, while appearing to win because it was just more efficient.

Wal-Mart's fuzzy math, and its rationalization for taking welfare, is modest compared to Cabela's, which has made its reliance on handouts a core part of its expansion strategy. In fact, Cabela's virtually boasts about its solicitation of welfare. In its 2007 report to shareholders, Cabela's declared:

> Historically, we have been able to negotiate economic development arrangements relating to the construction of a number of our new destination retail stores, including free land, monetary grants and the recapture of incremental sales, property or other taxes through economic development bonds, with many local and state governments. . . . We intend to continue to utilize economic development arrangements with state and local governments to offset some of the construction costs and improve the return on investment of our new retail stores.

Relative to the size of their businesses, the Cabela family is far greed-ier than the Walton family. Even if the actual Wal-Mart subsidies are 100 times the billion-dollar estimate that Matera and Good Jobs First calcu-lated, Cabela's has collected far more in subsidies relative to its size than Wal-Mart. In 2006, Wal-Mart took in $348 billion in sales, which is roughly 177 times more than Cabela's revenues. To be in the same league as Cabela's, Wal-Mart would have to have collected several hundred bil-lion dollars in subsidies since it first got on the dole more than three de-cades ago. And no one believes Wal-Mart got anything close to that in handouts.

It is not only general sales and property taxes that some of the rich pocket. In Atlantic City, the moguls who own the casinos arranged to take money from the poor. A state law directs that 1.25 percent of the amount casinos win from players be used to relieve urban blight and pro-vide housing and related assistance for the state's poor. More than $400 million, a fifth of the money raised from 1994 through 2006, has been diverted back to the casinos. Getting the law changed to allow this sub-sidy also involved persuading the legislature to eliminate one of the watchdogs of industry in New Jersey, the state Public Advocate.

The casinos used the subsidies to pay for 13,000 hotel rooms, parking garages, and even subsidized trips to the Jersey shore. Donald Trump's Taj Mahal casino hotel got money for new road signs. His Trump Plaza casino hotel will share in an $89 million subsidy for retail and entertainment space. Thus does the supposed billionaire take from the poor to magnify his profits.

The tribute Cabela's demanded from Hamburg amounted to roughly $8,000 for each man, woman, and child in town. Hamburg was not a unique example, but part of a strategy to build Cabela's stores across the country. Multiply the tribute in Hamburg by as many struggling little towns off the interstates as Cabela's has plans for retail stores and the figures balloon. Cabela's plans to build stores until, like Holiday Inns, it is everywhere. Imagine how many of those towns are run by burghers who could be persuaded to opt for hope and forget about reason. To become the dominant outdoor retailer Cabela's would need only to find a few dozen or, if it could, a few hundred towns whose political leaders were willing to pay tribute. By doing so it could cut the risks of expansion and gain an advantage over business owners like Jim Weaknecht who offered better service and lower prices. Mining local and state governments for tribute could even turn into a business more lucrative for Cabela's than actually selling sporting goods.

It already has.

In the three years after it had become a company with publicly traded stock, 2004 through 2006, Cabela's earned $223.4 million in profits. On the 10 stores and several distribution centers it opened outside Nebraska in those years it made deals for subsidies worth at least $293.7 million, a third more than its reported profits.

On the first 15 stores Cabela's built outside of Nebraska, in the years 1998 through 2005, it made deals for subsidies of about $25 million per store. The actual subsidies are certainly larger because many of the deal terms have been held back or are described in public documents in ways that only hint at their full value. Cabela's has fought to keep some of these documents secret. It wants government to force people to give it money, but it also wants to operate behind as thick a veil of secrecy as it can get away with, hiding full knowledge of how deeply it legally picks pockets.

Over time the subsidies Cabela's collects are getting bigger, not smaller. This is true even though each time any of the big three— Cabela's, Bass Pro, and Gander Mountain—opens a new retail mega-outlet the whole theory of a sporting goods store as a destination resort loses value.

When Bass Pro, for example, opened its own megastore in Harrisburg, less than an hour from Hamburg and at the confluence of busier interstates with more lanes, it surely cut into whatever desire existed for travel to Hamburg to shop at Cabela's. So, too, do the 11 stores that Gander Mountain operates in Pennsylvania.

The tribute local and state governments pay to Cabela's keeps on growing even though the market for hunting and angling is getting smaller, not bigger. One in six Americans goes fishing, the Census Bureau said in 2001, down from one in five just a decade earlier.

The first two Cabela's stores outside of Nebraska opened in April and September 1998 about 170 miles apart in Owatonna, Minnesota, and Prairie du Chien, Wisconsin. The known value of the subsidies was $4.1 million and $4.9 million, respectively. Even together those subsidies were but a small fraction of the Hamburg giveaways.

Less than two years after Cabela's launched the Hamburg store, it opened a slightly smaller store in Ft. Worth, not far from the heavily subsidized Texas Rangers stadium that taxpayers had financed for George W. Bush and his wealthy partners. The Ft. Worth store subsidy was $40 million, a fourth larger than the Hamburg giveaway. The next month Cabela's cut the ribbon at a much smaller store just 200 miles away in Buda, Texas, between Austin and San Antonio. The Buda store was 185,000 square feet, only three-fourths the size of the Hamburg store. The tribute, though, was at least $61 million, nearly twice the subsidy in Hamburg.

The granddaddy deal, though, was in West Virginia. Near Wheeling, not far from Pittsburgh, Cabela's built a store even smaller than in Buda, Texas, at just 175,000 square feet, plus a distribution center. Thanks to the generosity of West Virginia taxpayers, Cabela's will realize an astonishing $115 million for its skill not in the competitive market, but in manipulating politicians.

Cabela's reports to shareholders are unusual in how they account for costs. The company warns investors who read through the fine detail that its reports make it difficult, if not impossible, to compare its figures to other retail operators. Its uniquely uninformative disclosures benefit management by masking the boost the subsidies give to profitability. Even so, some stock market analysts have noted that Cabela's is less successful than other retailers at converting sales into profits.

My analysis of its reports suggests that at best Cabela's earns an annual profit of $12.60 per square foot of retail space. That means it captures about 3.6 cents out of each dollar as profit. At that rate of profit the whopping $115 million gift from West Virginia taxpayers roughly equals 52 years of profits from the store there. If the state were to get all of the sales taxes from that store, instead of letting Cabela's pocket that tax money, it would take more than 31 years to get back the $115 million.

To get an idea of just how generous the gift to Cabela's was, it is useful to compare it to state spending. The state could provide free lunches for 50 years to all the West Virginia children who are so poor that they qualify for that form of welfare. Given the power of religion in West Virginia politics, the politicians who made this lavish gift, and the wealthy Cabela family that sought it, might want to read Jeremiah 22:13: "Woe unto him that buildeth his house by unrighteousness, and his upper chambers by wrong."

These subsidies just keep rolling in, except in Nebraska. Cabela's has three Nebraska stores, but evidently has not sought any subsidies for them. In 17 other states, however, Cabela's was negotiating deals in 2007. All but one involved subsidies. Only some terms in a few of those deals are known. Even that limited information shows that if all these deals go through the subsidies will total at least $283 million. Among these proposed deals is $54 million of tribute for a proposed 150,000-square-foot store in the biggest little city in the world, Reno. That subsidy is bigger than those extracted from Hamburg and Ft. Worth, even though the store would be much smaller than the ones in those two places.

The day Cabela's Hamburg store opened in September 2003, Weaknecht stopped by to check out the competition. "If somebody had given me unlimited money to open a store, that's what I would have done, especially the huge inventory," he said. Only one aspect of the operation gave him a sense that he could compete against Cabela's. The salespeople he talked to knew next to nothing about rifles or fly rods or the conditions imposed on hunting licenses.

Looking back on it, Weaknecht wishes he had just closed his store that day. His sales soon fell more than 70 percent. He hung on for almost two years, his customers gone to Cabela's even though they could have saved money at Weaknecht's. "I refused to file bankruptcy," he said. "I just could not walk down the street and pass people I had screwed over by not paying them."

Nor could he imagine that in 2004, both President Bush and Vice President Cheney would campaign at Cabela's stores. The real customers were run off and only party loyalists with admission tickets allowed in. At four Cabela's stores, in separate appearances, the two politicians praised the chain and Cheney indicated it was his favorite place to spend money. President Bush extolled the jobs being created at the West Virginia store without a hint about the role of government in underwriting those jobs. They picked Cabela's in part for its audience, in part for the symbolism of connecting their campaign with the Second Amendment voters, but also because the Cabelas are among President Bush's top campaign contributors. Dick and Mary Cabela gave $11,000 to the Bush campaign. What they got back in the promotional value of these campaign visits was priceless, one corporate socialist helping another further their shared interest in avoiding the rigors of the market and instead taking from the many for their own enrichment.

Since he closed his store, Weaknecht has worked as an assistant manager for a regional grocery store chain. Cabela's actually offered him a job—$13.50 an hour to be a department manager, supervising people who make $8 or $9 an hour. Weaknecht holds a second job, too, working on his days off for his cousin's landscaping business. His wife, Julie, works, too, instead of devoting herself full time to their children. She holds down two jobs, as a teacher's aide and at a local department store.

The power of big retailers will crush most small businesses, Weaknecht believes. He sees it weakening the fabric of small towns. The owners of local enterprises have a vested interest in maintaining their communities and running the local government at a reasonable cost. The shift to chain stores may be inevitable, he believes, but what happened to him was not.

"If Cabela's had just come to town and paid their own way they probably would have put me out of business," he said. "But they didn't. This is not private enterprise. They are not building their business by their own means whatsoever. They are using the government for their personal benefit. What built America was the private businessperson who risked his own money and built his own business. In my opinion, that is what made America what it is, competition between businesses. We are completely losing that."

Weaknecht has a sort of grudging admiration for the Cabela family's Paris Hilton–level shamelessness in manipulating local governments for handouts instead of competing fair and square in the market. Weaknecht wants to believe any sensible citizen would reject welfare for the rich as both senseless and immoral. He believes that if he had sought a subsidy, the Hamburg town fathers would have laughed at his audacity. Yet his own experience tells him that the reality of business and politics has morphed into something else, something beyond the pale and yet very real. So long as he can earn his own way he will, even if that means four jobs for one family and paying off the creditors of his business so everyone he deals with is made whole. But being rich and collecting welfare, hundreds of millions of dollars of welfare? "I tell everybody the Cabelas are the smartest business people in the world," Weaknecht said, "because they pulled it off."

Not everyone has a hand out for subsidies, however. One company actively fights against them.

Chapter 10

JUST SAY NO

INFLUENCING GOVERNMENT IS ONE OF THE FASTEST-GROWING INDUS-tries in America. In 1975, Washington lobbyists collected less than $100 million in fees. Had their fees grown at the same rate as the economy, lobbyists would have taken in about $250 million by 2006. In reality, they took in 10 times that—more than $2.5 billion.

More than 35,000 lobbyists registered in Washington in 2006, double the number in 2000. Thousands more work the 50 state capitals and the larger city and county governments. These official numbers understate how many lobbyists are paid to influence government because many practitioners are not required to register. Until the end of World War II, no one was even required to register as a lobbyist. Only since 1995 have Washington lobbyists been required to disclose fees, and then not so fully as would allow full monitoring. Enforcement of the laws governing lobbyists are wink-and-nod except for the most outrageous conduct, and even that can go unchecked for years.

Lobbying pays fabulously well for those who succeed. Million-dollar annual salaries are common. Jack Abramoff sought a $9 million fee in 2003 from Omar Bongo, president of the small African nation of Gabon, just to arrange a meeting with President Bush. Bush and Bongo met in 2004. The fee was to be paid to one of Abramoff's multiple lobbying firms, the misleadingly named GrassRoots Interactive. It has never been established whether Abramoff collected this particular fee. However, he collected many tens of millions of dollars from other clients before he went to prison for fraud, including $45 million from Indian tribes who seemed to have little need of a lobbying firm and whose payments he tried to keep secret.

Abramoff held court at table 40 of his Signatures restaurant, which was strategically located between Capitol Hill and the White House. It offered "liberal portions in a conservative setting." The decorations included a copy of the pardon that President Ford granted to President Nixon. Diners sat down to custom Villeroy & Boch chargers and special lint-free napkins. They could rent lockers to store their favorite vintages, to be followed by after-dinner cigars from the Signatures humidor.

For select senators, representatives, and others in government the best part was that Signatures offered them a free lunch. And breakfast. And dinner. Abramoff gave his waitstaff a list of people who were not to be charged. Many of those who dined for free never left tips for the people who waited on them. That stinginess explains how the enterprising reporter Glen Justice was able to get from the stiffed staff records showing that 7 percent of the restaurant meals were given away to those Abramoff sought to influence.

Karl Rove, the man President Bush nicknamed Turd Blossom, House Speaker Dennis Hastert, and Representative Tom DeLay were often at table 40. The people for whom Abramoff said no bill was to be presented included Representatives Roy Blunt of Missouri, John T. Doolittle of California, Frank LoBiondo of New Jersey, and Senators Don Nickles of Oklahoma, Tim Hutchinson of Arkansas, and one Democrat, John Breaux of Louisiana. There were plenty of other favors. Abramoff arranged free trips in private jets to golf at St. Andrews in Scotland and prime American courses. Politicians watched Washington Redskins football games from his luxury box at FedEx Field. All one needed to enjoy these gifts was a willingness to be useful to Abramoff's clients, who were seeking their own free lunch from the taxpayers.

Nobody seemed to notice that government rules prohibit such gifts to those in office. Senators and representatives, for example, could receive no more than $100 worth of gifts from an individual in a year and no one gift could exceed $50. At Signatures a steak cost $74. Even a hamburger cost $12.

None of the politicians admitted to eating for free at Signatures. When DeLay's office was asked about a free meal there, an aide said he did not have any records showing that the Texas Republican ate there that day, a classic nondenial denial. Representative Dana Rohrabacher, a California Republican whose name was on the comp list, claimed that he often took Abramoff to lunch and picked up the tab, so there were no gifts. And so the excuses went from those officials whose staffs even bothered to return calls asking about the freebies.

The Signatures restaurant was central to a host of scandals. Abramoff pocketed nearly all the money from a children's charity. He seemed to work against gambling while actually promoting it in league with Ralph Reed. He engineered favors for a company that held women in virtual slavery on American-owned Saipan to make knitwear. The United States attorney pressing a criminal case in the Saipan case was mysteriously removed, a precursor of later scandals about the political uses of the Justice Department.

Abramoff arranged golfing trips for DeLay and others to Scotland that cost a quarter million dollars. Representative Bob Ney, an Ohio Republican, committed felonies to further Abramoff's interests. A rich Miami gambling ship magnate whom Abramoff had defrauded out of tens of millions of dollars was murdered. This is likely just the tip of the proverbial iceberg, but in an era when the Justice Department has been turned into a machine for partisan prosecutions, with a blurred if not blind eye to the crimes of friends of the White House, it seems likely that the evidence will melt into history.

In his student days, when Reagan was president, Abramoff had served as president of a national organization, the College Republicans. He had long and deep ties to Grover Norquist, Ralph Reed, and Newt Gingrich. In the 1994 elections, Gingrich led the Republicans to control of the House, ending four decades of Democratic Party control. Abramoff went to work for Preston Gates, the Seattle law firm founded by the father of Bill Gates. Preston Gates was almost totally allied with Democrats before Abramoff came along. By 2000, Abramoff had built Preston Gates into the sixth largest lobbying firm in the nation's capital. A firm known for its links to Democrats became renowned for its clients' extraordinary success with the Republican leadership in Congress. That year Abramoff moved on to became chief political rainmaker for the Greenberg Traurig law firm, raising its lobbying revenues in just three years from $3.5 million to $25.5 million.

In March 2004 the Greenberg firm fired Abramoff. It also issued a stinging statement trying, desperately, to distance itself from him. Greenberg Traurig acted just ten days after the *Washington Post* reported on its Sunday front page that Abramoff and a secret partner had collected $45 million in fees from Indian tribes. The fees were supposed to be disclosed, but were not. They were wildly out of proportion to the size of

the Indian casino industry. Most significant, the fees did not seem necessary given the paucity of Indian issues on the front burners of Capitol
Hill. The *Post* story became the talk of the town, partly because ever
since DeLay's rise to power lobbyists aligned with the Democrats were
finding it hard to get work and partly because of the extraordinary success of Abramoff clients in getting what they wanted from Congress and
the Bush administration.

The White House said in 2006 that hardly anyone there knew
Abramoff and released a log showing he had made two visits. Within
months a lawsuit pursued by Judicial Watch showed this was a lie. Judicial Watch is a nonprofit law firm that seeks to expose government corruption and that has been heavily funded by the right. In time its pursuit
of the case brought forth White House visitor logs showing that Abramoff
had visited the Bush White House at least seven times. His close allies
Grover Norquist and Ralph Reed had made more than 100 visits. Overall, Abramoff's team had nearly 500 contacts with the Bush White House,
including 82 with Rove or his staff.

After his firing by Greenberg Traurig, Abramoff would seem to be
an unattractive prospect for almost any employer. The leaders of his own
party were all busy distancing themselves from their once oh-so-close
friend. Yet within days of being fired, Abramoff and three of his associates landed at the premier lobbying firm in Washington. They joined
Cassidy & Associates, a firm founded by a Democrat who was a pioneer
in showing clients how to obtain a free lunch from Congress.

Gerald S. J. Cassidy grew up poor in Brooklyn. He started out as an
antipoverty lawyer. That got him work with the Democrats on Capitol
Hill, helping expose the awful living conditions of migrant farm workers.
Then Senator George McGovern, the South Dakota Democrat, developed a fantasy in 1975 that he could run for president again. McGovern
fired Cassidy to make room on the Agriculture Committee staff for another political operative, Bob Shrum, who stoked the fantasy.

So Cassidy opened a lobbying business. Among his first clients were
private colleges like Tufts University. Cassidy's firm invented the appropriation earmark, in which a specific amount of money for a specified
recipient is written into a spending bill. Instantly, Cassidy had plenty of
clients. A tsunami of greenbacks poured in.

Since then, appropriation earmarks have grown from a relatively few
items buried in the fine detail of the federal budget into an industry.
Campaign donations, favors, and carefully nurtured relationships mix

into a taxpayer-financed pork stew. The infamous $320 million earmark for a "bridge to nowhere" that would connect an island of 50 people with the nearby Alaska mainland is the best-known piece of pork.

Earmarks now finance everything from airport parking for private jets to a Kansas museum dedicated to prisons. A $37 million freeway ramp and road widening for Wal-Mart's corporate headquarters in Benton, Arkansas, accounted for more than a third of all earmarks for that state in 2005. Exxon Mobil, General Electric, and Microsoft have all benefited from earmarks in recent years, though their names do not appear in the statutes.

Many earmarks identify the beneficiary as a hospital, college, or non-profit association, but they are just the entity the money passes through on its way to IBM, Johnson & Johnson, or Ford Motor.

Religion has also discovered earmarks, a particularly curious development in taking from the many to benefit the few. The 108th Congress, which was in office during the 2004 presidential election cycle, gave out more than 450 faith-based earmarks to churches and religious charities. Back in the 1997–1998 Congress, fewer than 60 earmarks went to religious groups, my colleagues Diana B. Henriques and Andrew H. Lehren found by meticulously combing through the fine, and sometimes obscurely worded, details of budget bills. More than a hundred million dollars of cash and property or control of property, from forest land to an old Coast Guard ship, were given to Catholics, Mormons, and independent one-church operations. World Vision, a television-based religious charity, even got money for job training.

Thus does Caesar render that which is his onto the faithful, tearing down a wall that Thomas Jefferson thought crucial to the liberty of the people. "History, I believe, furnishes no example of a priest-ridden people maintaining a free civil government," he wrote in 1813.

Jefferson would be appalled at churches hiring lobbyists to arrange religious earmarks. In 1802, while serving as our third president, Jefferson wrote to the Danbury Baptist Association in Connecticut about the roles of government and religion. Referring to the First Amendment's purpose, President Jefferson wrote: "That act of the whole American people which declared that their legislature should 'make no law respecting an establishment of religion, or prohibiting the free exercise thereof,' thus building a wall of separation between church and State."

Cassidy is not a lobbyist for religious causes, but his success with earmarks has played a major role in turning the First Amendment right to petition government for a redress of grievances into a booming business instead of a political matter. The petitions of those who pay to be heard—by making campaign contributions, hiring the relatives of lawmakers, and providing jobs for those departing Capitol Hill and the executive branch agencies—get a full and often sustained hearing.

So what happens to the petitions of those who just want a responsive government? Those petitioners not seeking personal gain or offering donations? Those without the luck of a news event or celebrity backing to draw attention to their cause? Try getting a private meeting with your Congress member as a mere constituent and see how well you fare. Only rarely are the petitions of those who do not pay to play the basis for official action, except to drop them in the round file.

The growth of earmarks and of turning contact with lawmakers into a business has made Cassidy a demigod to those in the influence business. He is widely regarded as the premier lobbyist in the nation's capital. His personal fortune is well in excess of $100 million, including an imposing mansion on Chesapeake Bay.

Cassidy says he earned it all by working hard on behalf of his clients. Many carefully crafted campaign contributions, especially to Democrats, helped. So did bringing into his business people like Jody Powell, who was President Carter's press secretary, and Sheila Tate, who was Nancy Reagan's press secretary. Mostly, Cassidy made his fortune from the golden cake that is the nearly $3 trillion federal budget. He had slivers cut for his clients, who showered him with golden crumbs.

Because of Cassidy's long success, and the many who have come along emulating his approach, Robert G. Kaiser made him the focus of a 25-part *Washington Post* series on how lobbying really works. The series showed how there is only one party in Washington, the party of money. Cassidy allowed that it was not worth arguing whether the influence of the rich has grown mightily in Washington, while there are no lobbies for the migrant farm workers he had once championed, no lobbyists with big expense accounts to lobby for Joe and Jane Sixpack and their kids.

That an overabundance of money changes what matters was shown with Cassidy's reaction to part 17 of Kaiser's series. The installment had little to do with lobbying. It had a lot to do with bragging rights among those who measure themselves by how many zeros and commas adorn their net worth statement. Cassidy & Associates was sold in 1999 to Interpublic Group, a worldwide firm with 43,000 workers who seek to influence the public and governments through advertising, lobbying, polling, and public relations. Kaiser reported that Interpublic paid about $60 million for Cassidy & Associates. Cassidy was insulted, writing that the famously thorough and evenhanded Kaiser was both dumb and sensationalist. Why, as Cassidy complained, he got more like $80 million for his firm!

As the saying goes, many come to Washington hoping to do good and end up doing well. The federal government spends about $5 million per minute. Arranging to divert even a few seconds of this spending to a client will justify a job, and one who can capture a few minutes will live very well indeed. And, as we have seen, vast sums can be directed without any appropriation, just a rule or a policy that alters the flow of money through the economy.

In part because of Cassidy's pioneering approach, Capitol Hill staffs are now thick with people coming to Washington just to do well. The part about doing good is, for some, quaint. They want to work for a Capitol Hill committee or a lawmaker or an agency head just long enough to learn the ropes and get hired by the lobby trade. Starting pay is often $300,000. Expense accounts for those who make their clients rich off Uncle Sam are virtually limitless.

Cassidy operates in a very practical world, as Abramoff soon learned. As the long-simmering Abramoff scandals boiled over, the once popular lobbyist suddenly became a mess to be avoided. Anyone who was shown to have been close to Abramoff might be voted out of office. A few of his pals, like Congressman Ney, eventually went to prison. Cassidy got some nasty feedback about his new rainmaker. Senator Daniel Inouye, the Hawaii Democrat, told Cassidy he was not welcome so long as Abramoff was on his payroll. Three months after signing on with Cassidy & Associates, Abramoff got the boot.

David Ewald has had a very different career in lobbying, a trade he joined in 1986. He was 26 years old. He joined a firm started four years earlier by his father, Doug, a four-term Republican legislator. Ewald Consulting is not in Washington. Its offices are far down the political food chain in Minneapolis, the forty-eighth largest city in America. Still, the firm employs 30 professionals, some of whom manage trade associations too small to afford their own executive director and staff. But David Ewald spends most of his time lobbying for corporate clients.

For the past few years Ewald has crisscrossed the country to talk to state legislators, small-town mayors, and other local officials. But Ewald is no Cassidy wannabe, no provincial version of the Great Lobbyist seeking earmarks and handouts for clients. Ewald is the anti-Cassidy.

David Ewald's main job for the past few years has been stopping subsidies for Cabela's and Bass Pro. It has proved to be a very hard sell, so willing are politicians at every level to give away that which is not theirs.

He does this work not for some group of do-gooders, but for a corporation whose executives and key owners think more like Adam Smith and not at all like the Cabela family and Johnny Morris of Bass Pro. They are eager to compete, but on a level playing field, not one tilted in favor of corporate socialists who pose as capitalists.

The company paying Ewald to oppose subsidies is Gander Mountain. It ranks third among the hunting/camping/fishing chains in total sales. Unlike its two larger competitors, Bass Pro and Cabela's, Gander Mountain does not have a mail-order operation. Gander Mountain's retail store sales are greater than Cabela's retail sales. Gander Mountain has more than 100 stores, six times as many as Cabela's and more than twice as many as the privately owned Bass Pro.

What distinguishes Gander Mountain is not just management's ardent opposition to handouts, but also its willingness to spend shareholder dollars to fight giveaways to its competitors. The company came to this view after a brief flirtation with subsidies in Minnesota and Texas. The latter prompted an offer of free money so lavish that the allure could have blinded Mark Baker, the chief executive, to how chasing the free money could ruin the rest of the business.

When Gander Mountain moved its corporate headquarters into vacant office space in Minneapolis it got a modest subsidy. And it got another modest one when it opened an 88,000-square-foot store in Corsicana, Texas, an hour south of Dallas, in 2004. Then the developer of the Texas property said he could get Gander Mountain a great deal if it would open a store out west in Reno. And on the theory that more people than are already drawn by the casinos there would flock to Reno, the locals were willing to give away $54 million.

"It was crazy money," Baker said. It made absolutely no economic sense for the locals, even for a 150,000-square-foot store and even if it did draw more people across the border from California. The subsidy would be $360 per square foot, while the cost of construction would be perhaps $230.

The prospect of such money got Baker, who had spent years as the chief operating officer at the Home Depot, thinking about how subsidies distort business decisions. He had a plan for Gander Mountain and for the time being it was to open stores from the East and Gulf Coasts west to the Rockies.

"Reno was way outside our footprint," he said. "We had no distribution center to serve Reno, we had no recognition out there, and it would undo the plan for expansion."

It also got Baker thinking about how economic decisions should be made. "Why should some mayor or group representatives of some city or county decide who the right retailer is for their town?" he asked. "Government is not in charge of commerce. People should be making those decisions, not government. Customers get to vote every day and if you take care of customers they vote for you and if you don't then they vote for someone else. People have become totally confused about the role of government."

Baker told Gander Mountain's new developer, Oppidan Investment Company, to find someone to fight subsidies for Cabela's and Bass Pro. Oppidan chose Ewald.

Any thoughts Ewald had that this would prove an easy task vanished as soon as he hit the road. The city fathers who had a Cabela's or a Bass Pro on the hook were not just willing to give away millions, they were downright eager.

"You get in the back room with these guys," Ewald recalled, "and what they say is that they have to do it." One of the town fathers in Greenwood, Indiana, on the verge of a vote to give Cabela's $18 million for a store that would be just across a highway from an existing Gander Mountain store, told Ewald he had no choice. "Look, I totally agree with you," Ewald said he was told. "I wish we didn't have to do this, but otherwise we are going to lose this Cabela's to a town down the street."

Even in New Hampshire, a state famous for its antitax politics, Ewald found ending subsidies a hard sell. In one town there was a popular vote and, by a slim margin, subsidies won.

Ewald found himself astonished by this. These subsidies were not for research centers that would bring in people at high salaries or manufacturing plants with family wage jobs and lots of ancillary support. These were subsidies for retail, the end of the line for business where even if everything turned as claimed, the bang for the buck hardly qualified as a pop. *Pay Cabela's to open a store and maybe you'll get a gas station and an Applebee's,* Ewald thought.

The economic insanity of it made the work fun, but Ewald found it the most challenging assignment in his 21 years on the job. He had to devise clear arguments to counter the polished presentations by Cabela's and the developers representing Bass Pro. Ewald organized independent sporting goods stores, showing them how subsidies could wipe them out the way Jim Weaknecht had been, even if they owned several large stores with many tens of thousands of square feet of floor space. And he needed hard facts.

One idea was to question Cabela's claims about how many people would come if they built it. Sam Kennedy, a reporter for the Allentown *Morning Call,* came up with a simple way to test Cabela's claim that its store would draw 6 million visitors to Hamburg, Pennsylvania. On an October Saturday in 2004, a year after the store opened and on what should have been a busier than normal day, Kennedy counted cars in the parking lot. There were just 308 and only 68 of them had out of state tags. Even if people came four to a car, the store would have to attract an average of more than 4,100 cars per day to log 6 million people a year.

Two years later Ewald hired college students to check every Cabela's retail store. He picked November 4, a Saturday during deer-hunting season that should be just about the busiest day of the year for an outdoor sporting goods store. The results were nothing less than astonishing. Even assuming the stores were as busy every weekend as this peak season Saturday, and half as busy on weekdays, the study estimated just 2.5 million annual visitors to Cabela's Hamburg store, less than half the promised 6 million.

The average for the 17 Cabela's stores opened at the time was less than 1.5 million visitors per year. Ewald did a more detailed check of one of Cabela's Minnesota stores, counting both cars and people for an entire day. Based on the peak day study the store should have had a bit more than 1.4 million visitors per year. But the more thorough study from a normal day suggested only half as many visitors. In response Cabela's questioned the validity of the study and said that those customers with out of state tags on their cars spent far more than their numbers would suggest. Cabela's said in Hamburg that Pennsylvania residents accounted for less than a third of its sales, a claim that cannot be checked because in giving the subsidies to Cabela's most of the state and local governments did not require proof of success or an audit trail to check up on the claims.

Slowly Ewald began to record some successes. The governor of South Carolina vetoed a bill that officials said was drafted to lure a Bass Pro. Some politicians in Georgia, Kentucky, and Minnesota have started asking hard questions. And Ewald's client has stuck to its guns. Gander Mountain not only turned down several subsidy offers, it gave a million dollars back in Roanoke, Virginia.

The independent storeowners whom Ewald organized have also begun to complain about their tax dollars being used to finance competitors. Jeff Poet, whose family owns two large sporting goods stores in Michigan's Lower Peninsula, is trying to block any more giveaways in that state to Cabela's, which got $40 million for a store in Dundee. "It's just not fair," Poet said.

When Poet first talked to state economic development officials they were unimpressed. After all, giving away money is their job. So Poet and other storeowners adopted a three-pronged strategy. They told the public such giveaways were not fair. Then they complained to state lawmakers. And they made connections to people on the state boards that give the money away, or are crucial to such gifts, and started building relationships to make sure their side of the story was heard.

Yet the subsidies continue. Cabela's and Bass Pro each have tentative deals in the works for hundreds of millions of dollars of subsidies for "destination" stores that in many cases are only an hour or three from another such store.

The size of the subsidies keeps growing. The Reno store that Gander Mountain rejected, walking away from a $54 million gift, had by the summer of 2007 grown into a proposed gift of $83.7 million for Cabela's.

In Memphis, Bass Pro was negotiating to put one of its stores into the iconic glass pyramid that is supposed to connect the Tennessee city with its namesake on the Nile. Bass Pro is seeking tens of millions of dollars even though it already has a store just 20 miles away. "That the city is even talking about this is an indication of the desperation of local government politicians," said Tom Jones of Smart City Consulting. In Memphis and many other cities, Jones said, officials fear that the young will move away and time will pass their town by, so they will listen to anyone who promises to save them, no matter how foolish the plan or how senseless the economics.

Nowhere is that desperation more evident than in Buffalo, which blossomed when the Erie Canal opened in 1825, connecting Chicago and New York by water. But for the past half century Buffalo, an industrial city that relied on its strategic location on the Great Lakes, has been in decline. Bass Pro is negotiating to build a store there, though some locals think their city is just a pawn for some other deal. It would be built on the waterfront, right at the mouth of the historic Erie Canal, on land created when piles were driven into the mud in the months before Andrew Jackson became president. Who knows what costs lurk in such a spot.

Buffalo is a city awash in subsidized projects. Warren Buffett, who owns the *Buffalo News,* got $100 million in government giveaways to open a call center for his GEICO General Insurance Company, the one that uses cavemen and a talking lizard to pitch its products. A special subsidy zone had to be created just to lavish the money on Buffett.

The call center cost $40 million. So, basically, Buffett's company is getting back what it invested and then collecting a $60 million gift from local and state taxpayers. The call center may eventually create 2,500 jobs. If that happens the subsidy would equal $40,000 per job, which is more than a year's pay and benefits for each of the call center workers. The GEICO call center was not built in the city, where more than a fourth of the residents are officially poor. Instead GEICO chose to build in Amherst, one of Buffalo's affluent and overwhelmingly white suburbs. Buffalo has one of the highest unemployment rates among big cities in America, but there is no bus service that would enable its inner-city residents to get to the call center, one of many examples across the country of the subtle racism in job subsidies.

As the GEICO call center opened, another call center, owned by a Canadian firm, shut down. The net gain in jobs was zilch. Still, the *Buffalo News* wrote story after story about how the GEICO center was a wonderful economic development, while giving little attention to the one that closed. In this cheerleading mode, the newspaper even ran a breathless profile of a woman based on the premise that a job at a call center could be an excellent start on the path to an executive position. (The same paper also ran superb, in-depth looks at the failed promises of enterprise zones to create jobs in return for subsidies and other examples of taking from the many to enrich the few.)

James Ostrowski, a hard-line libertarian who has been fighting the subsidy culture of Buffalo, said it took him a few years to realize why the city, and Erie County, fathers were so eager for these deals. As the middle-aged lawyer talked to more and more of them, and read the fine print of those subsidy deals not shielded from disclosure, he began to see a pattern.

"There are about 50 people who make things happen here and they are all in on the subsidies," said Ostrowski. "Everybody is on the take in some fashion. We are drowning in high taxes, but if you are connected or wealthy you make a few phone calls and you get relief. The politicians just get to dole out money to enrich people and it gets them all sorts of favors. The wealthy give tremendous amounts to the politicians—tremendous amounts to you or me, but not to them—and then they get all these deals. Give $100,000 to the right politicians over a couple of years and get a $20 million construction contract or a $500 million deal that guarantees you make out even if the whole thing fails. All these families volunteer to serve on all these authorities—because they get so much back."

Buffalo has one of the lowest-price housing markets in the country. In 2007 the median price for a house in the city was $90,000, significantly lower than it had been in 1996. Yet one of the city's newest plans is to subsidize waterfront condominiums that would cost as much as $659,000 each. The property tax savings would total more than $100,000 over 10 years for each buyer. The real benefit flows to the developer, who can charge a higher price as people seek the bounty. The burden will be borne by those not able to buy luxury housing, including those too poor to afford a car to get a job at GEICO's subsidized call center in the suburbs.

This subsidy culture has so become part of the business and political leadership of Buffalo that the Bass Pro deal seems a normal part of the economic landscape. So what if, according to the deal sheet, it would get a historic waterfront site at the mouth of the Erie Canal? So what if its hunting lodge motif clashes with the carefully revived historic district of the city? So what if Bass Pro insists on freeway signs directing people not to historic downtown, but to its store? So what if Gander Mountain built its own store, with no subsidies, just a few miles away?

Bass Pro even talked the city into spending millions to move a light rail station a few blocks, making it harder for residents carrying groceries to their apartments, but easier for anyone riding the streetcar to pick up a hunting rifle.

Add up all the items on the deal sheet and the total subsidy comes to about $60 million.

The local government would pick up all the costs of making sure that site with the nearly two-century-old pilings is suitable for the Bass Pro store. And it would provide a marina so Bass Pro can display boats and let people take test rides. And Bass Pro would get to use the sales taxes from the store to pay its construction costs. And Bass Pro would control four parking garages, free to its customers but no one else.

Add it all up and the subsidy, depending on who does the estimating, would be between $90 million and $130 million.

The Bass Pro retail store would have 75,000 square feet. That is a subsidy of up to $1,700 per square foot, eight times construction costs for most such stores. The local government wouldn't get the sales tax money for years—Bass Pro will pocket the sales tax. But if government did get the sales taxes and applied them to the subsidy the taxpayers would in time be made whole—in about 60 years.

Crazy as those numbers are, the leaders of Buffalo keep negotiating and talking and offering more and more to Bass Pro. Subsidy economics have become so much a part of their DNA that they cannot bring themselves to just say no.

Subsidy economics has also become part of the scaffolding of the national economy. Sometimes you can benefit from a subsidy by just being in the right place, though seeking a little boost to increase the subsidy helps.

Chapter 11

BEAUTY AND THE BOUNTY

MIKE KEISER ACTED ON HIS OWN WHEN HE BUILT THE FIRST OF his stunningly beautiful golf courses on the remote Oregon coast. He did not retain one of the many firms that specialize in site consulting, a profession less about finding suitable real estate and more about knowing how to extract from the government part or all of the cost of any new job-creating investment. Keiser just put the word out to some real estate agents that he was looking to buy land by the square mile.

Keiser did not solicit government economic development agencies to woo him with offers of money, tax breaks, or other favors, either. That would have offended his libertarian views. Instead, Keiser did business the old-fashioned way: He put up his own money, in hard cash, and took on all the risk that his venture might be an utter failure.

Even so, without asking, Keiser ended up collecting a subsidy worth at least $12 million per year and probably more than twice that much. This subsidy is about to grow by about half. The reason is another subsidy, which he did seek. That Keiser benefits from a subsidy he did not even ask for shows how deeply embedded are new economic rules that take from the many to enrich the few.

In 1971, Mike Keiser found a niche in the greeting-card business and made a fortune growing it. With Phil Friedmann, his business partner, Keiser sold cards printed on recycled paper, catching the wave of the environmental movement. Recycled Paper Greetings allowed artists to sign their work, unlike the anonymous illustrators toiling for Hallmark. After a few years of modest success, the firm took the biggest plunge of all, switching from being one of many vendors represented by commissioned salespeople who supply mom-and-pop businesses to starting its own sales force. Almost overnight, sales boomed. Keiser became seriously wealthy.

What Keiser wanted was to play "dream golf." He favored the game in the style of the eighteenth-century Scotland of Adam Smith, before electric golf carts and narrow, perfectly manicured fairways squeezed into tree-lined country clubs. He had already built one golf course, on the shore of Lake Michigan near his family's getaway home. But like those who build a dream home and then realize it isn't what they wanted, that course fell far short of Keiser's ideal.

Fulfilling his desire required mildly rolling land on a coast, wind-swept, with few or no trees and sandy soil. As soon as Keiser saw the Pacific Ocean bluffs north of Bandon, thick with gorse, he imagined the shape of the land underneath. The owners wanted almost $5 million, but years had gone by with no takers. Keiser slept on it and the next day offered half the asking price. When the owners accepted, Keiser wrote a check.

Just two problems remained. Oregon has some of the toughest land-use laws in the nation, designed to reduce the gasoline consumption, commute time, and inefficient use of land that accompany urban sprawl. It took Keiser more than four years to get approvals to create his ideal golf course, including a hotel and clubhouse complex done in Corporate America Bland, which is to architecture as political correctness is to speech, sticking to neutral lines and tones that neither offend nor inspire.

The second problem was that the Bandon site seriously violated all three rules of real estate. The location was as out of the way as it gets in America without heading to Alaska. The nearest large airport was on the far side of Portland. Reaching Portland requires two plane flights from many cities, followed by hours behind the wheel to drive almost to the California state line just to play golf.

A few years earlier some fools had proposed a golf course that would have ferried players from Portland to the southern coast of Oregon in helicopters, ignoring both the enormous cost of those machines and their reputation for suddenly falling out of the sky. In time, though, a solution to Keiser's location problem would present itself as a free lunch.

When Keiser's plans became known, many in Coos County saw him as an economic savior. The area had fallen on hard times starting about 1980, ending more than a century of prosperity. Jobs vanished. Home-cooked methamphetamine ruined many lives. The schools provided the only escape from chaos for a small but significant minority of children.

William G. Robbins, the Oregon State University historian, titled his book on the changing fortunes of the area *Hard Times in Paradise.*

So many families moved on that the median age in Coos County rose from 28 in 1970 to more than 40 today. Half of the children who remain qualify for free lunches. The state says uncertainty about where the next meal will come from is a major local problem, one reason the local food bank helps 4,600 people a month in a county with 64,000 residents. More than 7,000 people are on a waiting list for 14 public housing units.

Local leaders seek grants to revive the old economy, hoping for subsidies to improve the little-used port at Coos Bay. They see an opportunity to offload shipping containers from China, if only the taxpayers will give Union Pacific more than $200 million to rebuild a spur line so antiquated that lumber trains must creak along at 10 miles per hour through Coast Range tunnels to the main rail line. But that dream began a quarter century ago, and the elusive dawn is still at least a decade into the future.

It was not always so.

For thousands of years the Coo, the Coquille, and other Native Americans prospered off the land and the sea. The climate was moderate; the forests thick with game sheltered by fir, hemlock, and myrtle wood; while the free-running streams and rivers made the sea flush with salmon. When the first Europeans arrived, right after the California gold rush in 1849, they found Coos Bay, the only natural deepwater harbor between San Francisco and Puget Sound. They cut down trees, some of which had sprouted before Columbus set sail for the New World, for bracing in mines and planks for housing in San Francisco. One of the 300-foot-long lumber ships of that era, the *Balclutha,* still lies at anchor in San Francisco, a reminder of when the winds alone powered cargo ships.

The newcomers also found coal, though the seams quickly ran out. Still, the discovery prompted some to call the area the "Appalachia of the West," a name that would take on new meaning after 1980 when the timber industry collapsed and the runs of salmon dwindled. The forests were rich enough to sustain a small population forever. But the owners of the timber companies wanted more profits now and so they cut faster and faster while the trees continued to grow back at rates set by nature. To hasten the harvest, new forests were planted like corn, with one kind of tree, not the diversity of nature. But still the cutting went on faster than the growing, until there was no more tomorrow to harvest.

Automation played a role, too, wiping out thousands of well-paying jobs in the mills. Today one mill at Coos Bay turns a baker's-dozen logs into finished lumber every minute. Monitoring the operation requires just eight people. The old Weyerhaeuser mill on the main drag in Coos Bay, where crews worked steadily, has been converted into a casino aptly named The Mill. Dealing cards and changing bedsheets, however, pays far less than slicing logs into lumber.

Like Keiser, Bandon area native Scott Cook is a born entrepreneur who sees opportunity all around. Cook finished high school in 1976, one of the last years of prosperity on the Oregon coast.

"When I grew up there was a job on every corner, there were family-wage jobs that paid $18 an hour, and if you were an entrepreneur there was opportunity here, you just had to pick it," Cook recalled.

His first summer out of school, Cook made the equivalent of $200,000 in today's currency. He fished for salmon, cut down trees, and drove a logging truck, even though he had only one arm, the result of an industrial accident when he was a hardworking lad of six. Two decades later, without a single accident or even a ticket on his record, the state took his commercial driver's license away, saying it was unsafe for a man with only one arm to drive a logging truck.

Cook and Keiser differ mostly in their choice of work and in luck. Cook took on blue-collar risks, like a tree falling at the wrong angle or a piece of machinery ripping off a limb. He lost most of the small fortune he had built after one almost perfect fishing trip. His 51-foot steel ship was full of fish and ice when a storm hit. The 40-foot waves beat a bulkhead with a bad weld into submission. Cook and his helper put on survival suits. That night, just before they jumped into the salty void, Cook told his helper, "I'm sorry I killed you." Somehow they both survived.

For the salmon fishermen of Coos Bay, times grew ever harder thanks to a host of government policies. The rules for commercial fishing ban barbed hooks and set a minimum length for fish. Having a single snapped-off barb on deck, even if every hook is clean, brings a stiff fine. So can a single fish just an eighth of an inch short of specifications. The government spends millions on ships and inspectors, and the fishermen believe the elaborate enforcement is how the inspectors justify their pay. Their zero-tolerance approach to law enforcement is far from the white-collar world of stock manipulators, pension thieves, and legalized loan sharking.

Further, decades of damming rivers for electricity and water storage

have cut into nature's bounty of salmon. For years the government miti-
gated this by running hatcheries, turning loose the young salmon known
as smolts to make their way as ocean predators. Now many salmon are
raised in floating cages, where the fish need no skill to hunt for their dinner. Because of salmon farming, the government is starting to talk about
shutting down the hatcheries. This is part of what it means to reduce so-
called discretionary spending in Washington and the state capitals. The
theory is that the market has provided a substitute for government-run
hatcheries, although that overlooks the fact that farmed salmon are not
nearly as healthful to eat as wild fish, even those that began their lives in
hatcheries.

The salmon runs in Oregon dwindled until, in 2006, there was no
commercial season. Don Yost, the harbormaster at Coos Bay for 18 years,
was ordered to seize the boats of seven salmon fishermen who had not
paid their dock fees. He refused, which cost him his job despite local uproar in support of this small act of heroism.

Cook laments these changes. "It's gone from family-wage jobs to
service industry; it's gone to just above minimum-wage jobs," he said.
"We are in a scenario now where our families, my children, can't afford
to live here anymore."

Meanwhile, Bandon has drawn economic refugees from Los Angeles, Orange County, and Silicon Valley. The locals call them Californica-
tors, people who sold their houses for a profit of a half-million dollars or
more and bought new homes on the Oregon coast to get away from the
stresses of suburban life. With few homes on the market in little towns
like Bandon, population about 3,000, prices soared. Matt Winkle, the
Bandon city manager, said if he came to town today he could not afford
to buy any home.

To Cook, the movement away from harvesting nature's bounty to
an economy built on golf is folly. "Our nation was built with timber, it
was built with fishing, it was built with natural resources," he said.
"We've been a natural-resource economy on the West Coast for generation after generation and, in just a short period of time, that's all gone
away. I think as a country we need that. . . . If we don't have that and
we stay strictly a service industry, I think we're going to fall apart."

Cook's family owns more than 300 acres of forest, enough land to
sustain them forever if they harvest it carefully. The land is up along
Johnson Creek, which flows freely and sustains salmon runs. Mike Keiser
wants to dam that creek. So does the city, which wants a reservoir for

the population growth it anticipates as more people retire there from California to live off their investments, pensions, and Social Security.

Building the earth-fill dam would mean Cook and his wife would lose their forest. Part of the site would be submerged and the rest would be cut off. And while they would be compensated, the Cooks have no expectation that they would be made whole. They fear they may get just pennies on the dollar. After being paid off they would be left at the mercy of the stock and bond markets, which are unfamiliar to them, instead of living off the land they know.

Keiser would pay his share of the cost for 200 acre-feet of water each year, a little more than 10 percent of the total. He needs the water for golf courses he wants to build south of town, miles from the Bandon Dunes Golf Resort on the north side, which already has enough water.

In joining the dam project, Keiser is seeking the very kind of government benefit that runs counter to his libertarian philosophy. The Cooks say they do not want to sell. Without eminent domain, Keiser would have to pay market price for the land he covets. Cook might well agree to a land swap, giving him 300 other acres of forest that he could harvest at the same rate the trees grow back. But with the market subverted, Cook will get the lowest price the government can justify if the dam project comes to fruition.

Government's power to condemn land, as Kim Blankenship learned when Jeep built its new factory in Toledo and took her garage for a bit of lawn, inherently means getting a fraction of the market price for real estate. As George Bush and George Steinbrenner and so many other wealthy Americans have learned, getting government to seize the land you want saves time and makes you richer.

Keiser is untroubled by the forced taking of another man's land for his benefit. "So long as the owner is fairly compensated," Keiser said, he did not see an issue.

Cook does see an issue. "It's morally offensive for government to take one man's land to benefit another," he said. "It's about guys with money making more money" at the expense of those who have less. "His project is no more important than my project, his family is no more important than my family."

But the dam project is small potatoes in terms of the financial rewards going to Keiser. So are some minor property-tax breaks he sought, worth less than $100,000 per year. The real benefit comes from a subsidy embedded in the scaffolding of the economy, one that showers Keiser with riches for just being there, though he has worked to maximize this subsidy. By Keiser's measure, the subsidy works out to about $37,000 for each full-time job at his Bandon Dunes Golf Resort. Including fringe benefits and tips paid to the workers, that is the average pay for these jobs. This subsidy is likely worth twice that much.

Keiser's dream has turned into pure gold. Even though Bandon is remote, each year it draws some of the wealthiest in the world. While many players come by car, the rich come in private jets. Before Bandon Dunes opened in 1999, about three private jets a year landed at the airport in Coos Bay, a 25-minute drive from the golf links. By 2006, there were 5,000 jets a year. Gary W. LeTellier, the airport director, expects 7,000 or more jets per year once a new terminal and parking aprons are finished in 2008 to serve all the Lears, Gulfstreams, Citations, and even Airbus personal jets delivering golfers to the Oregon coast.

This airport-construction subsidy for Keiser will cost $31 million, half from the ticket tax paid by commercial airline passengers and related air travel fees and half from the Oregon state lottery, which makes most of its money from the working poor hoping to strike it rich. It is a subsidy he sought and paid advisers to lobby to obtain. Without the airport expansion he would not be moving so quickly to add a fourth, a fifth, and perhaps more golf courses in the Bandon area.

The really big subsidy, though, comes from the policies Congress set on the personal use of corporate jets in 1985. When a corporate executive uses the company jet for personal flights, he does not pay anything. Instead the value of the trip is treated as a taxable fringe benefit, just like the personal use of a company car. But the way Congress values that trip means the executive pays only pennies of the real cost and then only in the form of higher income taxes. Taxpayers pick up one-third of the real cost because buying and operating a corporate jet is a tax-deductible business expense. Shareholders of publicly traded companies pick up the other two-thirds. That means ordinary folks who have put their retirement money into companies are dinged twice for this executive perk, once as taxpayers and a second time as investors.

In calculating the value of the fringe benefit that executives get, Congress leaves out huge portions of the real cost. First, the value is limited to what are called incremental costs, which excludes the basic costs of buying the plane, staffing it, and insuring it, but does cover fuel and landing fees. Then the government excludes the cost of "positioning" flights. For example, the head of one New York investment bank took the company plane to China on business, then sent it back to Chicago to pick up his son and fly him to a ski vacation in Colorado, and then had the plane return to Asia to pick him up. Only the two-hour flight from Chicago to Colorado was counted as a fringe benefit.

Many companies reimburse executives for the taxes they must pay on the fringe benefit of making personal use of such planes. Some even pay the taxes on the taxes, making the trips free rides in every sense of that word.

Keiser leases a corporate jet, a Gulfstream. But since his is a privately held enterprise, he bears the full after-tax cost of using the plane, in contrast to the subsidy for executives of publicly traded companies.

Some people, including those who claim they favor less government and oppose subsidies, argue that Keiser is not the beneficiary of this corporate jet subsidy. But even Keiser says he is. "Certainly from the recipient point of view," Keiser said, "I'm pleased that there is a subsidy and know very well that it is a subsidy that can be changed at any point in time. That is why we have a Congress, to look at things like that."

Keiser is not unique in benefiting from this subsidy. Disney World, the Super Bowl and golf courses like CSX's at Greenbrier in West Virginia also benefit from the personal use of corporate jets. What makes Bandon Dunes distinctive is that there is no other beneficiary for the use of the airport at Coos Bay. Commercial passenger traffic has been steady for years at about 100 passengers a day. And those corporate jets, except maybe three per year, are drawn by the golf links Keiser owns.

Such is the makeup of the American economy today that subsidies are built right into the framework. To Bandon and nearby Coos Bay, the subsidies seem like a godsend, creating hundreds of desperately needed jobs. But to the overall economy the subsidy is a drain, weakening the economy, because the subsidies by even the narrowest measure exceed the value of the new jobs. Add in all the costs of the subsidies, and the part-time jobs at Bandon Dunes, and it is still a net loser. And for what? For golf.

Each time an executive takes the company jet to play at Bandon Dunes you pay part of the cost. And the airport improvements, done solely to benefit Bandon Dunes, are also paid for when you buy a commercial airplane ticket or an Oregon lottery ticket. Perhaps we have not moved so far since the poet Sarah Northcliffe Cleghorn wrote about golf and inequality a century ago:

> *The golf links lie so near the mill*
> *That almost every day*
> *The laboring children can look out*
> *And watch the men at play*

While Bandon Dunes is a story of how subsidies, the largest of them subtle and hidden, benefit one man, there are whole industries that rely on subsidies for their profits. One industry shifts almost all of its labor costs onto taxpayers.

Chapter 12

FALSE ALARM

THREE DOZEN TERRIFIED CHILDREN RAN SCREAMING INTO THE ROSS Snyder Recreation Center in the depressed South Central area of Los Angeles. Arby Fields, just eight months into his job as the recreation director, stepped outside to investigate. Using his hand as a visor against the blazing July sun, Fields saw about 20 young men crossing the park, clothing draped over their guns. "I shut the doors and called the cops," he said.

Fields called again. And he called yet again. Finally, four squad cars arrived—three hours later.

Fields worked with poor kids in some of the most troubled parks in Los Angeles for 13 years. He heard shots fired three or four times a week. Hector Hernandez, the city's chief of park security, called them the "terrorized parks." Despite the dangers, police response was erratic. Sometimes the police arrived so fast it seemed that they had been parked around the corner. Far more often the response was frighteningly slow and, a few times, the cops never showed up. Guessing how long it would take the cops to arrive was like trying to predict the weather on a Tuesday next March.

Not being able to get a cop when you need one is becoming a more common problem across America. People who call the police for help are discovering that they may wait a long time for the cops to show up. Calls to 911 often are put on hold while music plays. In 1996 police answered calls involving property crimes within 10 minutes more than 34 percent of the time. That fell to 27 percent of the time in 2003, Justice Department research found.

Why is this happening? Has there been a massive surge in crime?

No. Crime is down, way down. Since 1980, the violent crime rate has fallen by a fifth. For property crimes the rate is down more than a third. Nor is it a problem of too few cops. America has more police today than in 1980. And the number of police officers per capita is higher today.

So if crime is way down and the number of police officers is up, why is it taking longer for the police to respond to calls for help? The answer is a free lunch being served to one industry—the companies that make, install, and monitor burglar alarms.

In many cities and suburbs, one of every eight calls for police service comes from a company that monitors burglar alarms. Taxpayers spent well north of $2 billion to respond to these calls, a subsidy to the alarm industry, which is spared that expense. More than a fourth of this subsidy goes to a single corporation, Tyco International. Tyco was at the center of the Wall Street stock scandals, with investors losing tens of billions of dollars and its chief executive, Dennis Kozlowski, and its chief finance officer, Mark Schwarz, going to prison for stealing more than $600 million. Tyco is also infamous for having its legal headquarters in Bermuda, even though its operations are mostly in America. This tax address of convenience allows it to profit from customers in the United States while not sharing in the burden of maintaining the government.

While Tyco is by far the biggest player in the burgeoning burglar alarm business, other big players include General Electric, Honeywell, and Brink's. This particular free lunch is so lavish that the taxpayers provide all of the profits the industry reports. Being able to collect huge sums from the taxpayers explains why other companies are trying to move into the alarm business, including cable television providers and some electric utilities.

As with many subsidies, this one is subtle. It does not appear in any government budget. No city council, legislature, or Congress voted to authorize it. Instead, it flows from a government policy that the burglar alarm companies exploit. But by listening carefully to the industry's television commercials the subsidy can be discerned.

Since 1980, the number of murders in the United States has declined by almost half. But from the alarm industry's alarming commercials, no one would know that. These commercials exploit the fear of crime promoted by local television news, which emphasizes violence out of all proportion to the actual risks. "If it bleeds, it leads" is the standard for local television news.

The commercials are effective. From 1995 to 2000, the number of homes with burglar alarms increased 50 percent, the industry's data show. A typical commercial depicts a lone suburban home on a dark and stormy night, a wild-eyed villain prying at a door. In one of these commercials the bad guy clutches a bowie knife between his teeth. Inside the house, the little woman, Hollywood beautiful, cowers in fear, arms around her little ones. Then the alarm goes off, turning on the porch lights. The burglar flees and the announcer's calming voice says that because the family bought an alarm system, "the police are on their way."

That's the subsidy. The burglar alarm company charges $29 a month and all it does is telephone the police. What people are paying for is to have uniformed officers show up, and that is expensive. The alarm company charges for a service whose real costs it fobs off on the taxpayers. Here is how it works: When an alarm trips, an electronic device automatically dials a monitoring station. The largest is run by a New Jersey firm called Amcest, which gets automated calls like this from across the nation. At the monitoring station, the call opens a display on a computer screen with details about the customer. The technician then calls the home to ask if all is well. If a predetermined question is not answered in the right way, or no one answers, the technician then calls the local police.

This is a lucrative gambit. The cost of monitoring is tiny. The cost of sending someone to check out an alarm is much greater. If the alarm companies checked out the alarms themselves their profits would disappear, the industry's own data indicate.

Of the $29 average monthly fee for monitoring, $22 is gross profit for the alarm company, according to Stat Resources, whose market research is cited by the industry as the most reliable source of information. Many small alarm companies hire another firm to do the monitoring, paying on average less than five dollars a month for this service.

This means that about 80 cents out of each dollar that customers pay for monitoring counts as gross profit.

Gross profit is not the same as net profit, which is what is left after deducting all costs. Still, burglar alarms are an exceptionally lucrative business. After meeting all expenses, the industry keeps almost 24 cents out of each dollar as profit, reports by Stat Resources showed. That is a much bigger profit than corporations overall, which keep as profit about a dime from each dollar they ring up on the cash register.

These profits are huge because the alarm industry does not pay its largest single cost, labor to check out alarms. The taxpayers pick up this expense. Each time the police check out an alarm it costs more than $50, the police in Seattle and other cities have determined. The average alarm goes off more than once each year. The police responded to about 38 million alarms in 2000 at a total cost to taxpayers of $1.9 billion.

The burglar alarm industry collected $7.9 billion from residential and commercial burglar alarm customers that year. So if the industry's estimates are reliable, it means that profits were almost $1.9 billion, almost exactly the value of the taxpayer subsidy in having police check out false alarms.

This subsidy is growing because ever more alarms are being installed each year, even though the number of burglaries is falling. Since 1980 the number of burglar alarms has grown much faster than the population as the price of alarm systems has fallen from about $3,000 to $600 on average. Many companies install alarms for free or a nominal charge when people sign a long-term contract to have their alarm monitored. There were 3.8 million burglaries reported in 1980, but fewer than 2.2 million in 2005, a 42 percent decline. Take into account the larger population and your chance of being burglarized is less than half what it was in 1980.

Having the police respond to burglar alarms may seem to be an appropriate public service. But only one in five residences has an alarm. This means everyone is paying for a benefit that four out of five people do not receive.

Worse, almost three decades of studies show that virtually all alarms are false. In many cities 99 percent of alarms prove to be false. In Seattle, for example, police in one recent year checked out 30,000 alarms. They made just 40 arrests as a result of this work. Each officer on the burglar alarm detail worked more than nine weeks to make one arrest. Other police work produces almost an arrest per week. This low arrest rate is not surprising, since even when an alarm is real the police are unlikely to arrive in time to catch the thieves in the act. The average burglary takes less than five minutes. Police on average arrive 40 minutes after learning of an alarm, the Salt Lake City police found.

Another reason that police burglar alarm squads make few arrests is that up to 60 percent of false alarms are caused not by burglars, but by the customers themselves. Not setting the alarm properly, leaving ajar a door that the wind blows open, and punching in the wrong entry code are common causes of false alarms. So are pets, severe winds, and momentary power outages.

It is not even clear that burglar alarms deter break-ins. Homes with a dog have the same burglary rate as homes with alarms, a study cited by the industry shows. And that holds true for any dog, even, say, a golden retriever, a breed equally likely to wag its tail at a burglar as bark a warning. A Justice Department study in Savannah, Georgia, found that having an alarm in a home deterred burglars. But just putting up a sign stating that a house has an alarm may be as effective. The most effective way to deter daytime break-ins, the Savannah study found, was to crack down on truancy, a policy that has the virtuous benefit of keeping youngsters in school.

As is so often the case with subsidies, they encourage waste by those receiving them. So long as Tyco and other big alarm companies can stick the taxpayers with their labor costs, they have no incentive to become more efficient by designing better alarms and better ways to detect false alarms.

Tyco had about 5 million alarm customers in 2004. That indicates Tyco's share of the false-alarm subsidy runs to about a half billion dollars each year. Looked at another way, Tyco's profits are inflated by a half billion dollars per year because of free labor by the police. That makes Tyco's profits close to 20 percent larger than they would be if it had to cover these costs. If Tyco had to bear the costs of this economic pollution, its stock price would drop to reflect the smaller profits. In this way, economic pollution enriches Tyco executives. Their pay is tied to the company's stock price, which is artificially inflated by this subsidy. This is yet another example of how government policies subtly take from the many and redistribute to the few.

Industry data show that the massive growth in the burglar alarm industry has come since burglary rates began falling after 1980. There are many reasons the number of reported break-ins are down, but one of the least appreciated involves a simple change in government rules, an example of how the rules that define a civilization can lessen crime and make people safer.

In the sixties and seventies, the federal government and some states, notably California, experimented with ways to make break-ins more difficult through building design. Carpenters built doors with different jambs, for example. And they studied what size windows near door handles made it hard to break in and just turn the handle, while still allowing light to flow in from outside.

This inexpensive research produced changes in building codes that made new construction less vulnerable to second-story artists, simple changes like the length of a dead bolt and how it was secured. These lock laws, as builders called them, also had an effect because they drove out the flimsiest locks. Architects and builders also acquired new knowledge on how design affects vulnerability to break-ins.

These government rules also affected who gets rich, but in a virtuous way. By setting minimum standards that drove out flimsy locks, the government no doubt harmed makers of those locks and steered business toward higher-quality products. But it did so by increasing safety, a long-established purpose of government. And it did not do so to enrich any group. The more important effect was in showing through research how the way that windows and doors are designed, and the materials used, can make a home more secure, even without incurring extra construction costs.

On the other hand, increased reliance on burglar alarms makes people less safe. At first blush that may seem odd, but the proof is right in the official government data. The more that police resources are diverted from activities that produce arrests, the more criminals get away.

"The time police spent on false burglar alarms could be put to better use on many other things, including homeland security," said Professor Erwin A. Blackstone, a Temple University economist who studied the burglar alarm industry subsidies.

In Los Angeles, for example, during a decade-long period, the police maintained a 100 percent commitment to responding to burglar alarms while cutting in half their commitment to each murder. As the number of alarms tripled, the number of hours police spent responding tripled, too. This growth continued until the equivalent of more than 200 police officers were assigned to what could have been accurately labeled the false-alarm squad. During those same years, the number of murders in Los Angeles doubled to more than a thousand, while the number of hours the police devoted to murder investigations remained almost flat. The result? For every dollar the police spent investigating murders, they spent $1.25 checking out false burglar alarms.

The beneficiaries of this spending policy were criminals, notably killers. When the police have identified the suspect they are convinced committed the crime, they count it as solved, even if they never make an arrest. Over time, the ratio of unsolved cases rose from one-fifth to half of all murders.

More significantly, the conviction rate fell. A study of more than 9,000 homicides found that just 16 percent resulted in a murder conviction. Add in convictions for the lesser crime of manslaughter and the tiny number of cases handled in juvenile court and the conviction rate was 30 percent. That is, 7 in 10 killers walked free, helped in part by the diversion of police to checking out false burglar alarms for Tyco and others.

Thus do the rules of government not just take from the many to enrich the few, but at the price of helping a majority of killers get away with murder.

The burglar alarm industry charges hefty fees for a service that costs it very little. Then the industry dumps onto the taxpayers the real costs of providing the very service it sells. This is economic pollution sold to people under the guise of making them safe. In fact, it makes them less safe.

While the alarm industry has found ways to profit by shifting costs onto taxpayers, another industry routinely commits crimes that balloon costs for customers. When one government official began looking into this subsidy, her family found itself under a microscope.

Chapter 13

HOME ROBBERY

ANYONE WHO HAS BOUGHT A HOUSE REMEMBERS THE RUSH OF EMO-tions when the moment finally arrives to close the deal. There is the excitement of owning your own home, the satisfaction of success, plus a touch of anxiety about whether you can really afford it—and whether you paid too much. All that is kept in check by the rapid presentation of documents to sign and initial.

Once the deed is done, the buyer receives an envelope with copies of all the documents and a list of the closing costs: fees for preparing documents and for filing them, payments to the appraiser and the termite inspector and perhaps one for a tax stamp. Among the bewildering array of little nips at your wallet of $15 here and $150 there, one item stands out as a very big bite—title insurance.

On average, the title insurance premium adds half of 1 percent to the purchase price of a home (except in Iowa, where it costs a lot less). As the price of real estate has ballooned along the coasts, the title insurance industry has jacked up prices, making that bite deeper. Americans paid $16.4 billion for title insurance in 2005, double what they paid five years earlier and four times what they paid in 1995.

Yet title insurance remains an expensive mystery. Why must you buy it? Who exactly is being insured? For what? Why does it cost so much? And why do you have to pay again when you refinance even with the same lender?

Answering those questions takes us inside a business that owes its riches entirely to the government. The product itself costs next to nothing but, because of the way the market is organized, competition pushes prices higher instead of lower and government regulations help hide the true cost. Here it is not Adam Smith's invisible hand of the market producing unexpected benefits through competition, but instead the manipulative hand of government helping the regulated insurers fleece the consumer.

A title proves ownership and it can come in different forms for different possessions. Many communities require that bicycles be licensed, a minimal form of proof that eases recovery if the bike is stolen. Every state has a reliable system to title cars and register outstanding liens that helps hold down the cost of car loans. Yet even though some cars cost more than houses, there is no requirement for title insurance on new cars. Until recently no such requirement existed for used vehicles, either, but the title insurance industry is working to create demand for such coverage.

Establishing rights to land is more complicated than it is for objects like bicycles or automobiles. For starters, there is the issue of where your property ends and your neighbor's begins.

In the United States property line boundaries often trace back to markers that are far from fixed: a bend in the river that may have moved over time with the watercourse, or a landmark rock so large that selecting slightly different reference points on its face results in different boundary lines radiating away from it. Some property records even refer to famous but transitory markers, like a once-renowned oak that was chopped down a century ago.

Even when surveyors mark plot lines from markers set out by the United States Geological Survey, imperfections arise because the Earth is curved while a surveyor's transit measures in straight lines. Mistakes are made, too. Then there is the random outbuilding that encroaches an inch or so onto a neighbor's property, or so he says. Or the easement for an underground pipe that runs right under your garage and needs replacement. And what of the rights to the oil, water, or minerals underground? Or the inheritor who shows up with a copy of his grandfather's will that says he was entitled to a share of the property, only no one told him when the ancestor died two decades ago because he was only seven years old? The land title insurance companies point to examples like these to make the case that the system cannot operate without them.

The land title companies are correct that a reliable system for tracking land ownership is crucial to building wealth, encouraging investment in property, and avoiding violent disputes. Hernando de Soto, the thoughtful Peruvian economist, traces much of the lack of investment in Latin America to uncertainty about land ownership and the failure of governments to enforce property rights. Through careful analysis of land title records in Egypt, Haiti, Peru, and the Philippines, de Soto showed that about 85 percent of urban dwellings are on land being used informally and thus subject to dispute about title.

He calls these buildings "dead capital" and estimated their value, worldwide, at more than $9 trillion. He is among those who favor systems to register land titles, saying this makes the property more valuable. When informally used land is registered with a named owner in Peru, its value doubles instantly. Within a decade such land grows tenfold in value as owners invest in buildings and equipment, creating value.

Much of the civilized world gets along just fine without title insurance. Australia, Europe, and Puerto Rico do not have it. Neither did Canada until the 1990s, when American title insurers started promoting their product to fill a need few imagined existed. In these places there are fewer title disputes per capita than in any of the 49 states that have commercial title insurance (Iowa being the exception). America could eliminate title insurance with simple reforms that would save billions of dollars in reduced litigation. Or we could keep the system, but place the burden of cost where it would be lowest, still saving billions of dollars each year.

De Soto's work shows the value in having a reliable way to tell who owns a piece of land and who has a lien on it. De Soto acknowledges that land title records maintained by government are not perfect. American land title insurance companies exploit this flaw in record keeping to sell a product that costs next to nothing at very high prices.

Based on all the names of land title companies operating in America, there appears to be a vibrant market with hundreds of firms competing for your business, which should mean efficient pricing. But when you follow the trail of ownership it turns out that five huge companies collect 92 percent of all the title insurance premiums paid in America: Fidelity National Financial of Jacksonville, Florida; First American Corporation of Houston; LandAmerica Financial Group of Glen Allen, Virginia; Stewart Information Services of Houston; and Old Republic International Corporation of Chicago. By operating through dozens of subsidiaries these five companies create the appearance of a vibrant and competitive market when in fact the five companies are so dominant that they collected $15.1 billion of the $16.4 billion in title insurance premiums paid in 2005.

The five major companies that are making billions off of this wildly overvalued insurance have too much at stake to allow reform. When a state insurance regulator tried to expose a costly practice, she became the target of a smear campaign orchestrated by one of the country's biggest title insurance companies.

Economists call the way these five companies control the market an *oligopoly*. It differs from a monopoly in that a scintilla of price competition may exist, though not always. With just a handful of players it is easy for companies to tacitly keep prices artificially high without colluding outright, which would be illegal.

The big five do compete, but not to sell at the lowest price and without the normal discipline the market provides to squeeze out inefficiency and lower prices. Title insurance is sold in a bizarre kind of market that economists call *reverse competition.*

Just like it sounds, reverse competition means a market that drives prices up, not down. In title insurance, this happens because the real customers are not the buyers of homes and other real property, although they pay the premiums. The real customers, from the perspective of the title insurance companies, are the people who steer business to them. That is exactly what the title insurance companies tell their shareholders and the Securities and Exchange Commission. Stewart Information Services of Houston, which collected $1.9 billion in title insurance premiums in 2005, reported that its "primary sources of title business are attorneys, builders, developers, lenders, and real estate brokers." It made no mention of the people who pay the premiums.

These lawyers, developers, bankers, and real estate salespeople want the highest payments they can get for referring their clients to a particular title insurance company, money politely called "referral fees." The more accurate description is kickbacks and bribes. Kickbacks and commercial bribes are illegal, so the title insurance industry has developed a complex and costly set of ruses to obscure them.

Erin Toll, the Colorado real estate commissioner, spotted the misconduct in 2004. She noticed that a new type of land title insurance in the state, sold only to buyers of new homes, had not resulted in a single claim in eight years. If no claims are made, is there any risk to insure against? It's not surprising that buyers of new homes made no claims. As with new cars, there was little reason to think that a builder would erect houses on land without clear title to it.

Toll found that the builders forced new-home buyers to purchase insurance at inflated prices from title insurance companies that the builders owned, something they called a captive company. The title insurance companies were mere shells, which bought the insurance through land title companies for a tiny fraction of what the home buyers paid, an illegal form of price gouging.

One of the big five land title companies, LandAmerica, tried to stop Toll's investigation. Company e-mails show Ted Chandler, the Land-America chief executive, authorizing his executives to use political influence to stop the investigation and to smear Toll.

LandAmerica went to higher-ups in Colorado state government hoping to shut Toll down. The company argued that Toll had a conflict of interest because her former husband, a lawyer, worked for the insurance industry, although in a segment unrelated to title insurance. The higher-ups backed Toll and told LandAmerica its complaints were baseless. LandAmerica was not deterred.

Peter Habenicht, LandAmerica's chief publicity agent, wrote in March 2006 that he would "dig for facts regarding Ms. Toll's stepfather, mother and sisters."

The company asserted that Toll had a conflict because her sisters were partners in a joint venture with LandAmerica in another state. That fact seemed to undercut their case. Assuming that Toll knew what her sisters were doing 2,000 miles away, her investigation demonstrated that she put her public duty ahead of her sisters' interests.

What disturbed LandAmerica the most, internal e-mails obtained by Congress show, was that Toll's investigation had sparked interest by regulators in 19 other states. In one e-mail Peter Kolbe, LandAmerica's senior vice president in charge of lobbying, discussed his efforts to get the National Association of Insurance Commissioners to "kill Erin Toll's captive insurance investigation."

Habenicht also crafted a damning letter that he planned to send to her superiors through his company's outside counsel that was intended to thrust a political knife in Toll's back without anyone noticing who had wielded the blade. In an e-mail, Habenicht described how the draft letter suggested impropriety by Toll but "does not get specific about her alleged conflicts of interests . . . rather it merely identifies them broadly. That changes the media game a bit. . . . Now one of the logical questions becomes 'What conflicts are you referring to, LandAm? Explain what you mean.' And then it gets gritty."

As part of its smear campaign, Kolbe called insurance regulators in other states. One of them, Paul Hansen of Minnesota, recorded the conversation. Kolbe began by saying that Toll "has extremely serious ethical conflicts with the entire insurance industry." He gave no specifics, but threatened, "If she doesn't back off we're going public." And if that happened, Kolbe said, "This is going to get real stinky real quick."

Hansen made it clear he did not believe Toll had done anything wrong. He also suggested that most state insurance regulators would see an attack on Toll as an attack on them. His own superiors, he noted, came to their appointed offices with extensive connections to those they regulated and to people in related fields like building and banking.

Kolbe backpedaled. "We've tried to raise it in a discreet way," Kolbe said. "If we were trying to hurt anybody, which we absolutely are not, we would have picked up the phone to the newspapers."

In addition to Toll's discovery that no claims were made or paid, what prompted her inquiry was the fact that very little of the title insurance premium paid by home buyers went to a real insurance company.

About 80 percent of the premium is kicked back to the person steering the business to the title insurance companies. In California in the years 2003 to 2005 the five big title companies kept only 8 percent to 12 percent of the premium for themselves.

These numbers show reverse competition at work. The competition is for referrals, not the best insurance at the lowest price. The mortgage broker, the banker, the real estate attorney, and the real estate agent bid up the price for steering business to one insurer instead of to another. The New Jersey Supreme Court recognized this when it held that the lawyer whom you think represents your interests in buying is really the agent of whatever title company issues the policy.

Even though kickbacks are illegal, they are thoroughly ingrained in the title insurance industry. Mike Kreidler, the insurance commissioner in Washington State, ordered an investigation based on what Toll found in Colorado. His office found a pervasive system of payments, some disguised and some quite open, and all illegal. His report found a "a clear pattern of inducements and incentives. Although details and form varied from company to company, it became apparent that the inducements and incentives represented similar patterns of behavior for all the companies."

Title companies paid for lavish open houses with catered food and drinks where real estate agents previewed properties understanding that whoever handled the sale would get their client to buy insurance from the host company. Kreidler found golf outings, ski trips, and $900 dinners. Some title insurance companies paid excessive sums for advertising in publications owned by real estate brokers. First American paid $23,000 in one such surreptitious kickback arrangement. Overall, First American spent $120,000 per month on shopping sprees, football game tickets, and other payments to buy business. A state report concluded, "First American offers a prime example of how illegal inducements can help a company attain superior market share."

Washington State found that LandAmerica "made extensive use of co-advertising, gift cards, providing food and drinks at broker opens and meetings, paying for meals and giving away sporting event tickets." Over the course of a year and a half, the company spent more than $25,000 to take real estate agents, bankers, and lawyers on chartered bay cruises paid for by unwitting home buyers.

There was also, and as of this writing still is, quite literally, a free lunch. The title insurance companies take turns picking up the tab for the monthly luncheons of Seattle's board of Realtors.

Everyone in the industry knows these payments are illegal, which is why they create shams to hide them. In Washington State the law allows gifts of no more than $25 per person per year. "There is nothing confusing about the limit," Commissioner Kreidler wrote. The insurance commissioner's office adopted a rule in 1988 to curb these illegal inducements and amended it in 1990. But the investigation showed that the industry was cleverly "skirting the law by creating new schemes and methods for providing inducements in order to obtain title insurance business."

The insurance regulators whose duty is to protect the public have instead mostly turned a blind eye to these payoffs. Even in Washington State, the solution was not to enforce the law, but instead to try a softer approach.

Commissioner Kreidler, who described himself as a champion of consumer rights, wrote that despite the "astonishing number of violations" what was needed to shake up the industry was a new set of recommendations and an education program. He said he felt it would be too expensive to punish the real estate brokers and the insurance companies for past crimes and helpfully suggested that the insurance commission should share some of the responsibility. That is to say, this consumer champion decided to do next to nothing, only to threaten that if deliberate and concealed illegal conduct continued, the law would be enforced some day.

Kreidler had good reason to fear that any serious enforcement of the law would begin a nasty fight. The title insurance industry says it employs more than 100,000 people. It is part of the whole real estate/insurance/lending complex that has long worked closely in the state capitals to shape government rules to serve its interests. A regulatory crackdown could easily spawn legislation cutting the budget for insurance regulators or, worse, passage of a subtle loophole that would make any future enforcement of the laws against kickbacks impossible.

Clearly the system of kickbacks and cover-ups is entrenched and self-sustaining unless the government steps in to control it. Douglas Miller, the chief executive of Title One, a title insurer in Minneapolis, refuses to pay people for steering business to him. "I've had many real estate professionals who were involved in these schemes tell me that they miss my company because our service was better and our fees were lower, but that they are now locked into the partnership and feel that they had no choice but to continue to refer 'their' business to these shams," Miller said.

Prices for land title insurance have not dropped in California, Colorado, Washington, or anywhere else, and the indications are that these practices continue. In paying all this money for title insurance, home buyers assume they are getting something of value. As so little of what they pay is in fact spent on insurance, that raises the question of just how much of the premium for land title insurance is actually needed to provide the protection the policy offers.

Title insurers say that the amount they pay in losses does not fully describe their costs. Unlike fire, automobile, and life insurance companies that pay a claim only after the event, title insurance covers unknown events in the past and so they spend some money on avoiding claims. They duplicate the official property ownership records at government buildings and organize them not by name but by plot, each company carefully guarding its duplicates of these public records. They collect new liens and easements as they are filed and add them to their archives, which they call *plants*.

So how much does this prophylactic cost? The American Land Title Association puts the figure at "millions of dollars each year." Measured against the billions of dollars collected in premiums, the cost would have to exceed $160 million annually to approach a penny on the premium dollar paid. Birny Birnbaum, an insurance economist who studied the kickbacks for the California insurance commissioner, said the costs are but a tiny fraction of 1 percent of premiums paid. *Forbes* says that with virtually all plots of land and buildings in America already in corporate databases, the cost of a title search is as little as $25 or less than two cents out of each dollar on the typical premium paid by home buyers.

If your boundary lines turn out to be different from what it says on your deed, or your new swimming pool actually intrudes into the neighbor's land, don't expect the title insurance company to defend you. The company may tell you to handle the litigation yourself. If you prevail, you can seek recompense from the title insurer, which no doubt will assert that your legal bills are excessive and therefore they will pay only what they consider to be reasonable costs. Or maybe you will have to sue the title insurance company, too.

The American Land Title Association acknowledges that little is paid out in claims. It tells consumers that "occasionally, when a title problem can't be cleared, the title insurance company pays a claim. The industry pays hundreds of millions of dollars in claims each year."

In 2005 the industry paid $748 million in claims. That is less than a nickel for each dollar paid in premiums that year. Add in the cost of total searches and that leaves about 94 cents for operating expenses and profits. The industry earned more in interest, dividends, and capital gains from its investments than it paid out in claims in 2005. For every dollar paid to the insured for their losses, the industry made $1.16 in investment gains.

The kickbacks are not hurting the title insurers, either. Stocks of large companies, over long periods of time, have historically earned investors an average total return of a bit more than 10 percent. Shares of First American, which has a quarter of the national market for title insurance, have earned a return of more than 11 percent annually since 1980, even though the company kicked back all but a dime or two of each premium dollar it collected.

What this means is that if you just loaned the title insurance company the amount of your premium interest free for three years and then got your money back, the investment earnings alone would easily cover the insurance company's overhead and the payment of any claims. If the company earns 5 percent on your premium, the first-year interest alone would be greater than the cost of paying claims. Give the company the use of your premium for two more years and you have covered all of the costs, except for those illegal, but never prosecuted, bribes.

The federal government helps the title insurance companies gouge customers by requiring disclosure of only the name of the title insurer and the amount paid on the mortgage application. By just adding a box that discloses in large type the portion of your premium that will be used to pay claims, based on the average payout of, say, the previous three years, customers would know when they are being charged a dollar for a product whose benefit is about four and a half cents. This kind of disclosure would be a cost-effective way to eliminate 85 percent to 90 percent of the cost of title insurance and it would at the same time reduce illegal behavior. Of course, it would come under attack as more costly government regulation, too. In reality, though, the cost would be infinitesimally small compared to the savings for buyers.

Another more elegant approach to stop this gouging is to place the burden of title insurance where it really matters—on the lender. Both the title insurance and mortgage industries acknowledge in their public statements that the lender requires that the title to the property be insured to protect its interests. The home buyer, however, bears the cost.

Adjusting the payment mechanism by making lenders buy title insurance would surely result in less money being spent on title insurance premiums. Banks, savings and loans, and credit unions are sophisticated about these issues, unlike the home buyer. They could negotiate with title insurers for better prices and they could buy in bulk. They could even decide to incorporate the costs of the occasional title problem that cannot be cleared into their cost structure, perhaps charging buyers directly for the portion of the title insurance that covers the buyer's equity in a home.

If banks insured themselves it would create a powerful incentive to be efficient and reduce liability and its associated costs. Then such insurance, which now costs on average about 51 cents per $100 of the purchase price, could well fall to a cost of just a tenth of a penny per $100.

Another way is to adopt the system used in Australia and Europe. Under these systems, the government checks its records to see if there are any liens or claims and notifies the seller and buyer when the title is clear. Fees are used to pay for checking the files and to fund insurance in the event a mistake is made.

Critics of government per se will no doubt think that this just adds to taxpayer expense. But the cost of such a system, which could be financed with fees paid by those selling their land, would surely be a tiny fraction of what consumers now pay, and thus it would be a net gain to the economy. Indeed, just eliminating the taxpayer costs of land title litigation for judges, court clerks, and recordkeeping might cancel out the cost of maintaining a proper land registry.

In Iowa there is no private title insurance. Instead, the state government runs the program. The cost is $500 on purchases of homes valued up to $500,000 and $90 for refinancing. Even those charges seem high. As the state improves the quality of its records, the number of claims should dwindle, allowing lower fees in the future.

Legislatures also can enact time limits on title claims. The law lets virtually all criminals, except murderers, escape prosecution if enough time passes before they are caught. In most states minor crimes must be prosecuted within 5 years and most felonies within 10. The same could be done with title claims, allowing some wiggle room, just as the criminal statutes do. For example, the law could start the clock on that seven-year-old boy only when he turns 18 or 21 and reaches his majority. Placing such time limits on claims would decimate payments from land title insurance while at the same time reducing litigation. No system will be perfect, but the goal of government policy should be to gain the most benefit at the lowest cost, not to enrich price gougers.

Until consumers demand reform from their lawmakers, expect to pay 10 times as much for land title insurance as it would cost if our governments enforced the laws on the books to protect consumers and end the costly excesses of reverse competition. And expect to pay about a thousand times the cost of a system in which lenders took out the insurance.

Next, let's look at government policies affecting our society's most valuable assets, our common property, and our individual debts.

Chapter 14

INDENTURED SCHOLARS

ONE OF THE MOST SALIENT FEATURES OF THE NEW ECONOMIC ORDER is exploding levels of debt. Young people and home buyers, even the government itself, face spiraling debt that is converting the ownership society into a debtor society with ever fewer reserves, either individual or joint. In turn this new debt load, combined with the sale of public assets like roads and water systems, means huge incomes for those positioned to take advantage of these burdens, all part of the new approach to using government to enrich the few.

For three decades, government has been cutting back on investing in the nation's most valuable asset, young minds. Adjusted for inflation, tuition at four-year public colleges more than doubled between 1980 and 2005, a period when incomes for the vast majority were essentially unchanged. Tuition rose from an average of $2,175 to $5,100. Add to this the costs of books, lab fees, meals, and either a dorm room or commuting to campus.

Seven out of ten taxpayers make less than $50,000 a year. For these families, even state college has become an onerous and often impossible burden, especially for families with more than one child. For those in the bottom half, whose average reported income is less than $15,000 per year according to the Tax Foundation, college is a goal too far, even for many smart and motivated students.

As recently as the mideighties, federal Pell grants to poor students covered 60 percent of the cost of attending a public college. That share has been nearly halved as Congress has cut the so-called discretionary budget. An estimated 200,000 young people do not attend college each year simply because they lack the resources. Many do not finish because they cannot sustain the cost for four or more years.

About two-thirds of college students who graduate are in debt, a prospect unimaginable in the fifties, sixties, and most of the seventies. Many owe more than their parents make in one or even several years. And this debt limits their options to develop themselves and to benefit society through important work, such as teaching, policing, and research.

Jason Clark learned to cook on the job. He wanted to do more than short-order work, so he sought formal training. Because his father is disabled, Clark had to finance his schooling on his own. He applied to the Pennsylvania Culinary Institute, a private, for-profit college, filling out applications for two loans totaling almost $30,000.

Six months after Clark graduated his first bill came, showing an interest rate of 13 percent. Clark did not recall agreeing to such a high rate or even signing a promissory note. Clark asked the lender, Sallie Mae, for a copy of the promissory note. He also asked for an extra six months before starting payments because he could not find work. Sallie Mae has never produced a copy of any note signed by Clark, but it did raise his interest rate to 18 percent.

Clark is just one of hundreds of thousands of students who borrow money each year to improve themselves through education. In all, students borrow about $85 billion *each year,* most of it at single-digit interest rates with repayment guaranteed by the taxpayers.

Nearly a fourth of these loans come from lenders, like Sallie Mae, EduCap, and Nelnet, that are free to charge any interest rate they want. Normally, the riskier the loan, the higher the interest rate. That is how lenders make up for loans that sour. But the interest rates that these lenders charge bear no relationship to risk that the loans will not be paid back. Thanks to Congress, these lenders operate almost risk free. Yet they are allowed to charge high-risk rates and to collect about $18 billion a year in government subsidies.

The reason their risk is small is that, under rules set by Congress, there are only three ways to retire these debts: pay them back in full, become totally and permanently disabled (and convince the lender that is so), or die broke.

Even if a student goes bankrupt, federal law prohibits the discharge of student loans, both those guaranteed by the government and those made on onerous commercial terms. Our Congress, in adopting these policies, has made the unstated assumption that everyone who gets a college education will succeed. That some people will become sick or injured, that others will fail to find work in the field they prepared for or will go into occupations that pay poorly, or will have a child requiring round-the-clock care, or any of a hundred other things that make life itself a risky venture, are not contemplated under this government policy.

To buy the lucrative business of students, many college lenders made under-the-table payments and other disguised forms of compensation to college admissions officers and others at Johns Hopkins, Columbia, and many other colleges and universities. Some colleges even solicited money from the lenders, promising in return to steer business to them.

Many students who were told they would pay interest rates of perhaps 6 percent or so found their loans were at two or three times that rate. At the Web site StudentLoanJustice.org hundreds of former students tell the same stories over and over again: how they were lied to, hit with thousands of dollars in collection fees for supposedly disappearing when finding them was as easy as dialing 411, and told they have to pay whatever interest rate the company picks, with no rights except to pay until they die. Under these one-sided rules, loans of $20,000 become $50,000 and loans of $30,000 balloon to more than $112,000. Is this any way to perpetuate a society?

While the government imposes harsh rules on students, it treats lenders with extraordinary leniency. The Education Department inspector general found in 2007 that one lender, Nelnet, had received $278 million in improper subsidies. The government let Nelnet keep the money. Sara Martinez Tucker, the undersecretary of education, told my colleague Jonathan Glater that seeking repayment would set a precedent that might require asking other lenders to return improper subsidies they had received. That, in turn, might drive out of business some smaller firms that make student loans, thus reducing competition. Translation: mercy for bankers, but not for borrowers.

That consideration goes to lenders and virtually none to borrowers is central to the creed of government as a source of greater wealth for those already rich enough to have money to lend.

For lenders, this government guarantee that they will be repaid produces phenomenal profits. Albert Lord, who ran Sallie Mae for years, built a fortune so large that he tried to buy the Washington Nationals baseball team. He built his own private golf course in Maryland, not far from Washington, using the riches he made off students to separate himself from them and the rest of society, just as the Sun King commissioned a palace in which his mistress could dine without having to even look at the servants.

Sallie Mae started out in 1972 as a government-sponsored entity to help students. That was under the old government policy of nurturing the middle class. Under the new rules of government as the helpmate of the rich, President Clinton signed legislation in 1997 making Sallie Mae an independent, investor-owned business known as the SLM Corporation.

What Clinton, and Congress, did not do was remove the stern loan repayment rules that show no mercy to student debtors. The result? Sallie Mae earned an astonishing 51 percent return on equity in the five years through 2006. This is more than triple the rate of return on equity earned by the banking industry.

Lord engineered the transformation to a private concern and arranged to obtain about 2 percent of the company, mostly through stock options. In 2007, when the kickback scandals and complaints from students and their parents about exorbitant interest rates finally began to get a hearing in Congress, Lord arranged to sell the firm for $25 billion. The buyers included Bank of America and JPMorgan Chase, banks that instead of competing in the market agreed to cooperate in this venture.

Jason Turner, a financial analyst, is typical of those who are embittered by what they see as a corrupt system that enriched Sallie Mae owners and others. He borrowed $16,000 in the eighties to attend college, but today with fees and deferred high-rate interest, Sallie Mae says he owes more than $50,000. Turner believes improper fees totaling more than $10,000 inflate that figure.

"It is impossible to get any documentation of the original debt or an honest accounting of how the current balance on the loan is calculated," Turner said, echoing a common complaint. Documents he was sent create the impression that the federal government is after him to pay off this debt, but a close reading shows that, in fact, the letters come from collection arms of Sallie Mae.

"My spouse and I have a solid middle-class income," Turner said, "yet we can't even pretend to think about buying a home because of these student loans. Al Lord gets to have his own golf course, but my child can't have a backyard to play in."

Another big beneficiary of the government's policy of requiring most students to borrow money to get an education and then shielding the lenders from risk is Catherine B. Reynolds, the head of a nonprofit foundation in McLean, Virginia, bearing her name. Despite its legal status as a charity, the Reynolds Foundation does business as EduCap and refers to itself as a company. It pays like one, too. Reynolds makes a million dollars a year from the foundation even though it has assets of only about $200 million. Her salary is many times what the executives of charitable foundations of that size typically make.

Her job comes with an unusual perk. This perk must be disclosed, but the foundation-cum-company did its best to obscure the perk, which it described this way: "Based on the recommendation of an independent security review, the corporation has implemented certain security measures including security-related services for officers and directors. The value of any services provided for any incidental personal use is treated as a fringe benefit to the recipient."

Could anyone reading that tell that the charity had bought a $30 million Gulfstream jet that Reynolds uses as her personal taxi?

EduCap can afford that perk and the big pay because of its skill at steering student applicants away from the lowest-cost aid and toward its expensive loans. EduCap hands out brochures that imply that it is hard to get government-backed low-interest loans, that they have inflexible payment terms and are too small to be of much help, none of which is true. The brochure instead touts what it claims are the benefits of its loans, including the false claim that they are more flexible, while ignoring the higher interest rates, the fact that these rates can be raised without warning, and the prospect of huge fees and costs.

The idea that young minds should be a source of immediate profit is among the most coldly calculated changes in government which, over the past three decades, have taken from the many to enrich the few. The idea that a borrower cannot escape a debt because of a government rule is unlike that of any other modern country. Indeed, in Western Europe, students who borrow money do so on terms related to their ability to pay, with investment bankers bearing more of the cost than nurses and forest rangers.

In America, the trend is toward more financial aid to the affluent and less to the poor, another example of widespread sacrifice for the rich. The nonprofit Education Trust compared financial aid to students at the top public university in each state during 1995 and again for 2003. It found that aid to students from families with incomes of more than $100,000 increased more than fivefold, while help for students from families making less than $20,000 dropped 13 percent. "Many of these flagship institutions have become, more and more, enclaves for the most privileged of their state's young people," the Education Trust concluded.

President Bush, who likes to refer to himself as the education president, vowed as a candidate in 2000 to increase Pell grants significantly. Instead, as president, his budgets cut Pell grants for poor college students in two ways. The maximum grant was reduced. In addition, funding was cut so much that each year as many as 375,000 students who qualified did not get Pell grants because the fund ran dry.

On another front, in at least a dozen states, government seeks to make the foolish, the addicted, and the poor pay the costs of making sure Johnny and Jane can read, write, and do their numbers. Some of the proposals seem fit for comedy routines rather than serious policy.

Governor Rick Perry asked the Texas legislature in 2004 to give billions of dollars of tax relief to homeowners, especially mansion owners. Under his plan the amount of money the state would have to spend on education would depend in part on the skills of women like Vanity, Destiny, and Rio, who sell lap dances at the Yellow Rose, a topless bar in Austin. In addition to a tax of five dollars on each admission at the nude dancing clubs, Perry wanted to raise taxes on beer and cigarettes and install video lottery terminals at gasoline pumps.

Governor Perry's proposal suggested that his own education came up short on 'rithmetic. His combination of onetime gimmicks and what he called "taxes on unhealthy behavior" would have raised $10 billion less than the property tax relief he proposed, forcing massive cuts in education spending after a few years. But then that was consistent with his budget. He was proposing over two years to cut state spending on education by nearly a billion dollars, despite a finding by a state commission that most Texas children did not have an education that prepared them for college. Making them fit for college would cost an additional $3 billion per year.

While Texas lawmakers rejected the Perry plan, California, Kentucky, Maryland, Missouri, Tennessee, Utah, and West Virginia are among the states that have shifted part of the cost of schooling to taxes on gambling and topless bars. In New York, George Pataki tried when he was governor to raise money for education by making video lottery terminals more widely available.

There is one final way that government policy discourages the poor and those of modest means from attending college, which in the short run saves the costs of educating them, but imposes a long-term drag on the economy. The application form for federal aid is so complicated that 1.5 million students who are eligible for aid do not even apply.

In contrast to these trends, across most of the modern world a college education remains so inexpensive that anyone with the necessary brains and discipline can earn initial and advanced degrees.

There was a time when college in America was free, or nearly so. But now the GI Bill and government policies that placed the costs of education on taxpayers, a benefit extended to the next generation, have withered in the face of demands by the wealthiest to reduce the burdens of government. As the costs of college have grown faster than inflation, and predatory lending practices have become common, the growth in advanced education has predictably slowed. More men earned doctoral degrees in 1975 than in 2005. The total number of PhDs grew only because the number of women receiving doctorates tripled to 23,000 over the same period. The number of bachelor's degrees earned by men grew just 18 percent during those years. The total number of four-year degrees grew by a bit more than half because so many more women earned degrees.

In a world of growing complexity and technological demands, short-changing higher education through rising tuition and high-cost loans is tantamount to a policy of reducing future economic growth so that the few today can have more. It is a kind of hidden tax on the future.

Chapter 15

SELLING THE FURNITURE

THE STUDENT-LOAN BUSINESS IS JUST ONE ASPECT OF A GREAT transformation in the balance sheet of America. When students graduate and start paying off their loans, many will find they cannot qualify for a mortgage to buy a home because of the money they borrowed in school.

Home ownership used to be the key to a secure future for the middle class, although African Americans, Hispanics, and other minorities were often excluded. Government programs after World War II encouraged widespread home ownership and low-cost housing. No more. Now home ownership is for millions a pathway to a life of endless debt.

Americans owned about two-thirds of the value of their homes in the sixties and seventies and owed the rest in mortgage debt, according to Federal Reserve data. In 1981 and 1982, for every dollar of home value in America, equity represented 70 cents. But by 2006, the equity share of homes had fallen sharply while mortgage debt grew to almost half the total value of American homes. In fact, for each dollar of equity people had added, they took on almost two dollars of debt.

Debt likely accounts for more than half of the value of homes in 2008. That is because in many communities, home values are falling, in part because the debt burdens are so high that the owners cannot cover the payments and there are no new buyers to take over for them at current prices. Many of these mortgage loans were made to people with poor histories of paying back their debts, and often based on inflated appraisals. The failure of subprime loans has become so widespread that it

MORTGAGE DEBT GROWS TWICE AS FAST AS EQUITY

	MORTGAGE DEBT*	EQUITY IN HOMES*	DEBT AS SHARE OF HOME VALUE
1980	$ 2,481	$ 5,400	31.5%
2006	$ 9,676	$ 10,945	46.9%
GROWTH FACTOR	4x	2x	

* In billions of 2006 dollars

Source: Federal Reserve Flow of Funds

wiped out many lenders and devoured two hedge funds sponsored by the Wall Street firm of Bear Stearns.

These rising mortgage payments in turn have contributed significantly to a profound change in the composition of household wealth.

From 2001 to 2004, the median net worth of all households rose only slightly. The median measures the halfway point. Half of all households had a net worth in 2004 of $93,100 or less, barely changed from 2001, when it was $91,700 or less. But it rose for the top half, with the greatest growth at the very top.

Within this overall picture, though, lies a major shift in the nature of American wealth. While the value of homes rose 22 percent from 2001 to 2004, according to the Federal Reserve, the value of household savings and investments dropped by 23 percent.

The falloff in household savings is reflected in the income Americans report on their tax returns. Fewer than half of taxpayers reported any interest income in 2004. In every income bracket, the portion of taxpayers with interest income was smaller than in 1994. Among those making $10,000 to $50,000, for example, the number of people reporting any interest income fell by a third from almost 35 million to 25 million. The amount of interest this group received in 1994, adjusted for inflation, was more than three times what they earned in 2004.

And it was not just cash savings at the bank or credit union that declined. For every income group earning below a million dollars, the portion of people receiving dividends from stock investments declined and so did the amounts of those dividends.

The more people must spend on mortgage interest, the less they can save or invest for use before retirement. That also narrows their cushion of support when the inevitable problem comes along, from a broken transmission in the car needed for work to illness or job loss.

In housing, current government policy also subsidizes the affluent and the rich far more than the poor and the middle class, helping the few far more than the many. Taxpayers who make $40,000 to $50,000 per year each save on average less than $400 from the home mortgage deduction, while those making more than $200,000 save on average more than 12 times that much, analysis of 2004 tax return data shows. Americans who make more than a million dollars a year save on average 16 times as much, nearly $6,300 each.

For every dollar the federal government forgoes in housing tax breaks for the poor, it spends a dollar and a half on housing subsidies for those making more than $100,000 per year, roughly the best-off tenth of Americans.

Peter Dreier, a professor at Occidental College who studies housing patterns, noted that "a wealthy corporate executive is more likely to receive a homeowner tax break—and to get a much bigger one—than a garment worker, a construction worker, or a schoolteacher. The current system subsidizes the rich to buy huge homes without helping most working families buy even a small bungalow. The real estate industry—homebuilders, Realtors, and mortgage bankers—has lobbied hard to preserve homeowner tax breaks, arguing that they are the linchpins of the American Dream. This is nonsense. Only one-third of the 52 million households with incomes between $30,000 and $75,000 receive any homeowner subsidy."

Dreier noted that Australia and Canada do not give a tax deduction for mortgage interest, yet they have almost the same rate of home ownership as the United States. That shows how ineffective the American policy is. Compounding this are changes in the tax laws that result in fewer than half of homeowners getting any mortgage interest deduction. And among even these families, a growing minority get no deduction for their property taxes because of the alternative minimum tax, a parallel levy to the regular income tax that hits primarily at families with three or more children who own their own home and make more than $75,000.

It is not just students and homeowners who are borrowing in a desperate attempt to get ahead of the game. Like the widow of the profligate husband who must sell the furniture to try to make the mortgage payment, we are almost all destined to lose the house anyway—in this case, the "house" or infrastructure we built to support our society.

If Wall Street offers to sell you a piece of the Brooklyn Bridge, it may not be a con. Across America, local and state governments are selling off pieces of the commonwealth. Colorado, Illinois, and Chicago leased toll roads to private investors, with bids coming in from all around the world. Citigroup, the Carlyle Group, Goldman Sachs, and Morgan Stanley are among those creating investment pools to acquire public assets. Their sales agents are out proposing to take over everything from the Brooklyn Bridge to the Golden Gate Bridge, as well as parks, parking garages, water mains, and even sewer systems. *BusinessWeek* estimates that a hundred billion dollars worth of public assets will be sold in 2007 and 2008.

Most of the deals to sell the furniture of modern society come with provisions exempting the investors from state taxes, while extending deductions on federal tax returns. When built, these public assets were our common property. In private hands, though, their value can be written off by the new owners to reduce their taxes. This erodes the tax base and shifts a burden onto everyone else.

Private investors are not alone in looking for safe, long-term returns from owning toll roads, bridges, and other income-producing properties. Pension funds for public workers are one of the major sources of money for these deals. Many of these deals include tax-sharing agreements so that the tax deductions all go to the taxable investors, not pension funds and other tax-exempt investors.

These sales of assets are typically used to provide a one-shot injection of funds for state and local governments. Just as officials squandered most of the money from the settlements with tobacco companies, which paid up so they could go on addicting people to nicotine, so too will the money from these sales of public assets go for naught.

The losers in this scenario are the taxpayers who bought and paid for these facilities. Now, more than a third of their value will be used to reduce revenues to the government, easing the burden on the wealthy investors and adding to those of everyone else. And they will have to pay for them all over again through user charges. And those tolls? Expect them to go up faster than government would have raised them.

Desperate as the sale of these assets is, there are worse things. Imagine, for example, diverting assets left to help poor children just so you can add to your own fortune. Next up, a modern mystery. But instead of a whodunit, this one is a whogotit.

Chapter 16

SUFFER THE LITTLE CHILDREN

CABLE NEWS STATIONS CUT BACK ON COVERAGE OF WAR, POLITICS, the economy, and other issues in the summer of 2007 to make time for nonstop coverage of an heiress who cried in jail for more than two days, until a tough law-and-order sheriff let her go.

A judge, unimpressed with photos of her carrying a Bible and declaring her piety, sent deputies to fetch her so she could finish her sentence. Her arrest was covered live from coast to coast, helicopters with video cameras following the squad car in which she cried all the way to the courthouse. When the 26-year-old woman finally emerged from a Los Angeles County jail, after serving half of her 45-day sentence for violating probation in a drunk driving case, her triumphant midnight appearance was also covered live.

Paris Hilton dressed for the occasion, wearing a smartly tailored jacket and form-fitting jeans, posing for the cameras as if she were a model on a catwalk. In a way, she was. Hilton was modeling a new line of clothes bearing her name, the glitzmongers who play reporters on television told viewers during endless reruns of that scene.

In all the years that tabloid television and actual tabloids have documented every aspect of Paris Hilton's life, none examined in any serious way the obvious question her conduct raises: What kind of family would produce someone so brazen, shameless, and self-absorbed? The answer reveals the most audacious free lunch of all, a fortune snatched away from poor children by Paris Hilton's grandfather, fattening his bottom line. Starving children got the leftovers.

The story begins during World War II when Conrad Nicholson Hilton was married to Zsa Zsa Gabor, the Hungarian beauty who took nine husbands, including an inventor of the Barbie doll. Gabor testified that Connie drove her nuts, going to mass every morning, disappearing on religious retreats, and constantly giving money to nuns who had taken vows of poverty so they could help the poor. She said her husband awoke from nightmares of going to hell, a not uncommon demon of rich men and women in the era before Americans began celebrating wealth for its own sake.

"He was always giving money to the nuns," Gabor testified years later. "I think he was overreligious. He had a terrible guilt complex."

Conrad Hilton would often discuss what to do with his money on long horseback rides in the Hollywood Hills and elsewhere with his lawyer, James Bates. Bates testified years later that his client frequently told him that his son Barron "has too damn much money."

Conrad revised his will 32 times, gradually leaving less to Barron and more for the poor. In his last will, out of a fortune worth more than a billion of today's dollars, he left Barron less than three million. He directed that after various modest gifts, and his final expenses, his wealth go to a foundation bearing his name. Conrad also wrote in his will guidance to Barron and the other foundation trustees, what he called "some cherished conclusions formed during a lifetime of observation, study and contemplation":

> There is a nature law, a Divine Law, that obliges you and me to relieve the suffering, the distressed and the destitute. Charity is a supreme virtue, and the real channel through which the mercy of God is passed on to mankind. It is the virtue that unites men and inspires their noblest efforts.
>
> "Love one another, for that is the whole law" so our fellow men deserve to be loved and encouraged—never to be abandoned to wander alone in poverty and darkness. The practice of charity will bind us—will bind all men into one great brotherhood.
>
> As the funds you will expend have come from many places in the world, so let there be no territorial, religious, or color restrictions on your benefactions, but beware of organized, professional charities with high-salaried executives and a heavy ratio of expense.
>
> Be ever watchful for the opportunity to shelter little children with the umbrella of your charity; be generous to their schools, their hospitals and their places of worship. For, as they must bear the burden of our mistakes, so they are the innocent repositories of our hopes for the upward progress of

humanity. Give aid to their protectors and defenders, the Sisters, who devote their love and life's work for the good of mankind. . . .

The message of charity and hope that Conrad Hilton wrote lost out to his oldest son's love of money. Ten days after his father died, Barron Hilton made his first move to capture his father's fortune for himself. He did so in a way that would give him more and the poor much less.

Lawyer Bates, the other trustee of the old man's estate, fought Barron, saying he was subverting his father's plan to deliver the maximum amount possible to the poor. "Barron Hilton does not come into this matter with clean hands," he argued in court papers, "and should not be allowed to defeat his father's intentions" by hiding information that would have allowed all of Conrad Hilton's stock to go to the foundation. Bates said Barron was seeking "unjust enrichment" at the expense of charity.

Before long Barron, at his own request, was suspended as cotrustee of his father's estate because he had a conflict of interest. Barron was simultaneously an heir, the chairman of the board of the Conrad N. Hilton Foundation, and chief executive of Hilton Hotels Corporation.

The issue involved a glitch in Conrad's will. The glitch concerned how much of the Hilton Hotels Corporation could be owned in combination by Barron and by the Hilton Foundation. A 1969 federal law limits how much of a corporation can be owned in combination by a family and its private foundation. Congress acted in the wake of many well-documented abuses. Rich families took tax breaks, short-changed charity, and then stuffed the money into their own already deep pockets.

When he died in 1979, Conrad owned almost a fourth of Hilton Hotels, Barron almost 4 percent. Together they owned more than 27 percent, while the limit was 20 percent. To comply with the limit, Bates testified, Conrad's will gave Barron an option to buy any shares that were over the limit, allowing him to pay for them over 10 years. The option, the will specified, was to be created at the moment the stock was distributed from the estate to the foundation and it was conditioned on the need to sell shares because of government-imposed limits, two facts that would become crucial.

Conrad went to his grave, Bates testified, believing that only a small portion of his Hilton Hotel shares might be sold to Barron under the option.

Barron had a plan. Ten days after his father died he moved to exercise the option. He argued that the option gave him the right to buy all of the shares in his father's estate, not just the number of shares needed to bring their combined ownership down to 20 percent. There was no way to meet the limit, Barron argued, other than to let him acquire all of the shares. However, it turned out there was a way and that Barron knew about it. So did his personal lawyer, Donald H. Hubbs. Hubbs was also the president of the Hilton Foundation.

The way out of the 20 percent ownership limit was to convert the foundation into a charity known as a *supporting organization*. A supporting organization makes grants just like a private foundation, but is not subject to the 20 percent rule. The reason is that it must give at least 30 percent of its grants to a specified list of charities. The law assumes that these charities will have an interest in looking out for any abuses, making them less likely and, if they do occur, will report them to the government. Since Conrad directed his foundation trustees to deliver "the greatest part of your benefactions" to Catholic nuns who serve the poor, the supporting organization made sense—to everyone but Barron.

Barron argued that there was no way to change the foundation into a supporting organization. However, a Texas lawyer named Thomas Broby had advised him on just how that could be done, although the other foundation trustees were not told this. When word of this came out the other trustees hired their own lawyers. The issue was finally presented to the Internal Revenue Service in Washington, which blessed it.

The foundation itself has been well run under the stewardship of Conrad's grandson Steve. It has focused its efforts, often working through Catholic nuns, on child poverty, access to clean drinking water, and preventing the diseases that cause much of the blindness in less developed countries.

Barron's strategy to enrich himself had a second front. He demanded that his father's shares be sold to him at a discount from the price they were selling for on the stock market. That was extraordinary because shares of stock that convey control over a corporation usually command a premium price. That is why, when a buyout of a company is announced, the price is usually higher than what the shares had been trading for, often much more. The premium recognizes the greater benefits the controlling shareholder has—compared to anyone who buys 100 shares from their broker—to pay himself a salary, use company facilities, and direct its operations.

Lawyer Bates fought back. The California attorney general joined the fight on behalf of the poor children. For a decade, litigation ensued over Barron's plan to shortchange charity and enrich himself. Barron's strongest argument was that while his father wanted his fortune to go to charity, he also wanted Hilton Hotels to remain in the family. That was the reason for the option, to thwart an unfriendly takeover. Barron and his allies insisted that the old man's desire that his "beloved Hilton Hotels" remain in the family get equal weight with his desire to help the poor.

When the case went to trial in 1986, Barron lost. The trial court judge ruled that the switch from private foundation to supporting organization defeated the option by eliminating the 20 percent ownership limit. Barron appealed.

Almost two years later the California Court of Appeals for the Second District reversed the trial court's decision. The appeals court focused not on the charitable intent, so eloquently stated in the will, but on its concern that Barron be allowed to buy his father's shares for "a reasonable and fair price that Hilton can find economically feasible" and that would not result in an unreasonably low value to the foundation.

The appeals court ruled that the option was created the day Conrad died. Both Myron Harpole, the lawyer for Bates, and James Cordi, the deputy state attorney general on the case, were stunned. The will stated that the option was conditional. It was created only if tax rules forced the sale of Hilton stock. And the option would come into existence, the will said, "at the time of the distribution" of shares from the estate to the charity.

The appeals court had found a way to serve up a free lunch to the rich at the expense of charity by rewriting Conrad Hilton's will. The appeals court ordered a new trial. Barron, his hand strengthened by the appeals court, proposed a settlement. He got one.

Barron received more than half of the value of the stock in his father's estate, about 250 times the amount specified as a gift in his father's will. In addition, he was guaranteed an income for 20 years. It started out at about $15 million per year and has since risen to about triple that.

And what of the stated purpose of Barron's case, that Conrad Hilton wanted the hotels bearing the family name to remain in the family? Just eight days after his granddaughter Paris took her fashion model walk out of jail, her grandfather Barron announced that he was selling Hilton Hotels to the Blackstone Group, a private equity fund. On top of the hundreds of millions he has already received, he will pocket $760 million, plus increased payments from the trust, all thanks to a free lunch served up by judges on an American court.

Chapter 17

TROJAN HORSE

A HEAVY MORNING MIST BLANKETED AUSTIN AS THE MEMBERS OF the House of Representatives made their way to the capitol, a Texas-size building made of a kind of granite called sunset red. They came to end a century of state government regulating the price of electricity and to create the dawn of what they told the voters would be a glorious new day. They promised that competitive markets would provide electricity cheaper and more efficiently than utilities regulated by the state government regulators had or possibly could.

Just outside the massive chamber doors, which stood like the gates of ancient Troy, each solon met a legion of lobbyists. All had played a role in shaping Senate Bill 7, making deals over this clause and that comma. All the corporate lobbyists embraced the final deal, but not two others, who stood out that morning.

One was Janee Briesemeister, a policy analyst for Consumers Union, publisher of *Consumer Reports* magazine. Lithe, free of makeup, and on the verge of middle age, she looked much younger and could have passed for one of the executives but for her plain suit, which even she felt was out of place among the fine raiment of the finance, legal, and utility crowd.

The other was Tom Smith, the executive director of Ralph Nader's Public Citizen in the Lone Star state. Smitty was a living icon of a consumer advocate. Short and trim, with wire-frame glasses, he walked and talked like a sociology professor with a bit of the scold in him. He wore a straw fedora, with wispy gray bumpers springing beneath the hatband and sprouting wild all the way down to his chin, symbols of his fiercely independent thinking about politics and power.

On this spring day in 1999 Briesemeister and Smith played the roles of truth tellers destined to be ignored and ridiculed, just like Cassandra and Laocoön in ancient Troy when the Greeks left their giant wooden steed outside the city gates.

Cassandra was cursed to always tell the truth, yet never be believed. Virgil recounted in the *Aeneid* that warnings came from within the wooden colossus the Greeks left before seeming to sail away:

> Oft the clashing sound
> of arms was heard, and inward groans rebound
> yet, mad with zeal, and blinded with our fate
> we haul along the horse in solemn state
> then place the dire portent within the tower.
> Cassandra cried, and cursed this unhappy hour
> foretold our fate, but, by the god's decree
> all heard, and none believed the prophecy

The priest Laocoön thrust a spear into what seemed like a marvelous gift to expose "a deadly fraud," only to be mocked (and later killed).

In Austin, a modern chorus of lobbyists drowned out Briesemeister's and Smith's warnings that Senate Bill 7 was not as it seemed. Smith was handing out flyers. One of the legislators could not resist a verbal jab at the man warning of economic disaster hidden in the bill. "Right, Smitty," the lawmaker said mockingly, "you're going to take on Steve."

The reference was to Steve Wolens, Democrat of Dallas, who was in charge of Senate Bill 7, which had passed the upper chamber two months earlier. Wolens had a reputation for devising creative ways to get impossible bills through the House, just as Odysseus came up with the idea of the Trojan horse to slyly enter Troy. *Texas Monthly* magazine once described Wolens this way: "Mesmerizing in debate, indefatigable in preparation, incisive in analysis, he is the House's most dreaded foe and most welcome ally."

By fiat, Wolens was about to transform electricity into a competitive business, or at least transform part of the electricity industry into what appeared to be a competitive business. This moment did not arrive by popular demand or by accident. The debate under the capitol dome in Austin, like those in half of the other state capitals, was the product of years of buying political influence by one man and the company he created: Ken Lay and Enron.

Lay sent teams of executives to meet privately with politicians and with executives of large companies that consumed electricity by the power plant. Its publicists beguiled journalists and stock analysts with equal fervor. Enron supported seemingly scholarly studies that advanced its cause. Enron's message excited the big industrial users, who had complained for years that they were charged too much. They said the prices set by state utility boards forced them to subsidize residential customers and small businesses. They had a point. In some states big customers not only were denied discounts for buying in volume, they were hit with premium prices.

The Enron executives promised that if they got their way, electricity would flow plentifully, and with lower prices, to these big buyers. How? The magic of markets. At the same time, Enron said, profits for the makers and sellers of electric power would rise, drawing new investment to build more power plants. It was a message that big business wanted to hear. It was a promise that, ever since *downsizing* entered the lexicon, had become all the rage in corporate America: more from less.

The problem was how to make politicians care. Voters did not care much. No candidates were whipping up voter rage over electricity prices, which had been falling for decades until they started to creep back up in the seventies. Hardly anyone cared about the arcane issue of how costs were split among industrial, commercial, and residential customers. Among the voters, no one was clamoring for competitive electric markets.

Enron offered a solution. It paid politicians to listen. Remember, as every politician says, his or her vote is not for sale. All that donations buy is access to officeholders: time to make a pitch and to get the donor's concerns in the forefront of the politicians. There is so much demand for contributions, and so little time to listen, that hardly anyone gets heard for free.

To make sure its voice was heard, Enron and its executives poured $5.4 million into campaigns for Congress and the White House in the last half of the nineties and the 2000 races, three-fourths of it to Republicans. Enron money flowed freely to state officials, too, especially in Texas, where Enron was confident that it could remake the rules by which electricity is sold. After all, Governor George W. Bush counted among his loyal friends the Enron leader he called Kenny Boy.

Donations also flowed from those paid by Enron, as well as companies currying favor with it. This made Enron's support even more valuable than the numbers about its own giving suggested. From his first run for governor of Texas in 1994 until he reached the White House, Enron was the single largest supporter of George W. Bush, donating $736,800. Of the next six biggest contributors to Bush, four were connected to Enron. Among them was Vinson & Elkins, the Houston law firm on which Enron relied most. Another was the parent of the Arthur Anderson accounting firm, which during the Depression rose to national prominence through diligent examination of an electricity industry scandal. In a few years the firm would come to its end because of its work for Enron in a remarkably similar scandal.

Lay also sent teams to meet with utility executives and leaders. Enron hoped to win them over. If they resisted, it tried to scare them into retreat.

One who heard their pitch was Jan Schori, general manager of the Sacramento Municipal Utility District. The burghers and farmers who prospered in the rich and flat lands around Sacramento, long after the gold rush had panned out, created the power district in the 1920s. They wanted an electric utility that would be responsive to their needs, focusing on reliable service at the lowest cost so their businesses would prosper. The utility district's prices typically ran a third lower than Pacific Gas and Electric Company, the corporate-owned utility with a monopoly in most areas of Northern California. As part of the utility district's tradition of service, Schori takes meetings with almost anyone seeking to do business with the agency, which collects about $6 billion from customers each year. One day, about the time of the Texas vote, Enron came calling.

Thinking the Texans wanted to sell some new financial service, Schori invited Jim Tracy, the utility district's chief financial officer, to join them. They gathered around a long table with metal legs painted black in an office that looks down on a grove of flowering cherry, ginkgo, and other trees, a sample of the thousands of shade trees that the district has given away over the years to help cool the area in summer and thus reduce demand for electricity.

The Enronites entered as if they owned the place. Years later Schori remembered thinking that they were so incredibly well dressed and so young; so very young and yet so confident, it was arresting. They said times had changed, that the smart move was to switch to Enron management.

Schori explained that the utility district was not a soulless business that could be bought, but a local government agency with directors elected by the people. The Enronites shifted their approach. They presented themselves as corporate Cassiuses inviting their hosts to join in a conspiracy to overthrow the dictates of regulation. A market revolution was necessary, the Enronites whispered behind the closed doors, for the good of the people.

When Schori made clear that there was no interest in joining this cabal, the Enronites turned to threats. "They told us that we had better turn our business over to them or in a few years they would come back and take us over," she recalled.

Tracy, the district's finance guy, marveled at the hubris. "They sat there and told us they could run our utility better than we could because they knew more than we did or ever could about electricity and markets."

Schori and Tracy felt neither intimidated nor angry, just bemused at the arrogance of the young plotters in their Dolce & Gabbana suits. They thought that these pups without a wrinkle among them had not a clue about the steady, solid work it took to actually provide reliable electricity at all hours in all kinds of weather no matter how much demand surged and fell from one minute to the next. And they were certain their guests, the ink barely dry on their masters of business administration diplomas, gave little thought to how much planning and judgment went into making juice flow every time a switch is flipped not just today, but a decade or two in the future.

While the Enronites had failed to intimidate the public servants in Sacramento, they struck fear deep in the hearts of Texas utility executives. By the time the Texas lawmakers gathered to vote on Senate Bill 7 it had become apparent that Lay and Enron had vast political capital to spend, especially with Governor Bush. Utility executives understood this sooner than most because their careers depended on winning the cooperation of government to set prices as profitably high as was politically possible.

Floyd LeBlanc, the chief spokesman for Centerpoint Energy, the utility once known as Houston Lighting & Power, put it best: The utilities fought Enron until they realized that Enron would win. Then they cut the best deal they could. It was a story repeated in state after state, from Maryland to Maine to Illinois and out on the West Coast.

Within a few years 26 states embraced the Enron way, passing laws that switched electricity to a competitive business, or at least creating the appearance of a competitive business. The specifics varied widely, except for one common element known as *stranded costs*. The utilities were guaranteed that power plants built under the old monopoly laws, but not yet fully written off on their books, would be paid off, typically by allowing the utilities to borrow the money and then add the cost plus interest to monthly electric bills for years to come.

Guaranteeing payments was a strange way to initiate competition, which by definition means winners and losers. It was as if the landlord of the only apartment building in town, confronted with new apartments under construction, persuaded the city council to force his tenants to pay off his mortgage even if they decided to move into newer quarters.

As Briesemeister and Smith saw it the utilities wanted to eat their cake and have it too. The utilities wanted the potential benefits of a competitive market, but with the guaranteed payments that came from a regulated monopoly. To the modern Cassandra and Laocoön this was not competition, but sheltered capitalism with guaranteed profits.

As events would unfold it would turn out that their predictions understated the economic damage that would soon be done not just to Texas utility customers, but also to millions of people and businesses from Chesapeake Bay to Puget Sound. There would also be a lucky few who made enormous fortunes.

It was stranded costs that Smith and Briesemeister warned most about that day in Austin. Just days earlier a House committee had taken up Senate Bill 7, the Enron bill, and more than 100 amendments were put forth, including some dealing with that guarantee the utilities wanted.

Representative Kevin Bailey, a Houston Democrat, voiced the loudest concern. "We've increased stranded costs considerably in this bill from the previous bill," Bailey told Wolens, doubling the figure to $9 billion. That was the equivalent of about $1,200 for each household in the state.

At one point Bailey suggested that Wolens, his fellow Democrat, was looking out for the bosses, not for the working people who are the party's base.

"The big boys have been backing up the truck and loading it up in this bill," Bailey said, while "the little guys aren't able. They don't even have a car to back up, and they don't have a trunk or the car to get anything in it."

The hearing room audience erupted in laughter.

Wolens was annoyed. "Mr. Bailey, you want to start discussing what the big boys have done on this bill? Because I will spend the next two hours—"

"No, no," Bailey quickly interjected, again drawing a laugh from onlookers as he tried to defuse the situation.

"Mr. Bailey, no, no, no, no, no, no, no," Wolens persisted, trying to talk over his counterpart. "Mr. Bailey, I'll let you complete, but I'll let you know I ain't taking that sittin' down or standing up. I have spent an enormous amount of time on this bill. I have spent more time than I ever thought I was going to be spending on it. And for you to suggest what the big boys have been doing on my time rubs me a certain way."

Bailey raised the question of whether there was any need to change the system for setting electricity prices at all. He cited a report by the Texas Office of Public Utility Counsel, the state's consumer advocate in electric rate cases. It predicted that sticking with the existing system of regulating electric utilities would produce lower prices, a drop of as much as 16 percent by the end of 2003.

It was unfair, Bailey argued, for residential and small business customers to pay almost all of the stranded costs while the big industrial customers paid little. After all, everyone had agreed that the big industrial customers would be the major winners in a competitive market for electricity because as sophisticated volume buyers they could negotiate lower prices for themselves. Bailey pointed to a chart showing a large purple area that designated how much residential ratepayers would pay in stranded costs. Then, he called everyone's attention to a little red bar, the tiny share that was to be paid by the biggest industrial customers.

"I'm not against paying the stranded costs," Bailey announced. It was how the burden was spread that mattered to Bailey. His words set off a flurry of activity by lobbyists. Terral Smith, Governor Bush's legislative liaison, immediately began twisting arms to kill the Bailey proposal. The industrial lobbyists joined in applying pressure to shove the costs onto consumers and small business.

What Bailey never did was take on Enron. Eight years earlier Bailey had learned how dangerous that could be for a Texas politician. Back in 1991, when he was a freshman in the legislature, Bailey would not go along with a bill that Enron, then a natural gas pipeline company, wanted. Soon Bailey's campaign manager was working for his opponent and Enron contributions were financing the opposition. Bailey eked out a narrow victory in the primary, but two years later Enron and its allies were again financing his opponent.

By 1999 no one in Texas politics with a lick of sense got into a fight with Lay or Enron. The company's coordinated drive to create a state government to its liking had put the candidates it backed into every statewide office, Republicans all. Thanks to Enron's money, Republicans controlled the Texas state senate for the first time since Reconstruction. Enron was not all-powerful, but it was not a force to mess with unless, like Smith and Briesemeister, no one paid attention to your predictions.

As the final debate on the bill took place in the House chamber in Austin, Briesemeister joined the other lobbyists in the gallery far above the floor. The stranded costs issue had gone through several permutations, but in the end residential customers were stuck with the biggest share of the costs at 40 percent and the commercial and small business customers had to pick up 30 percent. Still, the remaining 30 percent share placed on the industrial customers was better than their original hopes as shown by the little red bar on Bailey's chart. As Briesemeister listened to that final debate, she thought how it was not really a debate at all, just posturing. *How stage-managed this all seems,* she thought.

Late that day Wolens received a standing ovation from his peers and the corporate lobbyists in the gallery. The bill had not even passed, yet everyone was on their feet, congratulating Wolens, and themselves, for overthrowing a system that was not broken in favor of what Enron and Governor Bush said was the better way of letting the market determine the price of electricity.

When the vote was called, Senate Bill 7 passed by a tally of 142 to 4. Briesemeister felt sick. She was certain that the promises of lower prices would prove to be illusory, that for all of its flaws the existing system was less costly to consumers.

Sure enough, by 2006, Texas electric rates were more than 50 percent higher than four years earlier. Painful as that was, it was not the worst of it. For what the lawmakers in Texas and other states had created was not a market that Adam Smith would recognize, but a system to manipulate prices. And while the lawmakers mad with zeal remained deaf to the warnings, Enron knew it had enacted into law an economic Trojan horse. So did Wall Street. The soldiers of Mammon were poised to emerge and take their spoils.

Chapter 18

SIGHTLESS SHERIFFS

J AY INSLEE WALKED AS FAST AS DECORUM WOULD ALLOW. THIS WAS the Capitol of the United States, after all. The Washington Congressman was anxiously navigating the unfamiliar basement hallways located on the other side, deep below the Senate chamber. Inslee searched for a room where he was to join the five Republicans and the dozen other Democrats who comprised the Oregon and Washington delegations to Congress.

In his right hand, Inslee clutched a fax, its late arrival from the West Coast this March morning in 2001 the reason for his rush. When he finally found the right door, the meeting had already been underway for a minute or two. Inslee, an inveterate basketball player, quickly spotted the only open seat and slid his athletic frame into it. Directly across the table sat a man he had never met before, the new vice president of the United States.

The bipartisan gathering was to seek relief from the worst economic crisis to hit the West Coast in decades. Electricity prices had skyrocketed. A kilowatt of power that a year earlier cost $30 was now priced at $600. The old price reflected the cost of generating power plus a profit. Since the costs of generating electricity had changed little, the new price bore no such connection to costs. And strangely, even when the populace cut back on its use of electricity after opening eye-popping bills, prices stayed high, defying the bedrock economic principle of supply and demand.

California consumers and businesses saw their statewide electric bill rise from an annual expense of about $6 billion to more than $60 billion. It was the economic equivalent of the state raising taxes on a family of four by $7,000 a year. Electric bills were out of control in Oregon and

Washington, too. But no one was there from the California delegation. Cheney insisted on that.

Everyone in the room knew that electricity was an industry in transition, from prices set by state utility boards to a competitive market, even if they had no grasp of how the new price mechanism worked. The cause of the skyrocketing prices was a mystery to everyone but the few who understood what laws like the one passed in Texas, as well as the one California enacted, meant for making the few rich at the expense of the many.

Wasn't competition supposed to mean lower prices? And why would prices soar when the amount of power people were buying had grown at normal, predictable rates? And why did prices stay high, even rise, when people flipped switches off? To anyone with a basic understanding of economics it made no sense.

Some of the lawmakers worried that this was something far more ominous than an economic glitch that would pass in a few weeks. Constituents were calling on the phone, demanding that somebody do something. The volume of calls grew with each month's electric bills. And there was fear that the current March prices would soon look like bargains. Summer was coming and, with it, increased demand for power to run air conditioning equipment. But what to do?

This deep sense of unease prompted unpleasant thoughts, a few lawmakers in both parties would say privately many months later. They realized how easily this economic crisis could boil over into something much worse. California was riven by rolling blackouts, as well as brownouts, in which power flows at reduced voltage. People had been stuck for hours in elevators. Others could not get cash out of automated teller machines or even retrieve their debit cards. There had been accidents when traffic lights failed, some of which led to nasty disputes. Thousands of poor families, the electric bill suddenly burning up half their meager income, had their power shut off for nonpayment. It did not take much thought to realize that people would use candles for light and this would, inevitably, cause fires that would kill small children.

In the Capitol basement, the more senior delegates spoke first. They told Cheney about widows on fixed incomes who had to choose between going hungry or going without their medications because the electricity bill ate all their money. Someone mentioned a family whose electric bill was suddenly larger than their mortgage.

As one of the more junior lawmakers, Inslee waited his turn. He watched Cheney. The vice president's movements and words indicated that stories about little old ladies did not penetrate his steely resolve. What Inslee could not discern was whether the vice president did not believe the stories or—and to Inslee this would be worse—that Cheney did not care.

Representative Norm Dicks, a Democrat who represented Washington State's Olympic Peninsula, called electricity prices "the most serious financial crisis facing Washington State since Boeing laid off 60,000 workers in 1970." Back then things got embarrassingly bad for America. People in Japan sent baskets of food to help families of laid-off workers in Renton, Seattle, and Tacoma. Americans depending on charity as if they were third world peasants after an earthquake was a Cold War–era story that the Soviets and their friends played big for its propaganda value.

The talk in that Senate basement turned to small business. Grocers and ice-skating rink owners had complained that the cost of electricity to run their refrigeration units was ruinous. Some electricity-intensive businesses simply shut down. Many employers who used power for nothing more than lights and computers had stopped hiring. Some had laid off workers. Job losses in Washington State alone could reach 40,000, someone said.

Cheney did not express any concern about rising electricity prices hurting small business. Some in the room heard Cheney say "this is how markets work" and something about "froth in any market." Inslee had expected that the troubles of Main Street business owners would stir the vice president to action. *Old ladies going hungry don't move him. Okay. But how can he not care about small businesses?* Inslee thought.

What the legislators had asked for, at least some of them, was the imposition of price caps so that the price of electricity would be related to the cost of producing it. That was how the traditional regulation system worked. Utility rates were set based on the cost of producing power, including a generous amount of surplus capacity for peak demand times like hot summer days, plus a profit. The Federal Energy Regulatory Commission had the power to impose such caps if prices in any market, competitive or regulated, were not "just and reasonable." Nothing had happened to make it cost more than $30 a kilowatt or so to produce power, even if no one understood just why. Cheney said no to price caps. Period.

When Inslee's turn came he focused on the fax, whose late arrival had made him the last person to enter the room. The fax had come from Robert McCullough, a utility economist who rose to become a vice president of Portland General Electric in Oregon before he set out on his own. McCullough made his living as an expert witness in electric utility litigation, an area requiring knowledge of arcane economic and legal details and an ability to translate them into plain English. To many in the power business these skills made him a hated man. Overnight McCullough had gathered complicated official data from California and then reduced it to a single fact so revealing that when the fax finally printed out in Washington, Inslee had a *Eureka!* moment.

McCullough had analyzed the status of every electricity-generating plant in California the day before. Which ones were running, which were down for scheduled maintenance, and which were offline due to an unexpected breakdown or other reasons. What he found was not what one would expect based on textbook economic theory. Even though record prices were to be had for anyone with power to sell, the owners of generating plants were not cranking up every boiler and diesel motor they owned. Instead, a third of the electric power–generating capacity in California was offline.

To Inslee, a former small-town prosecutor, this cried out for investigation. Normally a small percentage of power plants would be down for maintenance or offline because of unexpected breakdowns. But a third? And when prices were running 10 to 20 times what they had been just a year earlier?

Some of those in the room would say later that what happened next was unlike any political negotiating session they had ever attended.

Inslee quickly made his points as he slid the fax across the table. Cheney, without reading it, slid the fax back, saying, "You know what? You just don't understand economics."

Inside, Inslee began turning white hot with fury, but said nothing. He did not even tell the vice president that his degree from the University of Washington was in economics, not that that would have changed anything. But while Inslee held his tongue, the questions in his mind gelled. *It's clear we are wasting our time. He has a closed mind. I understand economics; what I don't understand is letting people get screwed.*

When the meeting ended after 45 minutes, Cheney left via a side door. The lawmakers went out to talk to the few reporters present, including a Seattle television news crew. Representative Jennifer Dunn, a Washington State Republican whom the party often relied on to deliver scripted messages, said, "We shouldn't look for a trendy and superficial answer and give an artificial response like price caps." And she said the administration was doing all that it could. Inslee could hold his tongue no more. That is just not true, Inslee said—the administration plans to do exactly nothing.

Less than a month later the vice president met with Ken Lay, whose Enron had spent all those years, and millions in campaign donations, buying access to politicians so it could shape the new laws on competition to its liking. Cheney had many meetings with energy-industry executives and he fought to keep them all as secret as he could. He argued that to even reveal with whom he had met would somehow compromise the quality and independence of the advice he received.

At their April 17 meeting Lay gave the vice president a three-page memo that stated that "events in California and in other parts of the country demonstrated that the benefits of competition have yet to be realized and have not yet reached consumers." Lay's memo urged the Bush administration to reject any limits on what Enron and others could charge for power. "Price caps, even if imposed on a temporary basis, will be detrimental to power markets and will discourage private investment by raising significant political risk," the memo said, without specifying what political risk or to whom. The memo then made what would turn out to be a revealing observation about just how the rules on competition had been written. "Similarly, a return to cost-based wholesale rates will be extremely difficult," Lay's memo said, as consumers would learn years later.

Throughout this time both President Bush and Vice President Cheney and their aides blamed the crisis on California officials, whom they said had not allowed the construction of enough power plants and had mismanaged. They also blamed Governor Gray Davis, a Democrat, even though he was not the cause of the problem. However, his hapless responses, and his panicked decision to spend tens of billions of dollars locking in prices at what turned out to be the peak of the crisis, were major reasons that voters later recalled him. The voters replaced him with one of the richest men in the country, Arnold Schwarzenegger, an actor of such vast wealth that he is the only individual American to own a Boeing 747 jumbo jet (which he leases to Singapore Airlines).

In the months that followed, the Northwest delegation, and especially Inslee, pressed for an investigation. At every opportunity Inslee denounced the administration and attacked its integrity. The Federal

Energy Regulatory Commission did little at first, which was not surprising. Its chairman was Pat Wood. When Bush was governor of Texas he had named Wood to the Texas utility commission at Lay's urging. When Bush became president, he named Wood chairman of the Federal Energy Regulatory Commission, acting again at Lay's urging.

A few months later, Wood announced that the commission would impose price caps. That action, he emphasized, was exactly what Enron did not want. In most places the news was played like Wood really was his own man. But the price caps were modest and would allow prices to remain much higher than they had been, just not so high as to run a political risk of voter revolt.

The following February, in 2002, almost a year after the basement meeting and just weeks after Enron collapsed, Wood announced that the commission would investigate whether Enron had manipulated the energy markets. Ultimately this supposed investigation would produce a brief report concluding that "in perspective, the crisis remains an aberration from the competitive markets that have benefited customers both before and since."

Wood was a sightless sheriff, standing in the middle of a busy brothel while observing only the piano player, whose every missed note he claimed credit for pointing out. That Wood closed his eyes came to light only because someone else was unwilling to ignore it. The Snohomish County Public Utility District, which provides electricity in that Washington State county, was on the hook to pay $120 million to Enron for power it would never get. Its leaders suspected that Enron had manipulated power prices. The district lacked proof because, under Wood, anything that might show criminality was ignored.

One day the Snohomish officials learned that the government had tapes of every call placed by Enron traders. They asked for the tapes and were denied. They fought to get the tapes until they won. Then they spent $800,000 transcribing them. What they showed was worse than even Inslee imagined.

Traders talked about money they "stole from those poor grandmothers in California." They shouted with joy when a brushfire let off so much heat that the volume of electricity on a major transmission line had to be reduced, allowing Enron traders to jack up prices. "The magical word of the day is 'Burn Baby Burn,'" one trader exulted.

Other traders talked openly about how, when Wood imposed the minimal price caps, they got around them by selling electricity made in

California to Arizona or Nevada and then selling it back into the state to evade the caps. They talked about how the new president from Texas would be good for Enron.

When the Snohomish district made its transcripts public, the responses were revealing. Enron, gasping its last in bankruptcy, said it was cooperating with investigators. Wood's spokesman stuck to the Bush administration line that the crisis was a tale of California politicians failing to do their job without quite making the accusation. Ignoring the guilty pleas already made by several Enron traders accused of fraud and other felonies, Wood's spokesman, Bryan Lee, said: "The bottom line is, was this crisis all manipulation? Or was there an actual shortage that resulted in the supply and demand already being tight?"

Once the evidence of Enron's systematic criminal behavior became overwhelming, the Federal Energy Regulatory Commission appeared to finally act with regard for some interest other than Enron's. It ruled that Enron could be required to give up all of the profits it earned since 1997. The operative word turned out to be "could."

Wood's successor as commission chairman, Joseph T. Kelliher, said that any firm that extracted profit through market manipulations on his watch would be forced to disgorge all profits. That turned out to be more hollow than promise.

What seemed like a routine settlement came before the commission for approval in June 2006, two years after the transcripts showing Enron's trading desk was a vast criminal conspiracy. It involved Enron's claim that it was owed about $160 million by two small nonprofit utilities. To end the dispute, Silicon Valley Power, an agency of the City of Santa Clara, California, paid Enron $36.5 million for power it had agreed to buy but that Enron never delivered. Valley Electric Association, a cooperative in the rural desert west of Las Vegas, paid $14 million. Both payments settled issues from the period when Enron was engaged in criminal fraud.

What about Chairman Kelliher's vow that on his watch any profits from manipulations would be disgorged? Lee, his spokesman, said that policy remained in force. But, he explained, the settlement involved not profits, but a dispute over termination fees. Whether "the termination fee is an unjust profit," Lee said, "is something the commission has not weighed."

Congressman Inslee was incensed. "It's the equivalent of Bonnie and Clyde, having been arrested, demanding that the banks refund the money

they stole and the government making the banks give them the money."
Senator Maria Cantwell, a Washington Democrat, said the commission
"has abdicated its responsibility" to protect consumers and taken the
side of Enron and its creditors, "instead of looking out for the public
interest."

The settlement also drew complaints from a cement company that
has been billed $4.2 million for electricity that Enron will never deliver
to its Montana kiln operation. Jack Ross, general counsel for Ash Grove
Cement Company, said he was at a loss to understand why the commission staff agreed to the settlement. "We thought FERC would be an advocate for the consumer and we are an energy consumer," Ross said.
"We felt the staff decision was more aligning itself on the Enron side and
we were very surprised that they were so cozy on the Enron side."

The settlement with the two small municipal electric systems con-
tained a provision that showed just how cozy Kelliher's commission was
on the Enron side. It removed from the public record all of the notes,
letters, e-mails, and audiotapes that documented Enron's crimes. Para-
graph 12 of the settlement said that the commission staff agreed "to release the Enron Parties from all existing and future claims under any legal
theory or cause of action that: (1) Enron charged, collected, or paid un-
lawful rates, terms or conditions for electric energy, ancillary services, or
transmission congestion or natural gas in the western markets; (2) Enron
manipulated the western electricity or natural gas or associated markets in
any fashion, or otherwise violated any applicable tariff, regulation, law,
rule, or order relating to the western markets; (3) Enron was unjustly
enriched."

So there it was, five years after Cheney had told Inslee he did not
understand economics. What the Bush administration did understand
was that it could help its friends get rich, even if they were too clever by
half and lost it all. First Cheney could deny a problem existed, and decline to inquire. Then the administration could create the appearance of
an investigation while taking care to make sure nothing untoward would
be found. And finally, when the evidence of wrongdoing came out anyway, it could just seal the record, promising to never ask a question or
speak of these unpleasant matters again.

But wait. There's more.

Among the documents withdrawn from the public records under the
settlement were notes taken by an Enron lawyer named Mary C. Hain.

She worked at the hub of Enron's electricity trading operation. That was in Portland, Oregon, where Enron owned its only operating company, Portland General Electric. While far from conclusive, the notes indicate that Hain knew about wrongdoing or, at a minimum, considered a strategy to counter any serious investigation. Hain wrote:

no one can prove, given the complexity of our portfolio

look like we're forthcoming

answer questions, say nothing—answer questions, finger others

What makes these notes interesting is that the Federal Energy Regulatory Commission never questioned Hain under oath about her notes. Instead, it hired Hain as a lawyer in its office of administrative litigation. When word of Hain's hiring got around, Senators Dianne Feinstein, a California Democrat, Cantwell, and others asked questions.

Chairman Kelliher insisted there was no issue because Hain would not work on any Enron matters. Hain told the *Los Angeles Times*, which asked about her hiring, "I'm an extremely ethical person. I've felt that I've been that way my entire career, including the time I was at Enron." The value of the statement can be weighed in the context of the mob boss Joseph Bonanno, who in his autobiography boasted about what a moral and ethical man he was, at least in his own eyes. Hain said her notes were the product of two meetings in which she hardly knew what was being talked about because she was a regulatory lawyer and the others were traders.

Robert McCullough, whose fax showed that a third of power plants were offline when prices soared, said her hiring should raise a question about why the commission could not find someone else among all the legions of regulatory lawyers in America who was at least as good, if not better. "Apparent indifference to corruption," he said, "seems like a very poor qualification as a regulator."

Today Enron is gone. So is Lay, dead in July 2006. His fatal heart attack came after his fraud conviction, but before his sentencing. That means the record in his case, like the record before the energy regulatory commission, will be changed. His conviction will not stand. As for the market manipulations that cost energy customers tens of billions of dollars in electricity charges alone, and left California with debt it will take two decades to pay off, officially whatever did happen will never be spoken of again by regulators under the settlement.

Despite this, the story is not over. The damage Lay and Enron caused was not limited to criminal acts. Enron had laws written to suit its schemes. Those laws remain on the books. They continue to enrich the wealthy few at the expense of the many through auctions that are called markets but, as we shall see, act instead like bid-rigging systems approved by government.

Chapter 19

PAYING TWICE

A T THE CORE OF THE ARGUMENT THAT MARKETS ARE BEST LIES ADAM Smith's observation that, in a free market, prices will fall to the lowest level at which proprietors can stay in business. Professor Sarosh Talukdar of Carnegie Mellon University decided to look into how this applies to the auction markets for electricity.

Talukdar created an ideal market. His simulated market had ten electricity generating companies, each of equal size, selling power; and ten utilities, also of equal size, buying power. The sellers seek the highest prices, while the buyers want to pay the lowest prices possible. There was more than enough capacity to supply the market.

In this idealized market, prices would be expected to fall as buyers took only the lowest bids. Instead, prices rose. And as time passed and more trades were made, the prices the buyers had to pay rose higher and higher. The results astonished Talukdar, so he ran four variations of the market experiment to test the findings. The results were always the same. Prices rose.

This pattern of rising prices suggests strongly that the sellers were colluding. The classic way to raise prices is for sellers to meet in secret and agree to fix prices at higher levels than the market would set.

But in Talukdar's experiment, collusion was impossible. The sellers could not have met in secret to fix prices because they were not people, but simple computer programs called learning algorithms. The programs were so simple that high school students with a knack for software could have written them.

What the experiments showed was that sellers could jack up prices in this market because the buyers are forced to buy. If the price of a share of stock or a piece of land is too high, buyers can walk away. Not so electricity, where the utilities that distribute the power are required to supply it. In this auction, the sellers all paid attention to the prices offered by other electricity sellers, then raised their own prices to higher and higher levels. So long as no one broke ranks and undercut the market, the sellers overall got higher prices and fatter profits than they would in a competitive market.

This unstated coordination gave the producers of electricity what economists call *market power,* which means the ability to set prices higher than a competitive market would allow. Within less than a hundred rounds of bidding, Talukdar's experimental auctions resembled not so much a competitive market as a cartel, in which many sellers obtain monopoly power by coordinating their actions to artifically inflate prices. That is what OPEC, the Organization of Petroleum Exporting Countries, does openly when members collude on setting the price of oil by limiting production.

"Collusion is a crime," Talukdar noted, "but learning is not. My studies show it is easy to learn from the signals given by others how to get the benefits of colluding without breaking the law."

Professor Talukdar is a computer scientist, not an economist. He thinks as an engineer thinks. "In building complex systems, whether it is a manufacturing process or a jetliner," he said, "you have to have rigorous verification to see if what you designed actually works the way you intended. But that is not the practice with economists, who do not verify the design of trading markets. Economists have this faith in markets, that markets are always a good thing."

Defenders of the electricity auction system, especially the owners of power plants, insist that the system has produced lower prices than the old regulated system, whose rates covered costs and provided a virtually guaranteed profit to the utilities. But the figures they point to show that prices fell, not because of market forces, but due to the rate caps and freezes that government imposed. Numerous studies found no benefit to consumers. One Cornell University study concluded, "There is no evidence to support the general expectation that deregulation would result in lower electricity prices." Instead, the evidence points to competition resulting in the higher prices that Talukdar's experiment found.

Talukdar said that his experiments show that "the design of markets matters a great deal and the design must be verified to see if it really works as a free market." Frank Wolak, a Stanford University economist who favors competitive markets for electricity, said Talukdar is right. The design of markets matters a great deal, Wolak said, because "even small flaws in the design of markets can cause enormous harm to consumers in very little time."

The damage was, and is, huge. Marilyn Showalter, an advocate for publicly owned power systems, analyzed Department of Energy data. The data showed that in the 12 months ending in May 2007, electricity in states that adopted Enron-style laws cost $48 billion more than the average cost in states that retained traditional regulation, which ties prices to the costs of production. That is $132 million per day in excess costs that act like a tax on the customers paying the bill.

In adopting Enron's recommendations to create electricity markets, state legislators did not take into account many unique aspects of electricity that affect its suitability for market auctions.

In markets for stocks, pork bellies, airline tickets, and houses, potential buyers have the option to walk away if the prices are too high. A stock can be bought on another day. Bacon is not required for breakfast. A trip can be deferred, and so can plans for a new house. But utilities in California, Connecticut, Illinois, Maryland, Texas, and a dozen other states must buy power every day. Many corporate-owned utilities, under laws Enron drafted, were required to sell their own generating plants. They are forced to buy power in the electricity markets since they no longer produce electricity themselves, but are still required to supply all that customers want.

Unlike the stock market, where vast numbers of strangers buy and sell, the electricity markets involve a relative handful of buyers and sellers. In New Jersey, for example, just 10 generators won bids in 2006 to supply a third of the state's base load of power for the next three years.

In many markets, the buyers and sellers are related companies under a single corporate umbrella. When regulated utilities sold their power plants, the buyers were often unregulated sister companies owned by the same corporate parent. In such arrangements, if the unregulated company that owns an electric power plant gouges the utility, the result is big profits for the parent company, creating a perverse incentive to raise prices.

Finally, electricity trades repeat each day. Power is sold for specific time periods, often an hour or quarter hour, a day or two before it is needed. The short periods allow prices to be affected by changing demand from customers as they turn on air conditioners on hot afternoons or flip off lights at bedtime. Because auctions occur so often, those who generate power for sale can get an idea of what the market will bear by studying the weather report and historic patterns of demand. This is where the analysis of trading patterns that drove up prices in Talukdar's experiment comes into play.

Moreover, electricity markets operate in government-imposed secrecy. Individual stock investors can make sure they got a fair price by checking the prices paid just before and after their trade. But the Federal Energy Regulatory Commission and the electricity exchanges it authorizes stamp many trading records confidential, though some records are made public months or years later. Many times even this knowledge is misleading, however, as the markets include not just the owners of power plants, but brokers who act as fronts.

Finally, the very nature of electricity means that it must be produced, transmitted, and consumed in an instant. Automakers can cut production when vehicles do not sell. Investors who hold too much of a particular stock can sell it in blocks over time to get the best price. But electricity cannot be held in inventory.

There is one other crucial difference between electricity and stock markets. In electricity markets, every seller gets the highest price—*even when it is higher than the price at which they were willing to sell*. That is the rule in the electricity auction market: the highest winning bid sets the price for all.

Contrast this to the stock market. Someone who wants shares of a company buys them at different prices, perhaps $10 a share to start, and then, as word gets around that someone is accumulating shares, paying $20. The average of these prices may be $15. Not so with electricity. In electricity markets, everyone gets the highest price that is accepted. It is as if the stock market buyer had to pay $20 for every share, even the ones offered for sale at half that price.

Giving every seller the high price for the day, hour, or other time period creates a huge incentive to hold generating stations offline to restrict supply and thus drive up prices. This was exactly what was shown in the fax that Vice President Cheney refused to examine when he told Representative Jay Inslee, "You just don't understand economics." This system also creates incentives to apply what is learned, as Professor Talukdar showed, to rig prices.

Consider what happened on March 2, 2003, in the Texas electricity market. Power was being auctioned off in quarter-hour segments for the next day. Some power was offered for free, presumably by nuclear power plants, which must run at the same rate around the clock. Several dozen bidders then offered power at various prices.

The average of the bids required to supply all the power that was needed came to $83 per megawatt hour. But the bid that cleared the market, the bid that provided the last megawatt of power needed to meet demand, was more than $200. Under the rules for electricity markets, every generating company was paid the high bid of more than $200 per megawatt hour. The difference between the individual prices that the sellers offered and the price actually paid was $150,000. That money was extra profit for all but the top bidder.

In the auction for the next quarter-hour period, the bidding pattern changed. There were still generators offering power for free. But the high bid for the last few megawatts of power needed by customers was $990. Every owner of a generating plant got that price, even those offering power for free. The extra profit? More than $800,000 in just fifteen minutes.

The industry calls these inflated prices "hockey stick" bids because, when plotted on a chart, the prices show a long handle that rises slowly with a spike at the end like the blade on a hockey stick.

Official state reports identified only as "Company C" the bidder who set the price at nearly $1,000. Years later it was identified as TXU, which owns both the regulated Dallas electric utility and, through a sister company, a host of power plants. Although historically stocks of utilities were reliable but slow to appreciate, TXU has been one of the best-performing large company stocks between 2002 and 2007, showing just how valuable the pricing manipulations of "Company C" were to its bottom line.

The system was a perfect arrangement to get, not the lowest possible prices, but a free lunch through inflated prices, served up by government rules. Any one of the many TXU generating plants could make a high bid that produced windfall profits for the others. Because the power was sold to regulated utilities, which by law must provide whatever power customers demand, the price was just passed on. But customers had no idea that in some quarter-hour segments they were paying exorbitant prices. Why? Because all customers get is a monthly statement that adds up the prices paid for every fifteen-minute period into a single total.

Technology allowing residential and small-business customers to know what price they pay each moment for electricity has been available for decades. In the seventies, utility regulators in California and some other states said they would make it widely available to encourage people to reduce their use of power during periods of peak demand. Somehow, though, it just never happened. And without that knowledge of prices at each instant, customers cannot know when their pockets are being gouged.

The supposed markets for power enable price gouging in still other ways. California has 1,400 power plants, which ought to be more than enough for a vibrant market and, as Adam Smith observed, should drive prices down to the lowest level at which the businesses can afford to continue operating. But ownership of those California plants is so concentrated that just six generating companies can set an artificially high price for electricity virtually all the time, research by Carnegie Mellon University shows.

New Jersey and Illinois are among the states that conduct annual electricity auctions. In New Jersey, just 10 generators won contracts to supply a third of the state's base load of power through 2009. The price? It was 55 percent higher than the previous year's three-year bid.

In Illinois, prices also soared. Among the winning bidders to supply power? An unregulated sister company of Commonwealth Edison, the Chicago utility, both of which are owned by Constellation Energy. In essence, this is a system in which an unregulated company earns outsized profits from a regulated company, which in turn earns virtually guaranteed profits and, by law, can pass on the prices it pays for electricity to its customers. Think of this as the anti–Adam Smith policy.

That electricity is sold in what are called markets, but are really mechanisms to rig prices and cheat customers, has become obvious even to the large industrial and commercial customers who initially bought into Enron's campaign to make generating electricity a competitive business. They have seen their own prices rise, not fall. Robert A. Weishaar Jr., a lawyer for many big industrial customers, told the Federal Energy Regulatory Commission that his clients were being taken for a ride and damaged by commission policies that allow price gouging. "The 'markets' that are rolling off the commission's production line are not fit for their public purpose," he wrote.

The Federal Energy Regulatory Commission, however, rejected all such complaints out of hand. Under its circular logic, once it declares that a market for electricity has been created, whatever prices markets produce must by definition be fair and just, because markets produce fair and just prices.

Faux markets are not the only way that customers are having their pockets picked under current policies originally promoted by Enron. When competition began, most states that adopted the Enron proposals required utilities to sell their power plants. They not only allowed them to be sold to sister companies that were unregulated, they allowed them to be sold at bargain-basement prices.

Most plants were sold for the cost of construction minus the amount that had been depreciated, that is, the amount written off on the company's books. This was allowed even when the plant had actually risen in value. Said Lynn Hargis, who was a longtime federal government energy lawyer before joining Ralph Nader's Public Citizen: "Selling a power plant for its depreciated value is the equivalent of selling my grandmother's house for what she paid for it decades ago, less depreciation, while ignoring its real value. Nobody would do that."

For electricity customers it was even worse than that. The utilities demanded that they be paid in full for the value of the plants that they had not yet written off. These were the "stranded costs" in the Trojan Horse bill that the Texas legislature, and the legislatures of many other states, passed to mollify the utilities.

Across the nation, state utility regulators let the utilities sell bonds so they could immediately pocket in cash the value of the plants that they transferred to their unregulated sister companies. Then the cost of these bonds, plus interest, was added to electric bills. For residential customers of Centerpoint, the old Houston Lighting & Power, this will add an average of almost five dollars to their bills every month for 14 years.

Some of these plants were then resold at huge profits. Centerpoint sold 60 power plants that generate most of the power for the Houston area to a joint venture of four investment firms—the Blackstone Group, Hellman & Friedman, Kohlberg Kravis Roberts, and Texas Pacific Group. The price was less than $1 billion. Just eighteen months later, the four investment firms resold the plants for a profit of almost $5 billion. It was a deal that even by the standards of Texans produced awe, though no shock.

Sempra Energy, parent of the utility in San Diego, and two investment partners bought nine Texas power plants in 2004 for $430 million. Less than two years later, it sold just two of the nine plants for $1.6 billion. A group led by Goldman Sachs, the investment bank, bought power plants in upstate New York, Pennsylvania, and Ohio starting in 1998. It sold them in 2001 for a profit of more than $1 billion.

The prices of these and many other plants rose because of the easily rigged markets for electricity that make it possible for owners to inflate prices. Robert McCullough, the utility economist whose fax on price manipulations Vice President Cheney dismissed without reading it, said that from Maryland to Texas to California, the sale of power plants by utilities to sister companies had no benefit for customers. "The same energy is generated by the same plants, owned by the same owners, and sold to the same customers, simply at a vastly higher price," he said.

Ralph Nader said regulators should have required price protection to shield consumers from a "double-header corporate gouge, where the defenseless customer is paying twice for the same power plants."

But wait. There's more.

Paying twice for the power plants is not the only way that electricity customers are forced to double up their costs. Across the country, electricity customers pay taxes that are embedded in the rates they pay. Because utilities are legal monopolies, they must recover all of their costs from customers, ranging from the price of fuel and the chief executive's expense-account lunches to income taxes on profits.

These taxes do not always make it to government, however. When state utility boards set electric rates, they assume that the utility will file its own tax return. But often when the utility has a corporate parent, the parent files the tax return and the parent may not pay any taxes. When that happens, the utility and its parent company eat a free lunch at the expense of their customers.

The system that allows the corporate parents of utilities to pocket taxes has many defenders. Paul Joskow, a Massachusetts Institute of Technology utility economist, said, "For the customer, the result is the same." He meant that if utilities filed their own tax returns and paid the taxes, their rates would be the same as when they pass the taxes on to their corporate parents.

Mike Hatch, when he was Minnesota attorney general, said Joskow's argument is hollow. "Essentially, utility ratepayers pay the tax twice," Hatch said, "once through the utility bill and again through the lost revenue to government that means either higher taxes for them or fewer government services."

Hatch provided help to Myer Shark, a Minnesota lawyer who spent the last years of his life trying to recover $300 million in taxes, embedded in the rates paid by that state's electric customers, that never reached government. The taxes benefited Xcel Energy, which operates in ten states, though Shark sought recovery just in Minnesota. To Shark, who was in his nineties when he took on Xcel, pocketing taxes violated laws prohibiting "unjust enrichment" by legal monopolies like utilities.

"The law says that utilities are entitled to a just and reasonable return, but when they keep the taxes, they are earning an unjust and unreasonable rate of return because those taxes add to their profits," he said. Just days before he died in 2007 at the age of 94, Shark filed the last legal papers intended to make sure a court would decide his case and reject any efforts to dismiss it because he would not be around to argue further.

The champion at pocketing taxes was Portland General Electric, during the years 1997 to 2004 when it was the only operating business owned by Enron. Each year Oregon residents and businesses paid about $92 million to cover Portland GE's income taxes. But Portland GE, like virtually all electric utilities with a corporate parent, did not file its own tax returns. Instead, Enron filed the tax returns. Enron did not pay taxes, thanks to its use of hundreds of shell companies in the Cayman Islands and other tax havens. That meant that Enron pocketed an extra $92 million a year from Portland GE customers, a total of nearly $1 billion dollars during the years it owned the utility.

News that Portland GE did not pay taxes caused an uproar in Oregon. The state was so hard-pressed for money that some counties could not afford sheriff's patrols. The Oregon legislature passed a law in 2005 to require that any taxes embedded in utility rates be turned over to government. Not only did Portland GE fight the law, so did Warren Buffett, who had just acquired Oregon's other big corporate-owned utility, PacifiCorp. Both wanted to profit off taxes.

Buffett is a master at delaying the payment of taxes not for a little while, but for a generation. His MidAmerican Energy Company owns electric and natural gas utilities, with operations from Oregon and Utah through Iowa and east to Britain. It paid just 4 percent of its American profits in federal corporate income taxes in 2006, far less than most Americans paid on their incomes. On its overseas profits, MidAmerican paid a 21 percent tax.

MidAmerican will have to pay the rest of his American taxes, but not for a long time. It deferred $666 million in taxes in 2007. In 2035 it will have paid just half of those taxes. A tax not paid today but in the distant future is like getting an interest-free loan from the government, which is to say from the rest of the taxpayers. Imagine how rich you would be if you had bought a house 28 years ago, got an interest-free mortgage, and only now had to pay the price you agreed to so many years ago. Like Buffett you would be rich. When the government finally gets those taxes from Buffett's company it will get about 40 cents on the dollar. You will have to make up for those missing 60 or so cents through higher taxes, fewer services, or interest payments on more government debt.

This interest-free loan has not meant cheap electric rates. When it comes to charging high prices, Buffett plays hardball, extracting every dollar the regulators will allow his utilities to charge, as people in six Iowa cities discovered. For years Iowa had nine corporate-owned electric utilities plus a sprinkling of city-owned systems that sold power at lower prices. Then MidAmerican and another firm, Alliant Energy, consolidated the corporate-owned utilities into just two entities. Because consolidation lowers costs, people in Johnson City and five smaller towns tried, without success, to get lower rates, hoping this would both save them money and help local manufacturers create more jobs. Rebuffed, they organized to buy out MidAmerican and run municipal systems so they could get their power for less.

Buffett's agents immediately went to work to make sure electricity prices would not fall. His firm spent more than half a million dollars in Johnson City. It also filed a petition to lower rates, though more than four years later rates remain unchanged.

But Buffett's key move was getting legislation to thwart not just six towns but to punish the people in the nine cities with municipal power for giving advice on how to convert from corporate power to municipal power. MidAmerican drafted bills that would have made the existing city-owned systems pay taxes, prevented them from making changes as technology and the times always require, and blocked them from offering any new services, such as municipal Internet or cable television service. Buffett's lobbyists bluntly told the Iowa Association of Municipal Utilities that it would make the legislation go away on one condition: that the association stop giving advice to the six towns on how to switch to municipal power. Bob Haug, the association's executive director, told his members that the influence of Buffett's lobbyists showed how the state of Iowa had been transformed into "Iowa Inc." He said that given MidAmerican's grip on the legislature the association had no choice but to bow to MidAmerican's demand that it adopt a resolution promising to never help any Iowa citizens seek a municipal power system.

Carol Spaziani was a librarian in Johnson City before she retired. She became a leader of the municipal power campaigns. Spaziani said that she watched in amazement and horror both at how Buffett used government to enrich himself at the expense of others and at how eager state legislators and others were to bow to the will of his lobbyists. She said she was also struck by the inability of the news media to articulate the issues of a matter crucial to the local economy, and, when they were covered, how it was written up as a political dispute worthy of only a few words on the inside pages.

"On television I keep seeing this beneficent billionaire who is portrayed as someone we should all respect because he is so rich, and he has given so many billions to charity," Spaziani said. "What I don't see is coverage about how Warren Buffett is forcing people in Johnson City to pay more than we should for electricity, and how that means fewer jobs and hardship for people just so he can make more billions."

But wait. There's still more.

State regulators generally allow utilities to earn a profit of 10 percent or so. Yet despite this limit on profits, investors famed for earning much bigger returns, like Warren Buffett, are buying electric utilities. Kohlberg Kravis Roberts & Co. and the Texas Pacific Group, which teamed up to make those enormous profits buying Texas power plants, are in the game. The two firms worked jointly in 2007 to buy TXU, the big Dallas utility involved in the hockey stick bids. This joint venture came after KKR failed in its attempt to buy Tucson Electric Power in Arizona and Texas Pacific tried to buy Enron's Portland General Electric.

Why would investors famed for much bigger returns want electric utilities earning a solid, but modest, profit? The answer reveals how much government has become an ally of the rich in exploiting those with less.

After Enron bought Portland GE it raised rates, ending decades of cheap power. The revelation that it pocketed almost a billion dollars of taxes customers were forced to pay in their monthly electric bills turned many in Portland against both Enron and the local electric utility.

Then, in October 2003, the city's long Enron nightmare appeared to be coming to an end, thanks to Neil Goldschmidt, the most influential politician in the state. Goldschmidt was elected mayor in 1972 when he was just 32, the youngest mayor of a major American city. He went on to become transportation secretary under President Carter and governor of Oregon. He was instrumental in making Portland a vibrant, livable city, with mass transit, bicycle lanes, and ways for minorities and others to have a voice in city affairs.

Goldschmidt announced that Texas Pacific proposed to buy Portland GE, and that he would shepherd the deal through Oregon's Public Utility Commission. At his side stood two business leaders, Gerald Grinstein, the chairman of Delta Airlines, and Tom Walsh, a prosperous developer. The promise was of local leadership of the utility, although the investment money was coming from far away. Things soon took many unexpected, even salacious, turns.

Texas Pacific instantly persuaded state officials to seal most of the documents about how it would finance the purchase. It claimed that the information would be of value to competitors, a curious argument, since Portland GE is a legal monopoly that has no competitors. But Oregon's Public Utility Commission, whose members were so lackadaisical that the chairman was known to nod off during official proceedings, went along. Lawyers representing big industrial customers, consumer groups, and others could see the financial records, but only if they promised not to reveal what was in them.

Ann Fisher, a veteran utility lawyer who represented downtown building owners, was vexed by what she saw. So Fisher wrote an essay for *The Oregonian*. She wrote that the sealed files told a very different story than the public announcements about the purchase. Fisher took care not to disclose any specifics that might be of value to Portland GE's mythical competitors, but she wrote that from the viewpoint of Texas Pacific, a 50 percent profit was not out of the question. Her words suddenly turned an issue that bores most people into the hottest topic in town.

Soon after that, someone slipped the sealed documents to an exceptionally savvy reporter named Nigel Jaquiss. He had made a fortune as a Wall Street oil trader and then decided his children would have a better life if their father had a job he really enjoyed. Jaquiss reported for the local alternative newspaper, *Willamette Week*.

Using skills he had learned at Goldman Sachs, Morgan Stanley, and Cargill, Jaquiss plowed through the documents and determined that Texas Pacific had found a way to earn more than three times the rate of return that was authorized for Portland General Electric. The key was a complicated ownership structure with a lot of debt and very little cash, which meant that the real risk if anything went wrong would be borne not by the owners of the utilitiy, but by its customers. The public knew none of this, thanks to the official secrecy.

Such official secrecy in regulatory proceedings is becoming commonplace across the country. It fits the ideology that government is the problem, which it certainly is for some corporations when government acts as a guardian of the people against profiteers. It also has its attractive benefits for politicans, allowing them to do their work and even make subtle side deals to benefit friends without a spotlight on their actions. Keeping people in the dark also reduces the risk that the public will realize how much of its government has been twisted into a tool of the rich seeking to expand their riches at the expense of those with less.

The disclosures about the financial aspects of the deal followed an earlier story by Jaquiss that discredited Goldschmidt. It was the story of a secret that many of Oregon's business and political elite had known about, and many others had suspected or heard about, but that everyone had kept to themselves for more than three decades. Jaquiss showed how a few prominent Oregonians had even traded on the secret, getting official favors from Goldschmidt when he was in office.

The secret was that Goldschmidt, when he was mayor, repeatedly had sex with a 14-year-old girl, a neighbor whose mother was a close political ally. None of those who knew had stepped forward to protect the girl or to have Goldschmidt arrested for statutory rape. For years Goldschmidt paid the victim hush money. There was no indication that anyone among Oregon's elites ever shunned the child rapist, but plenty of evidence that some of those who knew turned to him when they needed to work the city, the county, or the state for official favors. Goldschmidt was, by all accounts, the man to see about getting government to help the rich and powerful, both fixer and kingmaker.

When Goldschmidt realized that the intrepid reporter Jaquiss had all the facts to break a story in the weekly newspaper, he went to *The Oregonian,* the largest daily paper in the state. He hoped that by giving the big daily newspaper a scoop he would get as friendly a story as possible, one that would not carry the sting that was certain to come from Jaquiss. It was a smart move. The next morning *The Oregonian* reported that when Goldschmidt was mayor he had "an affair" with a girl of 14.

The financial disclosures and the sex scandal eventually brought an end to the Texas Pacific bid. Jaquiss won an extraordinary honor for a reporter at a weekly newspaper, a Pulitzer Prize. The city of Portland tried to buy the utility, promising to pay more than anyone else, and then to lower rates, because as a municipal utility it would not have to pay big executive salaries or dividends. The corporate lawyers and executives who by then controlled Enron declined to take this high bid. Instead they had Portland GE issue stock, and it became a freestanding company, one that immediately asked for a hefty rate hike and a change in rules that shifted the risk of rising fuel prices entirely onto customers. As with Warren Buffett's hardball moves in Iowa, corporate power worked to make sure customers paid the highest possible prices for electricity.

What is significant about the Portland deal is how it exposes the willingness, even eagerness, of government officials who are supposed to be acting on behalf of the public to use official secrecy to benefit private interests. And even when Texas Pacific's fixer was revealed to be a sexual predator whose victim was a 14-year-old girl, the local elite did not turn on him, did not demand an inquiry, and did not queston their own complicity. Instead, the state conducted a long, costly, and ultimately failed investigation to try to determine how Jaquiss got hold of the financial documents. The state tried to pin the blame on Ann Fisher, who had acted honorably, and who had not been the source of the documents.

Fisher paid a terrible price for being honest. She lost her business clients. She has had a tough time finding new ones, as the tightly knit Portland business elite closed ranks.

And Goldschmidt? After laying low for months he resumed working for clients seeking subtle favors from government. But unlike his public announcement in the utility deal, Goldschmidt adopted a lower profile, working the telephones and backrooms.

Advocating competition, and then using government as a way to make deals shrouded in secrecy that promise enormous profits and few risks for those getting richer, is a core strategy for those who have discovered how easily government can be turned into a source of personal enrichment. Next, let's examine the career of one of the biggest beneficiaries of this self-serve approach to government.

Chapter 20

RISING SNOW

THAT MARKETS ARE SUPERIOR TO GOVERNMENT REGULATION LOOKS compelling on paper. Arranging symbols on pieces of paper with reasoned logic is, however, a much easier task than applying ideas in the real world. Human beings must act out the policies, bringing their strengths and shortcomings into play. They bring their own goals and ambitions and they must contend with external forces working under different assumptions.

The career of John Snow, the CSX railroad chief executive who became Treasury secretary for more than three years beginning in 2003, illustrates this dichotomy. The arc of Snow's career shows how the movement to weaken government while strengthening corporate power has enriched the few at the expense of the many.

John William Snow was born in 1939. He grew up comfortably in Toledo, where his father was a corporate litigator who enjoyed success despite being nearly blind. Mealtime in the Snow household was a family debating society with only one winner, which shaped Snow's remarkable skills at lobbying and flattery of those in a position to do him favors. Snow once told an interviewer about a valuable lesson he learned from the autocrat of the dinner table. "If you argued with my father, he was quite pleasant about it, but you would lose," Snow said. "Early on, I saw the tactical advantage of stating my views as hypotheses."

Snow graduated from college in 1962 and went to the University of Virginia for graduate studies in economics. It was a heady time. Two professors there, James Buchanan and Ronald Coase, were developing ideas about markets and government, for which each would later win the Nobel Prize.

Coase questioned established principles about who should pay for harm inflicted as a by-product of business. The idea that those who cause harm should be made to pay involved a subtle slip of the mind, Coase wrote in "The Problem of Social Cost," which every serious economics student reads.

Sometimes, Coase reasoned, society would be better off, or at least richer overall, if businesses were excused from paying for some or all of the damages they inflict on others. That concept would take on concrete meaning for Snow. He slashed safety spending at CSX by $2.4 billion between 1981 and 1993, conduct a judge called "willful, wanton negligence" that was "borderline criminal" in the death of Miami police sergeant Paul Palank. Yet the cost for what three other judges called a "flagrant violation of the public trust" was paid not by CSX, but was a free lunch the railroad obtained from the taxpayers.

Buchanan, for his part, argued that politicians often espouse good intentions and then act in their own self-interest. A similar pattern has been identified in how many chief executives run companies. Buchanan's insights also bore relevance to Snow's work, looking out for himself in his positions in both government and business.

Snow's 1965 doctoral thesis, a document with less intellectual heft than some papers written by college seniors, argued that government-sponsored training for auto mechanics contributed to an oversupply of these workers, depressing the future earnings of mechanics.

After teaching for two years and earning a law degree, Snow worked as a lawyer and a law school professor. He also held legal and policy positions in the Transportation Department during the Nixon and Ford administrations, where he worked on what was called "deregulating" the trucking industry. The resulting changes in regulation brought about numerous bankruptcies of trucking companies, which under the new rules were unable to earn what the government said was the necessary return to stay in business. More than a million truck drivers saw their wages plummet.

This work to reduce regulation brought Snow into contact with Hays T. Watkins, the chief executive of the railroad company that became CSX. Its properties included the Baltimore & Ohio Railroad, now best known as a square on the Monopoly board game. The B&O was also the first common carrier in America, its history going back to 1827, when mechanized transit began on this continent. Watkins was the driving force in shaping legislation that changed the rules on railroad regulation, another set of rules sold under the phony heading of deregulation.

Watkins hired Snow to be his chief lobbyist. Snow rose quickly as Hays groomed him to be his successor. Snow took on major operational control in 1981. He became head of the railroad division in 1985 and chief executive of CSX in 1989. Snow was not a railroad guy with knowledge of how to make the trains run on time, but a fellow who knew how to read numbers and schmooze government officials.

Watkins and Snow explained how they worked the government for profit in an interview when Watkins won an award from *Industry Week* magazine in 1982. Their comments showed that the real work they did was less running a railroad than manipulating government to serve their interests.

Once every two weeks, Watkins would drive his Oldsmobile Toronado the 105 miles from Richmond, Virginia, to Washington. Snow shared the driving. Watkins told the magazine that he was not a superstar at government relations like Reginald Jones of General Electric or Irving Shapiro of DuPont, who were previous winners of the magazine's award for excellence in government relations. Watkins said he hardly knew President Reagan because he spent most of his time with the representatives and senators, and their staffs, who set railroad policy, making 300 such visits in 18 months. The magazine described him as a habitué of the Transportation Department, as well as of the Interstate Commerce Commission and the Federal Trade Commission. That is, it said he spent his time where he could really influence what mattered to CSX.

Snow explained, "Hays has sensitized this entire corporation to government relations—right down to the engineer on a train. He has institutionalized it. If he were to leave the company, his approach would endure."

As Snow rose, he saw to it that government relations remained central. These skills were on display when he worked to prevent the sale of Conrail, the dominant freight line in the Northeast, which the government put together after the bankruptcy of the old Penn Central. The Consolidated Rail Corporation had more than 13,000 miles of track. The taxpayers had poured about $7 billion into keeping it going because it was so vital to the national economy.

The executive who ran Conrail, Stanley Crane, wanted an initial public offering so the market would set the price for Conrail, including its valuable rights of way and contracts to haul freight. That would mean more competition, which in turn could mean lower prices and demands for more capital investment to deliver freight faster and more reliably.

Snow wanted government to intervene in the market, exactly what his doctoral thesis—and his professors at the University of Virginia—opposed. Snow's most important ally was the federal government's Transportation secretary, Elizabeth Dole, the wife of Senator Bob Dole of Kansas and now a senator in her own right from North Carolina. Dole decided to let CSX and a competitor, Norfolk Southern, carve Conrail up to their mutual strategic advantage.

Under Snow, CSX budgets for maintenance and for inspection were cut and cut and cut. In the nineties, CSX spent less money on maintenance per mile of track than any other railroad. After a spate of crashes that killed 19 and injured more than a hundred people, a federal report said that CSX "employees were not reporting injuries due to fear of reprisals, such as formal hearings or harsh discipline for minor unsafe acts or mistakes."

Still, the safety cuts paid off. CSX made a dime per share in 1992, the year after Palank was killed. Five years later, long before the court found negligence, it earned $4.17 a share.

Little outside attention was paid to how CSX slashed maintenance and inspection crews, saying that mechanization and increased productivity reduced the need for many repair and inspection workers. A federal report found that half the CSX safety workers had been cut.

Congress was also cutting, reducing the number of Federal Railroad Administration inspectors. The agency has only 400 inspectors divided into five specialties to check up on 200,000 miles of track, 250,000 or so employees, and 20,000 locomotives that pull 12 million freight cars.

CSX also regarded the federal inspectors not as hard-nosed cops looking out for the public, but as friends. Consider the visit in 1997 by James T. Schultz, associate administrator for safety at the Federal Railroad Administration. The taxpayers paid to send Schultz to talk about persistent safety problems. CSX saw an opportunity to recruit Schultz. It hired him on the spot as chief safety officer, a job that also carried the title of vice president and a big pay raise. The move was so sudden that it raised some eyebrows and prompted an inquiry by the Transportation Department inspector general, who is supposed to be the official watchdog for the taxpayers. The inspector general concluded that there was "no evidence that Schultz violated any criminal conflict of interest statute."

This was just the kind of intimate connection between government and business that Adam Smith warned about. Markets that operate on official favors were not what Smith had in mind when he wrote of the invisible hand of the market. Putting a thumb on the scale is not productive in Smith's reasoning, though it may in the short run benefit the cheater.

Even so, the railroad had little to worry about. Federal law kept the fines modest, no more than $20,000 per incident, even if many people died and property damage ran into the billions of dollars. Measured against annual profits, the penalties were mere parking tickets.

When it came to paying Snow there was no stringency.

Snow made much of his plan to require everyone working for CSX to buy company stock. This was supposed to align the interest of employees with shareholders. As the price of shares soared in the early nineties, it seemed like a smart move. Then the stock price fell. Snow had borrowed from the company to buy his shares. The CSX board forgave the loans Snow had taken out to buy his shares and he gave them back, suffering no loss, unlike common shareholders. Company disclosures indicated the loans totaled $24 million. CSX said that number was in error, but would not provide what it considered an accurate figure. But what the loans and their forgiveness showed was that Snow had no skin in this game, bore no risk, had no alignment of his interests with those of shareholders.

Though legal at the time, Congress in 2001 made such loan forgiveness for executives illegal. When President Bush nominated Snow to become his second Treasury secretary, the White House was asked about the loan forgiveness. "Anything that was a common practice that was lawful is not, in the president's judgment, a disqualification," said Ari Fleischer, the White House press secretary.

The falling stock price did not align with Snow's salary, bonus, and other compensation, either. In the five years from 1997 through 2002, shares of CSX lost more than half their value. Snow's pay, however, soared by 69 percent. He made $6 million in 1997, but $10.1 million in 2001 and another $10 million in 2002.

Snow also benefited from an unusual pension deal that federal law allows. Most workers, if they get a pension at all, count only their base salary and the number of years they worked for the company. Snow got to count his base pay, his bonus, and 250,000 shares of stock the company gave him. And on top of this he received credit for 44 years of service even though he only worked at CSX for 25 years. Congress could, if it wanted, end such favoritism to executives by changing the rules. It could require that all pensions be based on the same formula as a condition for the payments to be tax deductible.

When Snow resigned to become Treasury secretary his pay for the first two months of 2003 plus his cash-out payments totaled $72 million. Meanwhile, 41 CSX retirees who had worked at the railroad's Greenbrier hotel and country club in West Virginia sued, saying they were deprived of life insurance benefits. James Hilton, a retired food storage supervisor, said that the life insurance benefit was routinely paid until October 2001. Then, he said, "out of the blue, CSX sent us this self-contradictory letter that says, 'We know you thought you had this life insurance benefit, but really you did not.' " One policy on the executive floor, another on the shop floor.

Snow's appointment was even too much for *Forbes*, which noted that at CSX "his performance was middling at best," while his pay was the highest in the history of the railroads.

As Treasury secretary, Snow promoted retirement savings and financial literacy (and anything else banal that the White House asked him to say). He did not practice what he preached. Snow's investment adviser bought almost $11 million in bonds sold by major players in the mortgage market: Fannie Mae, Freddie Mac and the Federal Home Loan Banks. It was improper for Snow to have such investments. Snow said he was not aware of the purchases because for more than a year he said he did not look at his own financial statements, as he told others they should. The impropriety came to light when a Treasury Department ethics official raised questions about the investments. A spokesman said Snow considered these investments "regrettable" and said they were sold at a loss of almost a half million dollars.

When Snow left Treasury he took on a new job, chairman of a private equity firm called Cerberus Capital Management. Few people outside of Wall Street have heard of the firm, but almost everyone has heard of some of its business activities. It is a regular in getting government contracts. Cerberus owns IAP Worldwide Services, the company that the federal government hired to send truckloads of ice to New Orleans, but that instead ended up scattered across the South, diesel engines idling to keep the cargo from melting. The same company also had a contract to fix up Building 18 at Walter Reed Army Medical Center, the one where soldiers complained of mold and rats and shoddy repairs.

Chapter 21

UNHEALTHY ECONOMICS

WHEN LINDA PEENO BECAME A PHYSICIAN, SHE TOOK THE HIPPO-cratic Oath, including a promise to patients to "keep them from harm and injustice." In time that vow began to weigh on Dr. Peeno's conscience. Her job was not to make patients well, but to make a company well at their expense.

"In the spring of 1987, as a physician, I caused the death of a man," Dr. Peeno told Congress in 1996. "Although this was known to many people, I have not been taken before any court of law or called to account for this in any professional or public forum. In fact, just the opposite occurred. I was 'rewarded' for this. It brought me an improved reputation in my job, and contributed to my advancement afterwards. Not only did I demonstrate I could indeed do what was expected of me, I exemplified the 'good' company doctor: I saved a half million dollars."

Dr. Peeno never saw her patient, a man who needed a heart transplant. Dr. Peeno examined "a piece of computer paper, less than half full. The 'clinical goal' was to figure out a way to avoid payment. The 'diagnosis' was to 'deny.' Once I stamped 'deny' across his authorization form, his life's end was as certain as if I had pulled the plug on a ventilator."

She stamped that death sentence at her desk in a 23-story marble office building in Kentucky; the patient was in California, a state where Dr. Peeno was not licensed to practice medicine.

What Dr. Peeno described is not an anomaly. It is only an extreme example of the predictable results of what government policy is doing to health care, a system that enriches the few at the expense of the many.

Nearly all decisions by health care corporations about providing care are routine. The companies would argue that all of their decisions are made in accord with the law. But that is mere cover, ignoring the bigger issue: whether the system is moral or even economically sound. The government rules shaping health care have created a whole industry of makework that drives up costs, denies care to some, makes it next to impossible for the already sick to get health insurance, and condemns others to needless pain and early death, while simultaneously making a few men and women fabulously rich.

From the perspective of the health care companies, these rules allow them to do business with only the more profitable patients, avoiding those most in need of care. In turn, that allows them to increase profits or lower premiums. Unless there is serious competition to expand by taking patients away from competitors, the preferred choice is bigger profits.

At its core, government policy makes health care a business. The purpose of business is to maximize profit. That is the appropriate standard for taking care of capital, but not people's health. Yet a strong push is underway to make health care even more of a business, backed with huge new federal subsidies to for-profit health care corporations. These subsidies are being lavished on for-profit health insurance companies despite studies showing that nonprofit health systems tend to provide superior care.

If health care as a business worked, it would be a success story to embrace. If it resulted in lower costs, more and better care, and longer lives, it would be just what the doctor ordered. The American system provides superb acute care, trauma care, and access to the highest technology. But by every other objective measure—cost per capita, health status, longevity, costs of paperwork, and economic pollution—the uniquely American approach to health care is a complete failure. We pay more, enjoy shorter lives, and are drowning in infuriating makework, filing claims and making appeals, while distorting the whole economy because one giant component is a commercial activity.

No other modern country regards health care as an insurance business. While some nations refer to their plans as health insurance, they mean that in the political sense, just as we call our basic old-age pension system of Social Security a "social insurance" program. No other country uses the word insurance in the business sense, which means to spread risks. The business sense of insurance includes the concept of examining claims to see if they fall within the contractual boundaries for payment, which was Dr. Peeno's job. This is how we ration health care in America, through contracts that limit care and exclude coverage—and by having tens of millions of people go without any insurance at all.

Because we tie most health care insurance to employment, this system is making us less competitive in the global economy. That is because no other country makes employers record the cost of health care for their workers on their books. Everywhere else this cost is part of the national ledgers just like the costs of police, education, and lifeguards.

In Europe, Japan, Canada, Australia, and New Zealand, people benefit from a system of *health service,* not health insurance. In many of these countries doctors still make house calls. The overwhelming majority of people who seek immediate care are treated that day or the next, which is also true in America. But the other countries do not spend vast sums on reviewing claims for payment and billing, a deadweight drain on the American economy that costs every man, woman, and child more than a dollar per day.

Individual purchases can make things worse, not better, as shown by our history with fire insurance. There was a time in this country when people paid commercial fire companies to protect their property. But instead of replacing lost property, as we do today, these policies insured that firefighters would fight any fire at your home or business. A problem arose when the house abutting yours caught fire. If that owner had paid a different fire company, or none at all, your fire company would not put out the blaze even though it was a threat to your property. Only when your building was ablaze was your fire insurance company obligated to act—and that could be too late. That system died when we recognized that fires are a public problem, not a private one. Our solution was to have government provide fire-protection as a public service. People relinquished having their choice of fire-fighting companies, but saw that government monopoly on fire-fighting service saved far more lives and protected property much more efficiently than the market did. Accident and illness are, like fires, public and social problems, not individual ones, that are mostly efficiently treated as public service.

In America we do not speak of police insurance, or education insurance, or, when vacationing at the seashore, lifeguard insurance. Rather, we pay taxes for police, education, and lifeguard services because these are essential services for a civil society. When we need a cop, we dial 911. How quickly the police respond depends on their judgment as to the urgency of the call compared to other demands for service at that moment. When a child is five years old, the government does not require proof of ability to pay before a child may start kindergarten. And when someone caught in a riptide cries out for help the lifeguard does not check a list to see if the person has paid in advance to be saved and also whether the coverage included Tuesdays before noon when the sky is overcast. But that is exactly what we do in health care, because we use a business model instead of a service model. In the process we also take from the many to enrich the few.

Complex bureaucratic systems to deny care based on subparagraph k at page 454 of a contract are also uniquely American. That does not mean other countries do not ration care. They do. But they do it as a matter of policy—as opposed to profit. These other countries place limits on care, such as not giving heart transplants to octogenarians. If you are in your eighties and need a transplant you may prefer our system, which will extend your long life a bit more. But the cost of that is paid in less care or no care for those much younger, who as a result are less likely to live to see their ninth decade. Rationing would be eliminated if voters were willing to spend enough on health care to cover every demand for service.

Adam Smith tells us "what improves the circumstances of the greater part can never be regarded as an inconveniency to the whole. No society can surely be flourishing and happy, of which the far greater part of the members are poor and miserable." His remark was not aimed at health care, yet it deals with the issue of how we allocate scarce goods in an imperfect world in which choices are inevitable.

No other country spends as large a share of its economy on health care as the United States. And that share is growing rapidly, crowding out other economic activity, especially investment in the next generation. Roughly every sixth dollar in the American economy was spent on health care in 2007. Our government has projected that by 2015 we will be devoting every fifth dollar to health care. In most modern countries health care accounts for less than one-tenth of their economies.

The inefficiencies of the American health care system also create jobs. However, that is hardly an argument for maintaining our existing health care system. If all we wanted was to create jobs we could ban giant earthmovers at construction sites and hire teams of workers with teaspoons to move dirt. Even if we wanted to treat health care as a jobs program, it would be better to put more nurses to work on hospital floors than to have so many clerks in the billing department.

The uniquely American system of health-care-as-a-business results in some poor countries having better health outcomes than the United States. America ranked thirty-sixth among nations in its rate of infant mortality in 2006. The Central Intelligence Agency estimated American infant mortality at 643 deaths per 100,000 live births, slightly worse than Cuba at 622.

That American infant mortality rate was actually an improvement. In 1960, we experienced 2,600 deaths per 100,000 live births. But the falling infant death rate slowed after 1980, even though medical advances continued. The rate virtually stopped falling in 1996, the year when Congress and President Clinton ended all basic welfare programs for the poorest children and mothers in America.

There is another awful cost to a policy of health care as a business: No one in the modern world ever goes bankrupt because of medical bills, except in the United States of America.

It is true that sometimes, for some conditions that are not life threatening, people in other modern countries have to wait weeks or months for treatment. But even people in America with health insurance have learned that scheduling appointments, getting referrals to specialists, getting insurance company approvals for those referrals, making appointments with the specialists, getting evaluated, and then finally getting treatment can also take months.

After the care is provided, an insurer can come back and say it made a mistake, demanding that the patient personally pay all their bills retroactively. That is far different from nations delaying some nonemergency medical services.

But no delay is comparable to the medical, economic, and moral harm done by a system in which at least 45 million Americans go without health insurance coverage. The American system is completely at odds with the Biblical morality publicly embraced by nearly every elected politician, which imposes a duty to sacrifice for the poor. Yet someone without insurance who gets cancer becomes eligible for government-provided care only at the point where they become permanently and totally disabled. That is to say, when treatment seldom will help and death is virtually inevitable, care begins.

And who goes without health coverage? By and large, families who work but earn a modest income. Among those making $65,000 or more, roughly those Americans in the top 25 percent income group, health insurance is nearly universal. But among Americans with less than average income, 57 percent are without heath care.

Health care as a business also imposes another drag on our economy, one that gets very little attention. It is the inefficient deployment of human capital caused by America's unique lack, among modern nations, of universal health care service. In the debates over the tax treatment of hedge and private equity funds, those huge unregulated investment pools, Congress has devoted plenty of attention to getting the most efficient deployment of capital so that we get maximum economic bang for the buck. Yet the inefficient deployment of human capital caused by treating health care as a business gets almost no attention from policy makers and, in turn, from the news media.

Many people who have a medical condition such as cancer, or who have a dependent with a condition, stick with their current employer because they have insurance whose payment policies they know. Under the Health Insurance Portability and Accountability Act of 1996, a new employer cannot exclude a preexisting condition from coverage. But every plan is different; every plan has its unique internal rules and policies. Changing jobs itself also involves a risk because one lacks seniority and the new job may not work out, which could result in unemployment. Under the 1996 law anyone who goes 63 days without a job loses some of their limited rights on health care coverage for preexisting conditions. All of this acts as a curb on efficient deployment of human capital. Government policy that discourages people from moving to new jobs that would make the most efficient and effective use of their skills is a drag on the economy, not to mention individual human happiness. Europeans, Canadians, Japanese, Australians, and New Zealanders never give a moment's thought to these matters because their health care is not connected to holding a job.

On the other hand, the lucky few who have positioned themselves to take advantage of the government rules are becoming fabulously wealthy under government policies that result in taking from the many to benefit the few. Government policy has replaced legal limits on pay with sky's-the-limit pay plans that have produced billion-dollar fortunes for the lucky few. It has made plundering public assets immensely profitable.

The idea of health care as a tax-free fringe benefit began with Roosevelt and the economic controls of World War II. But the drive to make health care into a part of corporate America through government giveaways began with the Nixon era. Those subsidies have grown from little weeds into a mighty forest of government giveaways to the few. Next, how health care started down the road to high costs, frustration, and riches for the few by taking from the many.

Chapter 22

LESS FOR MORE

FRED W. WASSERMAN WAS MAKING A PRETTY GOOD LIVING PROSPER-
ing in a career of his own design. He used what he had learned in
public health graduate school at the University of California at Los
Angeles to show doctors and dentists on the affluent Westside of that city
how to make their practices more profitable. As he drove between their
lavish offices overlooking the Pacific and their stunning homes in the
hills, he knew he would always do well, but it would take more to become fabulously wealthy. Then the federal government dropped a golden
opportunity into his lap.

Wasserman is a good place to start to tell the story of the reasons
Americans today find health care so expensive and so frustrating. He was
at the cutting edge of changes that transformed much of health care,
which had been dominated by nonprofit hospitals and individual doctors, into a for-profit industry whose largest customer is the government.

Over the past three decades our elected representatives created,
through a hodgepodge of laws, a health care system whose costs grow
faster than the overall economy every year. Greed goes unchecked. Theft
remains largely unpunished. While supposedly promoting competition,
government rules encourage behavior that contradicts market forces.
Wasserman grew rich playing by the rules the government set and then
managing successfully for more than two decades what government made
possible for him. But those rules set in motion a series of changes that
now cost us dearly in both money and access to health care.

Just as Wasserman was getting going in 1972, President Nixon told
Congress the country faced a health care crisis. Too many Americans

lacked quality health care and prices were rising too fast, he said. He pledged that his administration's "highest priority" would be the "reform of our health care system—so that every citizen will be able to get quality health care at reasonable cost regardless of income and regardless of area of residence."

Nixon said publicly that competition provided by prepaid group health care plans would lower costs. This allowed him to sidestep calls for the kind of universal health care every other modern nation was taxing its citizens to provide. In private, the Oval Office tapes show, he said something quite different.

In a prepaid group health care plan, employers pay a fixed fee in advance for all the health care their workers need. This was thought to explain why these prepaid plans had lower costs. Because every dollar spent on care that could have been avoided through preventative care was wasted, doctors supposedly had an incentive to keep people healthy. Dr. Paul Elwood, a Nixon administration official, coined the marketing term *health maintenance organization* to sell this idea to Congress.

Critics said the plans had low costs because they creamed the market, letting in mostly healthy people, especially young workers with small children, and avoiding employers with older, sicker workers.

Prepaid plans went back decades. The best known was started by Henry J. Kaiser, the multitalented businessman who made one of his fortunes during World War II welding together cargo ships in as little as a month at Marinship in Sausalito, Calif. Kaiser realized he could efficiently provide health care to his workers by hiring doctors on salary to give his workers any care they needed, charging the government a fixed price per worker.

John Erlichman, Nixon's domestic policy adviser, told the president in February 1971 that everyone on the staff except Vice President Spiro Agnew agreed that the administration should tilt toward health maintenance organizations. Erlichman had just discussed with Kaiser how the Kaiser Permanente system worked. Ignoring the "ums" and false starts, for the sake of clarity, here is how the conversation recorded on the Oval Office tapes went:

> Nixon: "Now you give me your judgment. You know I'm not too keen on any
> of these damn medical programs."
> Erlichman: "This—this is a private enterprise one."
> Nixon: "Well, that appeals to me."

Erlichman: "Edgar Kaiser is running his Permanente deal for profit. And the
    reason that he can—I had Edgar Kaiser come in, talk to me
    about this and I went into it in some depth. All the incentives
    are toward less medical care, because—the less care they give
    them, the more money they make—"
Nixon: "Fine."
Erlichman: "—and the incentives run the right way."
Nixon: "Not bad."

The following year Nixon signed into law a requirement that large
employers offer a prepaid group health care plan, a health maintenance
organization, or HMO, to their workers if they offered any health plan.

Nixon's law to use HMOs to induce competition guaranteed loans
and grants to HMOs so they would have the capital to grow quickly.
The market could not do this because by law HMOs had to be nonprofit
and, in some states, charities. In all, the federal government would put
hundreds of millions of dollars into developing HMOs.

Seeing subsidies move into a new health care market created by the
government, Wasserman decided to start an HMO. He took on a partner, Pamela K. Anderson. She had been his classmate in graduate school
and soon became his wife. It did not take much capital to get started.
They put together $27,000 in savings and a $10,000 loan. Most of their
capital came from a $169,000 federal grant. They called their nonprofit
health maintenance organization Maxicare.

Wasserman recruited his clients to work as Maxicare doctors. To
generate subscribers, he approached two of the biggest employers in Los
Angeles, the warplane makers Lockheed and Northrop. Both companies
were defense contractors, which meant Maxicare was really relying on
the taxpayers for subscriber fees. It also meant a generous flow of fees
because no one spends, or wastes, money like the Pentagon. Under Wasserman's able hands Maxicare prospered, quickly signing up hundreds of
thousands of subscribers and earning solid and growing surpluses, the
nonprofit term for profits.

As a nonprofit, Maxicare was subject to supervision by the state attorney general in his role as California's guardian of charitable assets. Any
money left over once Maxicare paid its bills was held in trust for the beneficiaries of the nonprofit and, ultimately, the public. The Wassermans
earned big salaries as health care administrators, but they could not get

seriously rich. Then, eight years after Maxicare's founding, a new opportunity presented itself. Once again it came from Washington.

President Reagan, declaring government needed to be tamped down so markets could work their magic, signed a law in 1981 that phased out the government loans and loan guarantees for nonprofit HMOs. Ever the entrepreneurs, Wasserman and Anderson decided to convert Maxicare into a for-profit business.

Back in 1981 few people thought they could make money converting a nonprofit into a business. Since then the markets-are-the-solution crowd has changed our concept of what is nonprofit, even what is public service, pushing more and more of our economy toward business. We now have a plethora of businesses whose revenue comes from the taxpayers, who typically collect much more than they did when the work was done by nonprofits and the motive was not profit, but public service.

Part of this trend that began in health care can be seen in the war in Iraq. From time immemorial soldiers did KP (kitchen patrol) duty and washed their own clothes, putting idle hands to work. Today we pay Halliburton and others, often under costly no-bid contracts, to feed soldiers. A Halliburton subsidiary was even paid $100 for each laundry load it ran for soldiers in Iraq; soldiers were refused permission to do their own laundry or even to pay Iraqis, who desperately needed the income. Likewise, in some cities sheltering the homeless has been turned into a profit-making business at horrendously greater expense than having this work done by volunteer organizations, including churches and religious charities.

The sale of nonprofit assets was not new, however. Under a legal principle in common law for four centuries, anyone can buy any or all of the assets of a nonprofit organization, including those of a charity. The rule was that the trustees had to agree to sell and that the buyer pay full value, in effect replacing the assets being purchased with cash or something else of value. Nonprofits rely on this principle when they buy and sell stocks in an endowment or when they sell their headquarters so they can move into another building. Say a buyer considered purchasing the Ford Foundation. Virtually all of its assets are in stocks and bonds. If the Ford Foundation wanted to convert all of its assets into cash, anyone could buy them. But it would make no sense to attempt to buy the Ford Foundation since it would be easier to buy the same portfolio of securities in the market.

There was no market at that time to determine the value of an HMO's assets, however. Despite this there were many ways that could have been used to establish the value of the HMO. Surplus (what a business calls profits), cash flow, or return on assets could have been analyzed to set a price. There were other reasonable considerations in setting the price, as well. What about the value of Maxicare's brand name? Its long-term contracts to serve subscribers? Or could its price be determined by something as simple as how much cash the nonprofit had in the bank overnight?

Wasserman and Anderson offered to pay $238,000 for Maxicare, roughly the cash on hand. The trustees accepted, even though the couple was not willing to pay even that tiny sum right away. Instead, they bought the nonprofit's assets for an unsecured, interest-only balloon note due in 15 years. The 8 percent interest rate was a steal because at that time big banks charged their best corporate customers a prime rate of more than 20 percent. And the loan was interest only for 15 years, when a balloon payment would come due.

Once that note was signed Wasserman and Anderson became seriously rich. Before long they made a deal with Fremont General, an investment bank, for $16.5 million, almost 70 times the value of the note that Wasserman and Anderson signed. Just seven years later, and after several acquisitions, the value of Maxicare shares had soared to nearly $700 million. Wasserman and Anderson had pulled off an amazing deal. With a cash cost of just $19,000 per year in interest payments, which were tax deductible, they ran a business worth two-thirds of a billion dollars.

No major newspaper or magazine wrote about the conversion deal at the time in any depth. The deal was too small to be on the radar of business reporters, few of whom back then possessed much understanding of the nonprofit world. But in health care management circles, the word spread fast. Others who ran nonprofit HMOs began maneuvering to get in on the easy money.

Among them was Robert Gumbiner, a California pediatrician and Korean War veteran. In the sixties, Gumbiner started an HMO called the Family Health Plan in suburban Orange County. On contract from the government, Gumbiner's organization provided prepaid government-financed health care for the poor at low cost. Over the years, Gumbiner expanded to serve retirees on Medicare. As his reputation for quality care and efficiency spread, so did his clinics. In time he had subscribers from Utah to Guam.

The idea of flat fees paid in advance offended many physicians in conservative Orange County, who believed in charging fees for services because they felt it made them beholden to no one. Some doctors shunned Gumbiner. A few called him a pinko. In time, however, his maneuvers would prove that Gumbiner was really a master capitalist—or at least a master at getting government to make him rich.

When it was legally a charity, Gumbiner treated the Family Health Plan like a personal cookie jar, engaging in deals that directed money to himself and close associates. Funneling money to yourself from a non-profit or a government agency that you control can be a crime. At a minimum is a civil offense called *self-dealing*. Gumbiner's conduct did not sit well with Evelle J. Younger, a former FBI agent who was the California attorney general.

When Younger's staff uncovered Gumbiner's self-dealing, they did not file criminal charges. Instead, they treated it as a civil matter. A settlement in 1977 required Gumbiner to return some money, but that was it. Despite his demonstrated proclivity for treating taxpayer and charitable funds as his own, all Gumbiner had to do to remain in charge of the millions of government dollars flowing through the Family Health Plan's accounts was promise to inform the attorney general of any major developments and agree to no more self-dealing. Even that gentle restraint did not last long.

About the time that Wasserman and Anderson acquired Maxicare, Gumbiner started negotiating to buy FHP's assets. Gumbiner and 17 other employee-investors agreed with the Family Health Plan board, which he controlled, on a price of under $14 million. The board also defined a charitable purpose for the money, a purpose that, at first blush, looked like a kindness to the poor. It was, but it was also a way for Gumbiner, who owned more than half the stock in the new for-profit company, and his fellow investors to further enrich themselves.

The money paid to buy FHP would create the FHP Foundation. Its charitable purpose was to cover copayments for prescription drugs and doctor visits for FHP subscribers who could not pay them. In an HMO, the key to profits is keeping people healthy enough that they rarely visit the emergency room, much less stay in the hospital. People with chronic conditions and illnesses, such as high blood pressure and diabetes, go to the emergency room or the hospital more often when they do not take their medications.

Poor people sometimes must choose between getting their medications and going hungry. Sometimes that copayment could mean losing the roof over their heads. In such a contest pills usually lose out. But with the FHP Foundation those concerns would be taken care of, the medicines issued and visits to the emergency rooms and stays in the hospital prevented. Thus Gumbiner's charitable purpose would be worth much more to his bottom line than the cost of these mini-grants to cover the copayments. There is a word for this conduct: self-dealing.

The circular flow of the money, and its effect on costs, would enrich Gumbiner by making his business more profitable, exactly what the settlement with Attorney General Younger forbade. But neither Gumbiner nor the FHP board saw it that way.

Gumbiner told me at the time that the price he offered for FHP was more than fair. He noted that Maxicare was three times the size of Family Health Plan. Yet he was paying more than 50 times what Wasserman and Anderson had paid for Maxicare's assets. That analysis ignored the issue of whether Wasserman and his wife had paid a fair price. Gumbiner also pointed out that the $600,000 in annual grants the FHP Foundation pledged to make to cover copayments was more than twice the value of the one unsecured note that Wasserman and Anderson had signed to acquire Maxicare.

The job of deciding the fairness of the deal in 1985 fell to the California Department of Corporations, whose office had no track record of looking out for charitable interests. Even so, the corporation commissioner's office could not stomach Gumbiner's deal, at least not the $13.6 million price. In the previous year FHP had taken in almost $15 million more in revenue than it spent on caring for subscribers, money that a business would call profit. Selling an enterprise for less than the profits earned in a single year fails the basic obligation of a trustee to be prudent. FHP's own analysis showed that FHP was worth about $216 million based on stock market values, an estimate that would turn out to be significant.

The corporation commissioner set the price at $47 million. That price was a big bargain for Gumbiner, a real loss to the taxpayers, and a tiny fraction of that $216 million estimate from FHP's own analysis. Still, Gumbiner complained that it was too much. The corporation commissioner then showed he could be accommodating, cutting the price to

$36 million. It was an easy decision since the commissioner was not giving up $11 million of his money, but the public's.

Among those who knew that Gumbiner was getting a sweet deal was Wasserman. He sued to block the sale. Wasserman said that Maxicare would pay $50 million cash without even inspecting FHP's books. Wasserman told me he would pay "up to between $60 million and $80 million" if he could just get a look at FHP's books. He suggested that if the facts warranted it he would pay even more.

At this point, the attorney general, the guardian of charitable assets, tried to step in. He pointed to the 1977 settlement that prohibited self-dealing and said that was precisely what the charitable spending on co-payments amounted to. And the attorney general said the price was much too low, citing four centuries of unbroken legal history in Western civilization that the only price for charitable assets was the highest price in the market.

Gumbiner countered that protecting charitable assets had nothing to do with it. He said Maxicare was simply a predator, a big fish trying to eat up the smaller fish like his Family Health Plan. Gumbiner argued that once Maxicare had swallowed the competition it could raise prices to subscribers. He said eliminating competitors undermined the whole idea behind the law that Nixon signed encouraging competition in health care. "If Maxicare prevails," Gumbiner said, "they would effectively establish a law that anybody wanting to convert would have to auction the assets, and then large companies would simply bid more than the fair market value to eliminate competition."

Gumbiner won. Ignoring competitive market principles and legal history, the corporation commissioner, and later a Superior Court judge, did Gumbiner an immensely valuable favor by rejecting Maxicare's higher bid. Gumbiner was not even required to match the higher offer. Remember that markets are supposed to be good for health care by instilling competition and economic discipline. But here the market was thwarted. The highest price did not set the market. Indeed, the market did not even affect the price.

The judge wrote that the legal standard "is not whether [the offer] was the highest lawful bid, but whether there was a fair value. Those are two different questions. . . . It may well have much higher value to a competitor than the fair market value. . . ."

Seven months later, after Gumbiner transformed FHP into a for-profit enterprise, the company sold shares at an initial public offering.

The stock sale set the value of FHP at $225 million, almost exactly what FHP's own analysis had shown was the real value of the assets that had been built up by the taxpayers and entrusted to Gumbiner. Wall Street's valuation meant that Gumbiner paid about 17 cents for each dollar of assets. Gumbiner's shares were worth about $115 million, vastly more than the new FHP Foundation received. Thus did one man use government to grow rich at the expense of the many.

A new attorney general, John Van de Kamp, appealed. Litigation continued until 1990 when a state appeals court also sided with Gumbiner. The reason why is instructive for anyone eager to get rich by slipping public assets into his or her own pocket for pennies on the dollar.

After Gumbiner settled with the state attorney general in 1977, he started working the state legislature. Gumbiner persuaded the California legislature and Governor Jerry Brown to undo the limits in the settlement with the attorney general. The legislature passed a law, which Brown signed, that changed FHP's status from a charity to another kind of nonprofit. And the legislation added an unusual feature that no one except FHP seemed to appreciate at the time—it allowed self-dealing. This special interest legislation slipped into the law books with no public debate, just as thousands of such favors are enacted each year in Washington and the state capitals on behalf of campaign donors.

Because of this state law, the appeals court ruled unanimously in 1990 that the attorney general no longer had jurisdiction to challenge Gumbiner's actions. Moreover, that law "legitimized self-dealing transactions by health plans," wrote the appeals court judges, Justices Paul Turner, Herbert Ashby, and Roger Boren.

Thanks to all three branches of state government—the legislature that passed the law, the governor who signed it, and the judges who blessed it—Gumbiner got his free lunch. The taxpayers got stuck with the risk and with the bill. And it was all perfectly legal, embraced by three judges—on the same court that enriched Barron Hilton—whose ruling contains not a single word of regard for the interests of the taxpayers who pay their salaries or the propriety of how the law was enacted.

While the judges in the Gumbiner case ignored how the taxpayers were being shortchanged, no one in the health care business did. It was as if the Army had sent its guards home and left the Fort Knox vaults open. Across the nation a new gold rush was underway by nonprofit executives eager to line their pockets with taxpayer money.

One of those who did exceptionally well was Leonard Schaeffer. He became chief executive of California Blue Cross in 1986, as the conversion movement was growing. Schaeffer effectively transformed the non-profit California Blue Cross into the for-profit WellPoint without paying a dollar for its assets, outdoing even Wasserman.

California Blue Cross was an elephant compared to Maxicare and FHP. It was also troubled, so strapped for cash that it had to sell its building to raise cash in a crunch.

Had Schaeffer converted the nonprofit sooner, he could have made a lot more than the $100 million plus that he eventually pocketed, perhaps a billion dollars or more. But by the time that Schaeffer acted the staff of Consumers Union, the publisher of the magazine *Consumer Reports*, was on to the deal. With a shoestring budget and a lot of moxie, the San Francisco office of the consumer group organized what public opposition it could to such a subtle and complex deal. The consumerists also posed inconvenient questions to for-profit enterprises about the conversion of assets held in the public trust.

Schaeffer knew the conversion deals were an outrage, a legalized theft of public assets, yet he defended his deal to create WellPoint. He adopted the same viewpoint as Gumbiner, who said he was paying more than Wasserman. Schaeffer wrote that "there was no law, regulation, or precedent that defined" the obligations of a newly formed public benefit entity. In 1995, his own deal still hanging in the balance, Schaeffer said:

> Before the conversion of WellPoint, the value of every single company that converted to for-profit status was significantly underestimated. . . . Almost all of the value created went to the management and boards of these companies. . . . FHP International, Foundation Health, PacifiCare, Take Care, you name it. These are companies that today are led by multimillionaires who achieved that status by virtue of receiving stock that was dramatically undervalued at the time of conversion.

In 1996 Consumers Union managed to get $3 billion for charity as the price for the conversion years earlier of California Blue Cross to a business. That was a lot more than the effective price of zero that Schaeffer had arranged, but it was still a bargain. All told, across a variety of deals, Schaeffer generated $6 billion for foundations. By that measure some might make him out to be a hero. But the prices paid were bargains. By the end of 2005, WellPoint was vastly more valuable than the charities it endowed, with assets of $51 billion and a net worth of about half that.

In an economy the size of the United States', a few bad deals for the taxpayers can be dismissed cynically as drops in the proverbial bucket. But the stories of how Gumbiner, Wasserman and Anderson, and Schaeffer got their free lunches are just a few examples of the early deals that set the pattern. Many more deals followed. Across the nation nonprofit hospitals, health maintenance organizations, and insurance plans were sold for pennies on the dollar. Billions of tax and charity dollars that were invested for the public's benefit were transferred to private hands. Every dollar less than true value paid for these enterprises was nothing more than legally sanctified theft, a transfer from unwitting taxpayers to the forces of greed.

Not everyone who passes by a bank whose front door and vault are open will rush in and scoop up the money. Some people will make themselves into the guardian of those assets. Others will call 911. Some nonprofit health executives refused to take advantage of the opportunity to line their own pockets, though the public may not appreciate what they did not do.

One of them is Howard Berman, who in 1985 left Chicago to take charge of the nonprofit Blue Cross/Blue Shield plan in Rochester, New York, widely regarded as a model for providing quality care at low prices. Later Berman consolidated Rochester with the plans in Syracuse and Buffalo, the other two sizable cities in western New York.

Berman calculated that if he converted the plan to a for-profit business the stock market would value the enterprise at $2 billion. That means he could have pocketed tens of millions of dollars by following the path laid out by Wasserman and Anderson, Gumbiner, and others.

So why didn't Berman go for the money? His answer is short and to the point: "It would be wrong."

What Berman saw was that shifting from an enterprise whose purpose was to serve people into a for-profit business would mean something worse than enriching the few at the expense of the many. It would also, inevitably, mean getting rich at the expense of people's health, not their betterment. Among other problems that Berman said would have followed a conversion of the health plan he ran would be spending a smaller share of health care premiums on actual care.

The year after Leonard Schaeffer turned Blue Cross of California into WellPoint, the for-profit company boasted that it had reduced its "medical loss ratio." That meant that a smaller portion of the premiums collected from customers was spent on their health care, and a larger share counted as profit. This effort to cut costs did not apply to Schaeffer's own compensation. His pay did not just jump; it went up like a rocket.

When Schaeffer ran California Blue Cross as a nonprofit, his pay cost subscribers $922,000, a princely sum for a nonprofit executive, one that pushed the limits allowed under nonprofit law. A decade later the for-profit WellPoint paid him $19.2 million, or 20 times as much. Then in 2004, when WellPoint merged with another insurer, Schaeffer received a $50 million payment simply because control of the company changed. And since he was also retiring, he got about $60 million more in deferred pay and cash-outs.

To WellPoint shareholders Schaeffer may well have been worth his money, but what about the subscribers? Their health status did not improve and claims weren't paid any faster, nor did premiums grow at a slower rate. In fact subscribers were paying more and getting less of what they paid for, a price hike as subtle as it was brutal. Physicians and laboratories, their fees reduced, saw the smaller "medical loss ratio" as nothing more than a pay cut.

That pay cut came with added costs, not just tightening up on fees. To reduce the reasons the health insurers could delay or refuse payments, the physicians and other providers had to hire teams of office workers to polish the paperwork they sent in to WellPoint, a deadweight loss.

Schaeffer said the fact that WellPoint was paying out less for medical care was due to forces beyond his control. He called it a sign of the market at work. "It's not our intent to upset or exploit physicians," Schaeffer told *Medical Economics*, a magazine on financial matters for physicians. "We've got to maintain a professional and business relationship that's mutually reinforcing. At the same time, lowering costs is the way of the world today and in the future."

Schaeffer's "way of the world" did not apply to his pay and that of the other health care executives. Schaeffer was neither unusual nor even the top dog in this game. Norwood Davis was paid less than $900,000 in 1995 as head of the nonprofit Blue Shield/Blue Cross of Virginia. When it converted to for-profit status, his successor, Thomas G. Snead, received $6.5 million just six years later, along with stock options valued at $16 million.

The top dog so far is William McGuire of UnitedHealth Group, which grew out of a small nonprofit Minnesota health insurer into the second-biggest publicly traded health insurance company in America. It became that despite the fact that Minnesota law prohibits for-profit health care, an annoyance the company got around by having a nonprofit front for its business. UnitedHealth Group covers about one in six Americans, most of them older and on Medicare. In 1999 McGuire demanded that his board give him stock options equal to 2 percent of the company's value. He also demanded a clause in his employment contract that guaranteed him his job unless he was convicted of a felony, a clause that would turn out to be very valuable to him.

McGuire's deal was much sweeter than Wasserman's. If the way McGuire ran the company made its stock price soar, he would become a billionaire perhaps twice over. And if his leadership resulted in a middling performance, the long-term rise in the stock market virtually guaranteed him tens of millions of gains because his options, like those of most executives, were good for 10 years.

The board of directors proved their devotion to McGuire by giving him the options, the job guarantee, and everything else he wanted, insulating him from the risks of a competitive market. They even agreed that when he made personal use of the company jet they would pay the taxes he would owe on that benefit, making his personal travels free. On the other hand, if McGuire failed, he was guaranteed his basic pay package and the options value due to the overall rise in the stock market. Flip a coin. Heads McGuire wins big or bigger. Tails, McGuire can't lose.

Theoretically the competitive market is supposed to restrain all expenses, including the chief executive's pay, so that, as Adam Smith wrote, labor and capital are rewarded with no more than the value of their contributions. Since for-profit insurers compete in a market that also has nonprofit firms, how can for-profit insurers afford the lavish pay of chief executives like McGuire and Schaeffer?

The answer is in what Schaeffer boasted about just a year after becoming a for-profit business—shortchanging subscribers.

The markets that Adam Smith wrote about were simple and straightforward, not complex pricing mechanisms, such as health insurance, that few people except actuaries and lawyers grasp. These contracts simply defy normal human understanding.

In Adam Smith's day corporations were few, allowed to exist for limited purposes and limited times, unlike the immortal but soulless entities of today that have the legal status of persons. Spending less on the very service promised is not a simple task. If a health insurer just cut payments, it could expect subscribers to go to other insurers. Insurers have devised elaborate mechanisms to deny health care and limit benefit payments, systems with their own intricate internal policies shielded by a mask of confidentiality that protects the privacy of patients and their doctors. Complexity is a friend of the insurance company scheming to fatten its bottom line by paying for less health care service.

The first strategy of corporate-run health insurance companies is to avoid marketing to employers and other groups where the need for health care is likely to be highest. Careful selection of customers to reduce risks can cut the amount that will be spent on health care by 30 percent. The second strategy is to find ways to pay providers less. Tough bargaining is legitimate. But the for-profit health care companies make the paperwork so complex that sometimes it's just not worth it for a doctor or hospital to get the full amount their contract requires.

The third strategy, as almost everyone in America has learned by sad experience, is to deny care. Subtle rules govern how the insured are paid for their medical expenses. Many of these rules are not posted anywhere. Physicians whom patients never meet, like Dr. Linda Peeno, make the decisions. Even if the rules were posted, most of them would make no sense to the average American because they are written to be opaque. The benefit statements health insurers mail to subscribers are about as decipherable as income tax forms.

Individuals, bipartisan Washington has been telling us since at least the Nixon administration, should shop for the best medical care, comparing prices. Competition remains the most widely recommended elixir for our ailing heath care system.

This idea ignores the fact that most people are not capable of assessing the skill of any physician, much less comparing the relative value of the price of one thoracic surgeon to another. Those with blind faith in markets are untroubled by this. Adam Smith did not share their faith that a complex market like health care would be fairly regulated by market forces. Smith's markets required full knowledge by both buyer and seller and no coercion to buy or sell.

Would you know how to shop for the pilot of the next jetliner you fly? Do we pay the pilot who lands his plane without a bump more than those who sometimes hit the tarmac hard? No. We trust that the government will set minimum standards of competency through licensing requirements, education, and testing. And then we entrust our lives to the airlines to make the expert judgment on which qualified and competent pilots should be in command of their aircraft and our lives.

When the random car crash or fall on the playground makes one writhe in pain, negotiating price is usually not on the agenda. If it were, the one in pain would be at a distinct disadvantage. While the conscious and observant can determine the relative prices and quality of tomatoes at a farmers' market, the prices for medical procedures are not posted anywhere. Indeed, insurers hold these prices, and the fees they actually pay, confidential. And in a hospital emergency room the only procedure certain to be performed is the wallet biopsy, an invasive financial procedure to determine whether the patient has insurance to pay the bill.

Health insurance does not cover the price of a service, but only a portion of the "reasonable and customary charge." This charge is different for each provider. Thus two people paying the same in premiums to the same health care insurance company can collect different amounts for the same treatment just because one chooses a doctor who charges lower fees and another picks a high-price doctor.

Examine a stack of for-profit health insurance financial statements and a trend emerges. Premiums increase faster than benefits. One study found that health insurers that converted to for-profit status reduced their medical loss payments by 10 percentage points. That is an extra dime out of each premium dollar for such necessities as increasing executive pay. Another study estimated that two-thirds of the administrative costs of for-profit insurers are spent on care denial.

Health care administration cost Americans $123.6 billion in 2003. That is an average of $412 per person just for overhead—paperwork, marketing, executive compensation and, especially, justifying denials of care. The total excess cost for administering the health care system works out to more than a dollar a day for each American. It is as if everyone from Bangor to Hilo got up in the morning, lit a match and burned a George Washington before breakfast—two on Sundays.

Americans spend nearly 6 times the average of what 13 other modern countries do on health care, according to a study conducted by the McKinsey Global Institute in 2007. The McKinsey study shows that 86 percent of this excess cost is in the part of American health care run as a business instead of a public service.

All systems have flaws, of course, and they attract people who try to beat the system. Government can also encourage, or discourage, such misconduct by its rules. In a health care system whose master is the bottom line, there are temptations that some simply cannot resist. The temptations are not just those passing open vault doors with no guards, though cutting back on guards makes it easier. One of the most damaging by-products of moving away from nonprofits and toward for-profit companies has been to encourage thievery.

Stealing from the taxpayers by billing for services not needed, not provided, or by mislabeling is rampant in the for-profit hospital industry. Despite this, the federal government's capacity to uncover such frauds dwindles each year. If allowed to do their jobs, government health care auditors pay for themselves many times over, something that is ignored by the ideology of "government is the problem." Also ignored when the ranks of auditors are decimated is the premise that taxpayers deserve to have their money dispensed honestly and prudently or not at all.

Health care thieves tend to be entrepreneurial and nimble, as Malcolm Sparrow of Harvard University has tried to teach a host of agencies. When government finds an area of white-collar thievery it throws a spotlight on the problem, Sparrow says, causing the smart thieves to scatter like cockroaches into the dark recesses where no one is looking. But typically the government does not move on to these dark recesses, but instead focuses its beam of light ever more sharply on the area of fraud it knows about, catching only those cockroaches too dumb to scram.

One of the biggest frauds, though by no means the worst in its audaciousness, took place at Columbia/HCA Healthcare. In the 1990s the company owned about 350 hospitals, more than 500 health care businesses, and numerous ancillary health care service companies.

Among those who grew rich as its stock ballooned in value was the Frist family, which founded the HCA (for Hospital Corporation of America) part of the business. The most prominent of the family is a heart surgeon, Dr. William Frist, the former Tennessee senator and one-time presidential hopeful. Richard L. Scott, who in less than a decade had built up the Columbia hospital chain from two Texas hospitals, headed the other half of the company. When the firms merged, Scott ran what became the world's largest health care company.

The company held itself out as a model for the increasingly cost-conscious world of health care, applying the competitive practices of corporate America to an industry still dominated by nonprofit institutions. But what really fueled its growth was fraud.

Under Scott, the hospitals schemed to collect billions of dollars from the taxpayers, insurance companies, and individuals by keeping two sets of books. There were self-dealing arrangements, kickbacks to doctors, and billing for services either not needed or not performed. The company even bought a rubber stamp, used at a Columbia/HCA hospital in Arkansas:

CONFIDENTIAL
Do not
discuss or release
to Medicare auditors

Kurt Eichenwald, an investigative reporter, discovered that stamp. With colleagues at *The New York Times*, he analyzed a huge pile of medical records to discern how taxpayers were being systematically cheated. The newspaper also reported that the big accounting firm KPMG abetted the fraud. At the same time that KPMG was helping Columbia/HCA cheat the government, it had a contract with Medicare to detect such frauds. Medicare even renewed KPMG's contract *after* its role in this fraud was reported in the newspaper. The federal manager overseeing the contract later told congressional investigators that she read the article but "had not taken it seriously."

The thefts came to light because of one honest man: an accountant in Montana, James F. Alderson, who was the financial officer for one of the chain's hospitals. One day a visitor came to show him how to set up two sets of books, one of them weighed down with phony expenses so that the hospital could extract more money from Medicare.

When Alderson refused to play ball, he was fired. That would have been the end of it, except that Alderson learned about a way that a private citizen can bring a lawsuit on behalf of the government. It is called a *qui tam* suit.

For years Alderson worked alone, unable under *qui tam* rules to tell anyone what he was doing. At one point, out of work and facing financial ruin, Alderson hired a former Medicare auditor named Nicholas L. Bourdeau to help him turn the complex billing records into something that would make sense to Justice Department lawyers and FBI agents. Bourdeau was astonished at what the stacks of boxes in Alderson's home held. "I couldn't believe what I was seeing," Bourdeau said years later. "I thought it was a Medicare auditor's worst nightmare. It was an organized system to take advantage of the Medicare system."

Years later three Columbia/HCA executives went to prison. Scott was ousted as chief executive. Penalties of almost a billion dollars were paid, part of the money going to Alderson as a reward for his service to the taxpayers. However, the government was so lenient that the penalties for this widespread, orchestrated scheme amounted to far less than the amount stolen.

Congress responded to these scandals by giving the FBI more than $100 million a year extra to investigate health care fraud. There had been little need for such an investigative budget when hospitals were mostly nonprofit.

The funding for FBI investigations may seem like a lot of money, but it is tiny compared to the size of the problem. In 2008 the nearly half a trillion dollar cost of Medicare and Medicaid combined will equal about $150 per month for every man, woman, and child in the country. By the same measure, the FBI budget to hunt for health care fraud works out to three cents per month.

Looked at another way, the cost of Medicare and Medicaid equaled all the income taxes Americans paid from January through July of 2004, but the FBI health care fraud budget equaled the income taxes Americans paid in about the first hour of the year.

With a $114 million budget for health care fraud the FBI was expected to produce big cases. Yet the FBI did so few health care fraud investigations that Congress asked the Government Accountability Office to find out why. The answer? The money was diverted. The FBI "was unable to track overall costs related to health care fraud investigations" and had "no effective mechanism in place" to detect fraud, the accountability office investigators concluded in 2005, nine years after Congress had ordered the crackdown.

The FBI did not even keep proper track of where it diverted the money. Its estimates of how the money was actually spent were "reported from memory," according to a congressional report. The FBI said it could not determine how a fourth of the money was spent, though perhaps the proper explanation would be to change the verb and observe that the FBI *would not* explain.

In health care fraud the chances of getting caught are tiny and the financial penalties typically are just a cost of doing business, not a deterrent. "It's a bizarre world," says Jim Plonsey, president of Medicare Training & Consulting, a cost-report specialty firm. "There is an incentive to abuse the system and wait for Medicare to catch you. And there has been no penalty for doing it."

At least one state, New York, institutionalized fraudulent payments in the name of efficiency. Health care industry literature is filled with studies on how computerized billing systems can save money by cutting back on paperwork jobs. But in New York State one out of every five dollars paid this way—with a computer ordering checks cut because it is too costly to have a human review the invoices—goes for services that were not needed or not performed, an investigation by *The New York Times* found. The state comptroller said that estimate sounded just about right.

All of this, from the bargain basement prices paid for HMO assets, to spending fewer premium dollars on care so CEOs can get rich, to the spread of organized Medicare fraud, to the FBI's dishonest behavior, grows from the idea that market forces were the efficient way to rein in the escalating costs of health care and that competition would work its magic to deliver a high-quality product to consumers. The idea, Nixon's tape recorded voice shows, was a fraud from the beginning.

Instead what we got is a horribly distorted marketplace where the health care companies, engorged by unchecked greed, ration health care. That is a crucial point to keep in mind when opponents of *universal health service* assert that the health care systems in other countries ration health care. Our corporate health care system does, too, and at vastly greater expense. We deliver the best care to those able to pay a high premium or who have one paid for them, like our representatives and senators, while delivering paperwork, delays, anxiety, and sometimes death-for-profit to those of less than grand means.

Americans are less healthy even though we spend far more, according to the 2007 McKinsey Global Institute report cited earlier. McKinsey compared 124 countries. It found that our system's inefficiencies and waste costs us an extra half trillion dollars a year. This excess cost works out to $1.3 billion every day. The study concluded that $75 billion of this was due solely to the fact that these other countries had public health systems. Despite what we are spending, we live shorter lives than the Canadians and the Britons.

Our expensive, inefficient health care system is also making us less competitive in an increasingly competitive world. Toyota rejected offers from Alabama and other states for extremely generous subsidies and tax breaks in 2005 that basically amounted to giving the company a free factory if it would locate there. A nearly free factory, Toyota concluded, was worth less than avoiding the continuing cost of health care for the factory workers. Health care costs the Detroit automakers more than the steel in cars. By some estimates health care accounts for as much as $1,600 of the cost of a new American car.

Toyota chose Canada. And there lies a secondary component to the Toyota story. As health care costs head toward a fifth of the American economy by 2015, they are squeezing out other spending. One of the big losers is education. That, too, played a role in Toyota's decision. Canadian factory hands are so much better educated that Toyota estimated the costs of training workers there would be significantly less. Toyota could rely on verbal instructions and written manuals with Canadian workers, rather than color-coded cards it would need to train some of the reading-challenged workforce in the southern states that had offered subsidies.

The business of health has created a massive makework program, run by health insurance companies, whose purpose is to justify denying care. That in turn has forced physicians, hospitals, laboratories, and others to employ their own armies of paper pushers to fight for payment, not to mention all the grief and anguish endured by individual patients and their families.

Now a new industry is emerging: consultants who examine claims denials to help people fight for payment. That service is a boon to the individuals it helps, but just another deadweight loss to the economy.

In short, our government's blind faith in the wisdom of the market has created the most expensive and inefficient health care system in the world without making us healthier. Among those who have denounced this system's waste and how the market gives us less health care at higher prices is Robert Gumbiner, the Orange County doctor who grew rich from FHP, the health maintenance organization he bought for a fraction of its value.

"The present orientation towards greed is a national catastrophe, as far as I can see," Gumbiner said when he sat down for an oral history project sponsored by the University of California. "The feeling is, it's okay to be greedy and it's okay to exploit your fellow man just to line your pockets. To me, there is something wrong with that."

Gumbiner spoke these words after he had become ill and FHP was sold. It is not without irony that Gumbiner sued over the sale, saying he was cheated. To make FHP more attractive in a sale, Gumbiner charged, Merrill Lynch investment managers handling the sale fired a third of the doctors. The progressive medical policies that made FHP attractive to subscribers were stopped. No chance to cut was overlooked. The investment bankers, he charged, even had all potted plants in offices gathered up and put in a dark closet to die to eliminate the cost of watering them.

"Quality and investment return are antithetical," Gumbiner concluded, "because in order to generate short-term profits, the company cannot put money into research and development, new long-range concepts, management training, and all the things that will build a long-term successful organization. People who strictly have investors' return as their motive are not interested in long-term corporate guarantees."

Well put, Dr. Gumbiner.

Next, a look at how the Bush White House and Republicans in Congress worked behind closed doors to funnel hundreds of billions of dollars in subsidy money to for-profit health care companies—and hide what they were doing.

Chapter 23

HOOKED ON DRUGS

O N THE GROUND FLOOR OF THE CAPITOL, NEAR A BUST OF RAOUL Wallenberg, lies an unmarked corridor. A guard stands watch, making sure no tourists enter. Beyond the guard the drab, eerily silent hallway meanders through the building until it ends at a set of cream-colored, saloon-style swinging doors.

Not just tourists were unwelcome. So were some members of Congress. This is a room for those whom the man who controlled it for five years called "the coalition of the willing." The willing, in this case, meant a willingness to engage in a particularly underhanded scheme to take from the many to benefit the few while appearing to do the opposite.

This room served as the private hideaway for Representative Bill Thomas of California, who ruled the House Ways and Means Committee with an iron fist from 2001 until he left Congress in 2007.

Thomas was known for three things. First, he was so faithful in delivering President Bush's messages on tax cuts and Social Security privatization that even his Republican colleagues called him the White House mailman. Second, he was shrewd, a tactician of the first order. Third, he was a short-tempered bully who was voted the meanest man in Congress in a *Washingtonian* magazine poll of Capitol Hill staffers.

Thomas's imperiousness got out of hand one Friday in July 2003 when a pension bill came before the Ways and Means Committee, which controls the nation's tax laws. The Democrats were not allowed to see the latest version of the bill until the hearing began. To stall for time, they employed a parliamentary trick. They ordered that the bill, all 200 pages of it, be read into the record. Then all but one of them retired to an anteroom to plot strategy.

Thomas grew increasingly annoyed as he sat on the dais. Before long he called the Capitol Police to evict the Democrats. Thomas later tried to lie and deny his way out of it, saying he only wanted to restore order because of some foul language by the one Democrat left behind in the hearing room, Fortney "Pete" Stark, another combative Californian. Five days later on the House floor, at the urging of his party leaders, Thomas confessed. He admitted that he indeed wanted to break up the minority party's meeting. He took action that he described, tears running down his cheeks, as stupid, but not wrong.

As much as Thomas was a partisan, and even though decades of worsening partisanship on both sides have made Congress less and less functional, the real split on Capitol Hill is not between the Ds and the Rs. The real split is shown by who was welcome in that hideaway Thomas kept beyond the saloon-style doors.

The dominant group is thick with politicians like Thomas. In public they speak of free enterprise and the virtues of competition. Behind closed doors, however, they work to create a paradise of corporate socialism for the few. Their reward comes when their days as lawmakers are done and they can easily move on to new careers that pay extraordinarily well, helping industries and individual companies pillage that "largesse out of the public treasury" that Ronald Reagan often talked about.

These are the Washington corporatists, whose hearts bleed for every company and industry complaining that the rules, and often the market, are unfair. Every issue must be filtered through the lens of big business profits, as if that were the only aspect of a sound economy that matters.

Except for the better newspapers and the dry policy magazines, the press ignores this public Jekyll and backroom Hyde dichotomy most of the time. Even when the contradiction between public positions and backroom actions are reported, the presentation tends to be devoid of human drama and lacking a larger context about the influence of the political donor class on government decision making. From reviewing thousands of pages of news clips going back to the late nineteenth century, it is clear that the definition of news has changed. Today a politician is far more likely to get attention for personal acts that belie a public image of a virtuous life than for promising to protect voter's purses while working stealthily to pick them. And that goes triple for television, which most people say is their primary source of news.

The minority group in Washington is composed of Republicans and Democrats who agree on almost nothing except their Adam Smithian belief that business is at all times engaged in a conspiracy against the public that ought not to be aided by government policies.

At one end is Representative Ron Paul, a libertarian Republican from Texas. He believes that the income tax violates the Thirteenth Amendment prohibition against slavery because the government requires people to do the work of filling out their tax returns. To Paul that is a form of involuntary servitude, while filling out a form for, say, a driver's license is not because you are not required to have a driver's license (unless you want to drive).

At the other end is Senator Bernie Sanders of Vermont, the only socialist in Congress, though he caucuses with the Democrats. Sanders rails about a government that lavishes welfare on corporations, but not on children born into poverty.

While their views run the gamut from left to right, these politicians share a belief that government should be run mostly to maintain the people and their liberties and that corporate interests are too powerful, too doted upon. And while they are not pure in their approach, their leanings tend to be away from corporate interests and toward the people. We will call them the peoplists.

So it was that one late September morning in 2003, one television camera was present to record a clash between the corporatists and the peoplists. It took place in that hallway where a Capitol police officer stands guard beside the bust of the Swedish diplomat who saved many Hungarian Jews from the Nazi death camps before he was "disappeared."

Events began with a bit of impromptu political theater staged by Representative Charles Rangel, a New York Democrat who usually aligns himself with the peoplists, though at times he has been known to perform duties for Wall Street, home of the greatest cathedral in the House of Mammon. Rangel is every bit as partisan as Thomas, but much more affable. Rangel had been named to a conference committee to work out differences between the House and Senate versions of a bill giving older Americans a prescription drug benefit program. Thomas was also on that bipartisan committee.

President Bush, who wants to end Social Security as we know it, sponsored this drug plan. That might seem an ideological non sequitur for a Republican president who calls himself a fiscal conservative. Yet Bush proposed the greatest expansion in socialized health care for the elderly since Medicare was enacted in 1965. It looked like a smart way to win the votes of older Americans, the group most likely to turn out at the polls.

The proposal brought forth all sorts of support and opposition. But the prescription drug benefit bill was not so much a divider of Democrats and Republicans as a perfect illustration of the divide between the corporatists and the peoplists. It was also a window on subsidy politics in Washington and why so many who pose as protectors of the public purse are so willing to raid it.

The bill was written in a way that looked out first for the interests of drug makers and health insurance companies that sell prescription drug plans. The elderly were simply a tool to that end. The effort to conceal what was really going on was multipronged.

One key provision prohibited the government from negotiating for the lowest possible prices. Negotiating for low prices when buying in bulk is standard practice. That is what Veterans Affairs does. That is what every business owner does. So does every other industrial nation for their universal health care plans for their citizens. Negotiating for the lowest price would seem to be an obvious choice for those in both parties who talk about running government like a business, promising voters that if elected they will work tirelessly to replace waste with efficiency.

The corporatists said that negotiating for lower drug prices was an abuse of government power. They called negotiating a euphemism for government price controls. And they said it would mean less money to invest in new drugs, delaying advances in pharmaceuticals.

To the peoplists, the ban on price negotiation was a stealth plan to make the drug benefit so costly it would cause the whole system of socialized medicine for the elderly to collapse. This political paranoia was not without some basis in fact.

On the first issue, no company wants to discount prices. Companies cut prices only when the discipline of the market forces them to take less. Adam Smith would not have approved of government staying the invisible hand by having government pay anything but the lowest possible price. "The natural price, or the price of free competition," Smith wrote, "is the lowest which can be taken, not upon every occasion indeed, but for any considerable time together. . . . [It] is the lowest which the sellers can commonly afford to take, and at the same time continue their business."

Getting top prices while dealing in volume guarantees fat profits, even by the famously lush standards of the pharmaceutical industry, which ranks second only to the military-industrial complex companies in profitability. Huge and easy profits for both drug and health insurance companies meant that the price of their stocks would rise. That, in turn, meant that the stock options given to executives would soar in value. And as a side benefit it would, in time, enrich some lawmakers and their staffs when they left the public payroll to seek work in the private sector. But first the bill had to garner 51 votes in the Senate and 218 votes in the House before any of this could come to pass.

Rangel was in a jovial mood that September morning when he met with a pack of journalists, including a camera crew from CNN. Rangel explained that he was the one House Democrat on the conference committee named to work out the final version of the prescription drug bill. He said that while the bill's supporters would tell him where to go, they would not tell him where to go to attend the conference committee meetings. But Rangel had an idea about where he could find the conferees. Camera crew in tow, Rangel waved the entourage past the guard and down the hallway.

They came to a halt outside the swinging doors. An ornate chandelier lit the salmon-hued room beyond. Voices could be heard. Heads and feet were visible above and below the doors. Thomas's staff peeked out from a side door to find out who had descended on their boss.

"I'm charging the room," Rangel said, mugging for the camera. He knocked; the scene quickly became a parody of the old *Saturday Night Live* "Land Shark" skits.

Even though he had been alerted that it was Rangel outside, Thomas called out, "Who is it?"

"It's the postman," Rangel replied with glee. The journalists and Rangel aides in the hallway guffawed. Thomas told Rangel to enter.

Inside were Thomas; Senator Max Baucus, a Montana Democrat; and two politicians from Louisiana, Senator John Breaux, another Democrat, and Representative Billy Tauzin, a Republican. They were corporatists all.

Baucus and Breaux, looking sheepish, mumbled hellos.

"I'm here to negotiate," Rangel announced.

"This meeting," Thomas replied, "is only open to the coalition of the willing."

Baucus, Breaux, and Tauzin slipped out a side door. Then Thomas begged off, leaving Rangel standing with a handful of reporters in Thomas's den.

The locations of meetings were not the only things the bill's backers were hiding. The Bush White House said the drug benefit would cost $400 billion in the first 10 years. That was an important number because some conservative House Republicans said they would not vote for the bill if the costs exceeded $400 billion, a number with no apparent significance other than being round.

Cybele Bjorklund of Rangel's staff suspected the number was low. She asked Richard Foster, the Medicare chief actuary, for his analysis. Foster said he had the numbers, but that his boss, Thomas A. Scully, the Medicare administrator, would fire him if he told what he knew. Scully later denied he had threatened Foster with firing, but did admit he tried to keep the cost figures secret. But then an e-mail, written by one of Scully's aides to Foster, was leaked. It showed that he had threatened Foster with dismissal for insubordination if any numbers got to Congress: "Please work up the numbers and share them with Tom Scully only, no one else," the e-mail said, adding, "The consequences for insubordination are extremely severe."

In the summer and fall of 2003, Scully told everyone the $400 billion figure was solid. He even wrote a letter to the editor, published in *The New York Times* a few days before the vote on the drug bill, which stated flatly, "We are spending $400 billion."

Even so, when the bill came up for a vote on the House floor, it was in danger of going down. Many members suspected the cost was higher, but they lacked the data needed for debate. The vote began at three in the morning on November 22. Under House rules votes can take no more than fifteen minutes. House Speaker Dennis Hastert and his whip, Tom DeLay, kept the vote open for almost three hours, the longest vote in the history of the House.

The time was used to get votes through cajoling and threats. President Bush made predawn calls to some representatives. Off the House floor, the drug industry lobbyists were thicker than ants on sugar, their numbers estimated by some at more than 1,000, a figure that strains credulity; but if a careful count turned up a third that many, it conveys a sense of the resources poured into the effort.

"Bribes and special deals were offered to convince members to vote yes," Representative Nick Smith, Republican of Michigan, later wrote to his constituents. "I was targeted by lobbyists and the congressional leadership to change my vote, being a fiscal conservative and being on record as a no vote. . . . Secretary of Health and Human Services Tommy Thompson and Speaker of the House Dennis Hastert talked to me for a long time about the bill and about why I should vote yes. . . . Other members and groups made offers of extensive financial campaign support and endorsements for my son, Brad, who is running for my seat. They also made threats of working against Brad if I voted no. . . . I told all those urging a yes vote the same thing: this bill will lead to explosive new costs and huge unfunded liabilities that will unfairly burden future generations."

Later, in a radio interview in Kalamazoo, Smith told listeners that an unnamed Republican leader told him, "Some of us are gonna work to make sure your son doesn't get to Congress."

Nearly a year later the House ethics committee admonished DeLay, who admitted that he offered to endorse Brad Smith in return for his father's vote. The ethics committee also chastised Nick Smith for telling his constituents what happened in such bold language because that "risked impugning the reputation of the House" with statements that "failed to exercise reasonable judgment and restraint." In such ways do those whose job is to protect the reputation of Congress reveal that their real job is to protect Congress from the consequences of voters learning the truth about how it really operates. On many matters, the representatives act like servants in the House of Mammon, squabbling over how much free lunch to serve up to their masters that day.

Smith, whose son lost the election a year later, turned out to be right in his belief that the bill was more costly than the supporters were saying. The prescription drug bill was legislation by deceit.

Foster, the Medicare actuary, had given Scully the 10-year cost estimates, as requested, months before the vote. The estimate was $500 billion to $600 billion. Later, it would come out that even these numbers were misleading because of the time period used to make the estimate. Foster was told to estimate costs from 2004 through 2013, even though the drug benefit would not become available until 2006.

The Bush White House finally put out the real numbers, but not until more than a year after the vote. The estimate was made public in February 2005, three months after the president won a second term in an election where he campaigned for the votes of older Americans, citing the prescription drug benefit. The real cost? Was it $400 billion, as promised? Or even the estimate of up to $600 billion over 10 years that Scully hid from Congress? No. It was $720 billion. That is 80 percent more than the number Scully and everyone else working under White House direction insisted was solid.

Chances that the House would have passed the bill with its requirement to pay the drug companies top dollar had the $720 billion figure been known? Zero. Value to the drug companies of hiding the costs? Many tens of billions in profits beyond what the market could ever provide, not to mention all the increases in executive and lobbyist pay. Contribution to the president's winning a second term? Priceless.

One way to look at the ban on the price negotiations provision in the drug benefit bill is how it affects the flow of funds through the economy. The government will pay far more than the market would require for these drugs. That means the drug companies will make above-market profits, further enriching their executives, whose compensation is tied to company performance, whether it results from the market or government gifts. So what the bill produced was a redistribution scheme. It takes tens of billions of dollars each year from the many and funnels them to the few. Those little weeds of subsidy to Wasserman and Gumbiner grew into fortunes for Schaeffer and McGuire and became mighty forests of giveaways.

The cost of this plan is so high that it will soon force change. It may be that the ban on price negotiations will be set aside. It may be that taxes will be raised to pay for the benefit. And it may be that the costs will kill Medicare, which many of the peoplists believe was the real purpose of hiding the costs. By their reckoning, the rising costs will force a crisis that will end in an effort to kill Medicare. That seems hard to imagine given the political clout of seniors and of the drug industry, but without a doubt the costs will create instability and a battle over the future of Medicare, its outcome uncertain.

However the future turns out for Medicare and for seniors who need prescription drugs, those who hid the facts did very well. Before Scully was named to head Medicare in 2001, he was the chief lobbyist for the Federation of American Hospitals, an organization of 1,700 for-profit hospitals. A month before he ordered Foster to withhold the real cost figures from Congress, Scully somehow obtained a waiver of ethics rules that bar high-level officials from negotiating for private-sector jobs that conflict with their official duties. When he ordered Foster to withhold information, Scully was already negotiating with law firms and investment banks for his next job. Three weeks after the drug bill passed with

220 votes, two more than needed, Scully resigned to take a new job. President Bush held a ceremony to honor Scully, saying "I appreciate Tom Scully, the administrator of the Centers for Medicare and Medicaid Services, for his good work."

Scully's new job: as a lobbyist working out of the Alston & Bird law firm, whose roster of drug company lobbying clients runs from Abbott and Aventis through Merck to ZLB Behring.

A few weeks later Miles D. White, chairman of Abbott Laboratories and the trade association called Pharmaceutical Research and Manufacturers of America came to Washington for an announcement. White said that the industry had hired Representative Tauzin, the Louisiana Republican who was part of Thomas's backroom "coalition of the willing," to pass the drug bill, as its new chief lobbyist.

"This industry understands that it's got a problem, it has to earn the trust and confidence of consumers again," Tauzin said, White agreeing with him. In his new job as chief Washington lobbyist for the industry that will collect $720 billion in 10 years because the government is barred from negotiating for lower prices, Tauzin will do quite well. His salary, it was widely reported, is more than $2.5 million per year. And to keep on getting free lunches from the taxpayers, Tauzin will have a budget of more than $100 million a year to lobby Congress on behalf of the drug companies.

Chapter 24

"I'M BEING TRAPPED"

TO APPRECIATE HOW GOVERNMENT POLICY IS ENRICHING THE AL-
ready rich and putting everyone else at risk, it is worthwhile to visit
Greenwich, Connecticut, the richest little town in America. For
most of a century, it has been favored by the wealthiest for three reasons.
Greenwich is an easy commute to Manhattan. It offers acres of space for
mansions along with views of Long Island Sound unmarred by industrial
reality. Most important, other rich people live there.

In the Roaring Twenties, when huge fortunes were made in unregulated stock markets, Greenwich was home to the brand names of industrial America. They included the mattress maker Simmons and founders
or heirs to fortunes made in oil, steel, sugar, banking, and even con-
densed milk. Among the old-money residents was Senator Prescott S.
Bush, grandfather of George W. Bush.

Greenwich residents vied to show off just how much opulence they
could afford. *Vanity Fair* reported that in 1910 an heir to the Phelps
Dodge mining fortune "had a sixteenth-century Tudor manor house
taken apart in England; then, wainscot by wainscot, peg by hand-carved
peg, it was packed into 688 numbered cases, shipped across the Atlantic
to Greenwich, and re-assembled."

Among the magnificent homes of Greenwich, the one that is most
revealing of the community's aspirations is a replica of the Petit Trianon,
the private palace at Versailles that Louis XV built for his mistress in the
1760s. The original later became, ever so briefly, the hideaway for his
son's teenage bride, Marie Antoinette. The Petit Trianon was built in an
age when government policy determined one's economic fate. The land,
and much of the commerce, was secured for the already rich by French

law in such a way that success in life depended almost entirely on one's choice of parents.

The Petit Trianon was designed to separate the royals from everyone below them. One of the unusual features of the original made the servants invisible. A mechanism connects two rooms through the floorboards. On the lower floor, the dining table was set with the finest food the royal chefs could prepare. The table was then to be raised through the floorboards into the *salle à manger*. This would allow the royals to eat, drink, and be merry without any contact from those of lesser station. Before the table could be finished, however, a revolution intervened.

Still, in its social purpose the design is not unlike that of the luxury boxes at commercial and college sports stadiums. These boxes connect to private corridors so that the rich need not encounter those of lesser station, at least until they leave the sports palaces for their waiting limousines.

Today a new race is on to build mansions whose servant quarters equal in size, though not opulence, the mansions of old. Homes of 20,000 square feet, one with an antique carousel and another with its own indoor ice rink, are all around in Greenwich. There may be some limits, however, as the hedge-fund manager Joseph M. Jacobs discovered. Neighbors complained about his proposed 39,000-square-foot family home. The house was too large for a plot of only 11 acres, they said. Jacobs gave up.

The town's parking spaces are filled with exotic cars, including the occasional Maybach 62S, the $400,000 German sedan. The merchants of Greenwich sell the same baubles found in the finest stores in Manhattan at the same prices. These merchants also pay the same rents per square foot. Office space, however, rents for more than on Wall Street or midtown Manhattan: such is the demand created by the hedge-fund trade. Greenwich has become to hedge funds what Madison Avenue is to advertising.

There is no official definition of a hedge fund. It refers broadly to any pool of money invested aggressively. The word hedge comes from the idea that some of the money is invested to limit risk, often by buying options so that if a particular investment suddenly loses most of its value, the fund can unload its shares at a minimum price.

Because of hedge funds, the fortunes made in Greenwich today more than compare to the riches of those who competed to build the great mansions of the Gilded Age and the Roaring Twenties. But they derive from something far less substantial, and much more dangerous, than mining, manufacturing, or even banking.

There are just 23,000 households in Greenwich. The Forbes 400 list includes four Greenwich billionaires. There are certainly many more. Steve Forbes assembles his list on the cheap, getting maximum publicity for the least possible expense on journalism. While widely cited, the list is so poorly constructed that it has often included poseurs while failing to identify the majority of families whose net worth statements come with three commas. In Rochester, New York, where I live, for example, Forbes lists a single billionaire. Yet public records, interviews with those whose job it is to know where major wealth lies, and conversations with some of the wealthiest reveal that there are at least four billionaire families in the Rochester area and probably seven.

That Greenwich has more billionaires than the four that Forbes lists is certain for many reasons, but just one fact will suffice. It is how much hedge-fund managers make. *Alpha* magazine, a trade publication for these unregulated investment pools, reported that the top 25 hedge-fund managers made on average $570 million each in 2006. That is not their combined total pay, but the average compensation *per manager.*

The highest paid hedge-fund boss that year was James Simons. He calls his company the Renaissance Technologies Corporation, though the name belies its practices. Simons runs a kind of supersophisticated arbitrage operation from his offices in Manhattan and in East Setauket, which looks toward Greenwich from Long Island. Simons made $1.7 billion in 2006, a fact that is known because the hedge-fund managers like to brag about their success as a way to attract new investors.

The rarified world of hedge funds may seem distant. It is not. Just because you never wrote a check to a hedge fund does not mean you are not invested in one. The chance that you contributed to the gargantuan payday of at least one hedge-fund manager is 100 percent. If you live in America you are in a hedge fund. But what is far more significant is that you are at risk for losses, possibly decimating losses, when a single hedge fund, or the entire industry, encounters the inevitable losing streak.

The concern that a hedge fund could put a big dent in your net worth, or even wipe you out, comes from no less an authority than Alan Greenspan. He had the Federal Reserve intervene in 1998 during the unraveling of a single hedge fund, Long-Term Capital Management. By today's standards it was not even a big hedge fund. Yet the Federal Reserve and Treasury Department intervened a decade ago because Greenspan feared that this one fund's recklessness had the potential to cause a worldwide economic collapse.

Hedge-fund managers make their money by taking risk. In theory, the more risk, the more reward is needed to compensate for it. But there is no lockstep matching of risk to reward, as Simons likes to tell his clients. One can take on lots of risk for little or no reward. And a host of studies shows that, over time, managers cannot beat the market. That is what a government study concluded in 1962. This was an affront to many on Wall Street who assume that, as professional investors, of course they can beat the market. It was left to legendary investor Benjamin Graham to explain in a speech to securities analysts that "neither the financial analysts as a whole nor the investment funds as a whole can expect to 'beat the market,' because in a significant sense they (or you) are the market." It is this fundamental aspect of investing that inspired the low-cost index mutual funds, the first of which John Bogle devised while a graduate student, an idea that grew into the Vanguard Group of mutual funds.

So if hedge funds are beating the market, then other factors must be at work that let them defy the principles of economics. Could it be that unscrupulous employees are paying for inside information, say about news that will drive the price of a stock up or down once it is formally announced? That would be illegal, but logical. After all, people have been known to commit murder for hire for less money than an hour's interest on a hedge-fund manager's pay.

Hedge funds are deeply intertwined with banking because hedge funds succeed only by leveraging the money investors give them with borrowing. Long-Term Capital at one point had $5 billion from investors, against which it had borrowed $95 billion more. Stock market investors can usually borrow 50 cents for each dollar of stock they own. These guys put up one buck and borrowed $19 more. Not even the bankers realized what they had done until a series of unpredictable events ate away at the strategy that Long-Term had devised, revealed a risk they had not contemplated and that they certainly had not hedged against. The coup de grace came from the Russian government, which in 1998 stopped paying interest on its bonds and returning capital to buyers whose bonds had matured.

Hedge funds are not like the mutual funds that most Americans are familiar with, many of which engage in lots of trades in an effort to produce greater returns than the market as a whole. Over time these actively managed mutual funds produce results no better than the market because they can't. Certainly this or that fund manager can go a long time beating the market, winning gushing coverage and attracting more money to manage. But those managers who consistently underperform the market offset these winners. They are less visible, getting little attention in the business press and virtually none on the television financial shows. Add up the performance of everyone and you can get only one result—society overall gets the market performance.

Hedge funds also are not like private investment pools or venture capital pools, which put money into existing or new companies to make them successful in the hope of turning a profit. Hedge-fund managers buy and sell stocks, bonds, pork bellies, scrap steel, stock options, interest rate futures, and anything they think they can make money buying and selling. With rare exceptions, they are not investors, but speculators.

James Simons employs about 80 PhDs at Renaissance Technologies, which has 200 employees in total. Many of his workers write computer programs that spot anomalies in the market prices for stocks, commodities, options, and even the expected rate of interest a week from next Thursday in Timbuktu. The computers then execute trades to capture these gaps in prices, which are often momentary.

If this sounds like gambling, it should. Hedge funds trace their history to a math professor who figured how to make money gambling in Las Vegas. That is a neat trick, since every game comes with rules that give the house an advantage or add a fee, called *vigorish,* guaranteeing that overall the house wins and players lose.

Back in 1962 this professor of mathematics and statistics at the University of Southern California, Edward O. Thorp, published a book called *Beat the Dealer.* Thorp showed that anyone smart enough to keep track of all the cards at a blackjack table, and who always made the choice with the greatest probability of winning, would walk away a winner. The gains were slim, though. A card counter could take the house for as much as a nickel for each dollar bet, but more likely it would be less, as little as a fraction of a penny.

The Vegas casinos quickly caught on to this strategy. They persuaded the Nevada regulators to let them toss out anyone suspected of counting cards, a rule in force everywhere there are casinos in America. At Binion's, a downtown gambling house started by a man who was convicted of one murder, charged with two, and suspected of blowing up an FBI agent, some card counters were beaten within an inch of their lives. At least once the punches extended an inch too far.

Professor Thorp was smart enough to know there were other ways to apply his statistical knowledge and eliminate the risk of violent reprisal. Seven years after publishing *Beat the Dealer*, Thorp started an investment firm called Convertible Hedge Associates, later renamed Princeton-Newport Partners. Thorp and a half dozen or so associates used early computers to look for differences in the price of stocks, buying low on one exchange and selling high on another.

It was classic arbitrage with a high tech boost. The professor quickly proved that he could beat the stock market, too. Some years his investors reported gains of nearly 50 percent while the market moved in single digits. It was also easy pickings. Back in those days, most stocks were owned by individual investors, the opposite of today when mutual funds, pension plans, charitable endowments and, more recently, hedge funds hold most of the shares. Professionals are much more efficient traders than amateur investors. Back then most shares were traded through face-to-face negotiation on stock exchange trading floors. Gaps in prices were the norm.

Increasingly, trades are automated, software programs deciding when to buy and when to sell. And price gaps are measured not in the blink of an eye, but at the speed of light. That was what prompted Dave Cummings to move his TradeBot Systems from Kansas City to New York, as discussed in an earlier chapter. He improved profits by shaving 19/1,000 of a second off the time it takes a sell or buy signal from one of his company's computers to reach the automated trading market.

The key to Professor Thorp's success at gaming the stock market was a little loophole in the rules governing investment funds. Most Americans own stocks through mutual funds, which are plain vanilla compared to the 31 financial flavors in a single scoop of the hedge funds run by Thorp and those who followed his path. Mutual funds are regulated. Under the government's rules they can trade as often as they want, but they have to trade with money that investors gave them, not funds borrowed at the bank.

The loophole through which Thorp slid his profits was not available to most Americans. The loophole exempted his hedge funds from the rules against using borrowed money. The rules also specified that hedge funds were open only to the already rich. The theory behind this exemption was that anyone who is seriously wealthy must either be so-phisticated enough not to need protection from financial predators or so rich that they could survive big losses.

Back in 1982, the threshold for being eligible to invest in a hedge fund was a net worth of at least $1 million and an annual income of $200,000. Only a tiny fraction of 1 percent of households qualified. To-day the only real barrier to opening an account at a hedge fund is whether the investor has enough money to make the recordkeeping worthwhile for the fund managers.

This wide-open and unregulated world has attracted plenty of ge-niuses and serious investors. But it has also drawn financial sharks. Cases alleging that more than 60 supposed hedge funds were really swindles were brought by the federal government between 2001 and 2006.

During the stock market bubble in the late 1990s, hedge funds began to attract growing numbers of the newly rich as well as charitable en-dowments, including those at Harvard, Yale, and other wealthy institu-tions of higher learning. As much as $300 billion from state and local government pension funds is invested in hedge funds, putting every tax-payer at risk because they are obligated to provide the pensions earned by civil servants even if the funds are lost through bad investments.

The promise of hedge funds is that they make money in any market, up or down. This made them even more attractive after the collapse of the Internet bubble on Wall Street in 2000, which wiped out $7 trillion of wealth, a sum greater in real terms than that lost in the 1929 crash. By 2007 the broad stock market gauges had only begun to return to their previous highs, and that was without considering the effects of inflation. But many hedge funds during those years generated double-digit returns. The long sag in stock prices made many investors more susceptible to pitches promising a big upside in any market.

Investing in hedge funds quickly took on an aura of financial sophis-tication in wealthy circles. Anyone living in the tonier neighborhoods of Manhattan, Washington, Los Angeles, Silicon Valley, and the other great centers of wealth in America was sure to hear at every business lunch and wine tasting from those whose hedge-fund statements showed fat profits despite a languishing stock market.

Those who made out best, however, were not the hedge-fund in-vestors, but the managers. Hedge funds charge stiff fees, under a system known as two and twenty that some of them trace back to Queen Isa-bella of Spain and Christopher Columbus. Isabella was no fool. She did not sell her jewels to pay for the explorer's journey. Instead, Isabella made the city of Palos provide for free the use of two ships for a year as tribute. She raised some of the money for the 1492 voyage from bankers in Italy. And she made a deal with Columbus that would make him rich, but only after the Queen got back her investment and most of the profit. Columbus died a wealthy man (although not before he spent some time in chains, something the royal court dismissed as a little misunderstanding).

In the modern version, most investors pay 2 percent of the amount in their account each year as a management fee. Hedge funds that turn a profit then take a fat slice off the top, every fifth dollar of profit. This is not unlike the Texas Rangers deal that made George Bush wealthy. Instead of 2 percent, Bush and the other general partner got salaries. And instead of 20 percent of the profits, they got 15 percent.

For comparison, some Vanguard mutual funds charge investors less than a dime per $100 invested. So on a million-dollar account with no change in the balance, Vanguard would be paid $900, the typical hedge-fund manager $20,000. And if the account doubled in value the next year, Vanguard would charge $1,800 while the hedge-fund manager would pocket about $240,000.

Simons charged even higher fees. His management fee was 5 percent annually. And he keeps 44 percent of the profits. Why would anyone pay such fees? Because even after paying fat fees to Simons, a former government code breaker, they made a lot of money. A thousand dollars invested in 1990 in the Standard & Poor's 500 index, which covers about 85 percent of the value of all American stocks, would have grown to less than $5,000 by 2005. The same sum put with Simons would have become $77,000.

Simons does not tell anyone, including his investors, precisely how he does it, but the broad strategy is known. Those computer programs his PhDs write look for pricing gaps or anomalies in the market and then these arbitrageurs act decisively. Simons has let loose one detail about his strategies. He stays away from exotic derivatives, like those that promise to pay the square root of the change in the value of the Australian dollar compared to the Thai baht between today and six months from now.

What makes such huge returns possible is not just computer programs that spot pricing gaps. What fuels hedge funds is debt. Lots and lots and lots of debt. Hedge funds and banks have become joined like algae and fungus to form financial lichen. And just as attractive lichens can be poisonous, so can this financial symbiosis, with its attractive investment returns, turn toxic.

A home buyer who makes a down payment and then borrows four times that amount with a mortgage is using leverage. Because hedge funds are not regulated, as mutual funds and banks are, much of what they do is secret. But from the few cases where records have become public it is known that UBS, the big Swiss bank, has a policy of lending to hedge funds at a ratio of 30 to 1.

That kind of leverage is what allows tiny pricing gaps to produce billions in profits. If an investor has to put up only a dollar to invest $100, and whatever the hedge fund bought doubles in price, the investor makes out like a pirate capturing a galleon laden with gold. Even after paying the two-and-twenty fees, the investor's one dollar has grown to $77.

Of course, if things go badly, the investor can be wiped out. Banks foolish enough to lend so much can also suffer huge losses. If the banks have no idea how many intertwined, cross-connected deals their money is in, and something unexpected goes wrong, it could wreak havoc with the global financial markets.

Being free from the regulations that govern mutual funds is in itself a form of subsidy, for it allows hedge funds to take risks that may be borne by others. The easing of government rules on bank lending is another form of government favor that benefits the few. And then there is the 1999 federal law that repealed the Glass-Steagall Act, a New Deal–era law that required commercial banks, which make loans, to be separate from investment banks, which underwrite stocks and bonds. The Glass-Steagall Act was a barrier to mingling the money in people's checking and savings accounts with the risky capital used in underwriting new stocks and bonds. Only time will tell if the replacement law, the Gramm-Leach-Bliley Act, will lead to the temptation that spells ruin for people who just wanted to pay their bills by check or save a few dollars for a rainy day.

While hedge funds come in all sizes, styles, and quality of managers, they have in common an eagerness to acquire, however briefly, any asset that can produce a profit. One way to make a profit is by creating tax shelters that make profits appear to be losses.

Tax sheltering is one of those activities that civilized people usually carry on behind closed doors. Hedge funds are legally organized offshore, the favorite spot being the Cayman Islands. A narrow spit in the Caribbean, the Cayman Islands are home to more bank deposits than the financial capital of the world, New York. Of course nothing is really there except a brass plate in the lobby of a law firm and a secretary whose job is to gather up any mail and periodically send it off to the real hedge-fund offices in the United States. But by going offshore, the hedge funds get secrecy from the American tax authorities; accounting rules that let them build up huge fortunes while reporting no income; and, for the income the hedge managers do report, a tax rate of just 15 percent, less than half the top tax rate on wages.

Most hedge-fund managers have never even been to the Cayman Islands, making the headquarters arrangement a farce. They put their businesses there, at least on paper, because of its extreme secrecy laws. Anyone can operate in secret through a Cayman Islands shell corporation. All it takes is paying a small fee to the island government and bigger, but still modest, fees to the local lawyers. They work bankers' hours and live very well. This secrecy is as useful to Al-Qaeda, Hezbollah, and drug lords as it is to hedge-fund managers. But the doors to one room in the House of Mammon were thrown open by a lawsuit that revealed how hedge funds flout the law. It even came with a real-life *Perry Mason* moment.

The revelations came from Long-Term Capital Management, the hedge fund that nearly caused the global finance system to melt down in 1998. Federal tax auditors concluded that the firm had cheated the government so brazenly that stiff civil fraud penalties were warranted. The hedge fund took the government to court, insisting its tax deductions were all proper.

One July morning in 2003, in the Federal Courthouse in New Haven, a few miles from Greenwich, a career government lawyer faced off against one of the hedge fund's partners. The two men seemed ill matched for a game of intellectual chess. Charles P. Hurley was a career trial lawyer for the Justice Department, tall and ramrod-straight but otherwise just another government-issue lawyer in a cheap suit. The witness was Myron S. Scholes, who shared a Nobel Prize for devising a technique to value stock options. He brings to numbers the same kind of elegance that Titian brought to painting.

At issue was whether some securities the hedge fund bought for $4 million could generate $375 million in tax benefits. They came via a long and complicated history of tax dodges involving offshore leasing deals that were themselves tax shelters for Advanta, Electronic Data Systems, the Interpublic Group of Companies, Rhone-Poulenc Rohrer,

Wal-Mart, what is now Bank of America, and the computer-leasing arm of General Electric. Scholes's challenge was to find a way to recycle these securities so they could be used a second time to short the government.

Under questioning by his own lawyer the day before, Scholes had coolly explained that he knew the securities had to have economic substance beyond their value as tax deductions in order to qualify as a proper tax shelter. Without this rule smart people could just move symbols around on pieces of paper, fabricating deductions until business profits appeared, to the taxman, to be losses.

Hurley's first question sought to impeach Scholes. "Am I correct that yesterday you described yourself as a layperson in regard to taxes?" Hurley asked.

"I said I was not an expert with regard to taxes," Scholes said, setting the tone by quarreling with the question.

"You did, in fact, write this book?" Hurley asked, pulling from behind his lectern a copy of *Taxes and Business Strategy*, a $130 text used at Stanford Graduate School of Business whose primary author was Scholes.

Again and again Mr. Hurley went to the book, quoting from chapter headings and plucking a detail from page 457, each answer revealing the sophisticated knowledge Scholes possessed yet about which he claimed to lack expertise.

Hurley framed many of his questions to elicit a simple yes or no. Scholes would argue with the question, then navigate a maze of potentials, prospects, possibilities, and expectations before coming to a one-word conclusion.

Hurley: "I think the answer I wanted was in there—no."

Scholes: "Yes, and I wanted to explain why."

At one point, Scholes parsed a seemingly simple question into three parts, two of which had two subpoints each, and turned it all into a seamless soliloquy that lasted more than two minutes, without a single pause or "um," before reducing his own words down to one: yes.

After many rounds like this Hurley shifted tactics. He eased up in his style and began taking apart various dimensions of the potential profits and risks in the tax shelter, all the while pacing back and forth at the lectern, his suit coat buttoned, his right hand deep in his pocket. He appealed to Scholes's ego, flattering him at key moments, Scholes lapping up every syllable of praise.

Scholes explained how he had become aware of these securities with enormous potential value as tax deductions and how he had worked hard to imbue them with economic substance, ordering analyses, soliciting legal opinions, and even flying to London to meet with one of the three owners to make sure, he said, that they were not people who would bring disgrace on Long-Term Capital.

Finally he came up with a solution, more convoluted and subtle than his answers to simple questions. It involved letting the three Londoners and the San Francisco tax boutique that brokered the deal, Babcock & Brown, become investors in Long-Term Capital, even though the firm had been closed to outside investors. Neither the Londoners nor Babcock & Brown wanted to put up any money. And neither was willing to assume any risk that the hedge fund might fail. So Scholes arranged to lend them millions of dollars. The interest rate was lower than Long-Term Capital could have gotten on its money by placing it elsewhere. Then he used his expertise as one of the creators of the Black-Scholes method for valuing stock options to write several contracts whose options clauses guaranteed that these investors could not lose money.

After 14 months, the Londoners cashed out and walked away with a 22 percent profit after paying Long-Term Capital $900,000 in fees. Those fees were the key because they gave the whole deal economic substance apart from the value of the tax deductions.

Scholes practically boasted about how he had figured all this out. In her back-row seat, his wife, Jan, herself a Babcock & Brown principal, began to fidget. She, and others on the benches, could sense that the long-winded answers were blowing down a house of straw. Scholes swaggered on, oblivious.

Hurley asked about the money Scholes had spent getting expert advice on the deal. Scholes confirmed that to make sure the tax shelter was sound, Long-Term Capital had paid more than $500,000 to the Shearman & Sterling law firm in New York for an opinion letter that found his deal had economic substance. Long-Term Capital paid $400,000 more to King & Spalding in Washington for an opinion letter on another part of the deal.

Scholes said that Larry Noe, the tax director of Long-Term Capital, received a bonus of between $50,000 and $100,000 for his efforts. Taken together, the opinion letters and Noe's bonus had eaten up all, or nearly all, of the $900,000 in fees that gave economic substance to the tax shelter.

Then came the coup de grâce. Hurley slipped in a question about whether Dr. Scholes had sought, and received, a bonus of several million dollars imbuing the tax shelter with economic substance so it would survive an IRS audit. Scholes confirmed that he had, but emphasized that it had been paid in extra partnership shares, not cash.

Counting his bonus, the tax shelter cost far more than its economic value of $900,000 in fees, eliminating any economic substance.

"I'm being trapped here," Scholes blurted out, the famously smart man realizing he had walked right into the trap set by someone of lesser station but not blinded by greed. Scholes had finally grasped what his wife and everyone else in the courtroom had seen coming for a half hour. Because of that bonus, the deal had no chance of turning a profit, as the judge, Janet Bond Arterton, would later confirm in her decision rejecting all of the "disingenuous choices" Long-Term Capital made in its scheme to cheat the government.

The hubris of this Nobel laureate illustrates how those blinded by money can rationalize the absurd. The bigger the potential gain, the greater the temptation to cheat.

The rise of hedge funds has come at a time when there have been big increases in stock trading just before news that leads to stock price changes. Could it be that some hedge-fund employees are paying for inside information, which is a crime? Given that with sophisticated computer programs, big money can be made on tiny movements in stock prices, could it be that some hedge-fund operatives are not taking advantage of price gaps, but creating them? And are the Wall Street cops, the too-few investigators for the Securities and Exchange Commission, as sophisticated as the hedge funds? How would they know about what the hedge funds, all wrapped in secrecy and offshore accounting, are really doing?

Here are two things we do know from the documents made public in the Long-Term Capital cases. First, the fund's 16 partners were themselves leveraged, putting up $250 million and borrowing $500 million more, which created the appearance that the entire $750 million was their own money. That means when the hedge fund had borrowed $100 for each dollar investors had put up, for the accounts of the partners that leverage was 300 to 1. Second, UBS, the big Swiss bank, has a rule limiting loans to hedge funds to a ratio of 30 to 1. Despite this, an internal memo revealed that UBS made loans to Long-Term Capital at leverage the bank estimated to be 250 to 1.

Leverage can be a good thing. It can help families buy a house or a car or start a business. But leverage is also addictive. It can easily become the crack cocaine of hedge funds. Centuries of economic history show that those who try to leverage the world bring themselves to ruin—and often drag others down with them.

And what is the social or economic value in allowing hedge funds to operate in secrecy, borrowing other people's money? Hedge funds are making a few people spectacularly rich, but they add nothing of value. Each trade that puts a dollar into the pockets of Simons and his investors is a dollar someone else lost. Trading is a zero–sum game.

At the same time, borrowing 10 times, 100 times, even 250 times as much money as investors actually put at risk means that everyone is at risk, including the vast majority on the losing sides of these zero–sum games. This is economic pollution. Risk does not darken the sky or make the water smell, but spewing it unnecessarily into the system degrades the financial system for everyone else. And if something unexpected goes wrong, it can bring ruin to the many.

A lawyer working with Quellos, a financial boutique that works closely with hedge funds, sat down to coffee with me and explained that the firm had identified 26 different risks that come with owning a stock. For a fee any of those risks, up to 25 of them, could be hedged away, the last needing to remain or the problem that destroyed the Scholes tax shelter would arise, the lack of economic substance. Hedging—buying a financial instrument to protect against risk—comes at a cost. Hedging away 5 or even 25 risks could wipe out any potential gain. But there is a deeper risk here, not unlike that in new drugs or chemicals that find their way into the environment. By hedging away so much risk, what new risks are created?

Seeking answers to that question has produced some intriguing academic research. But the real answer will come like the collapse of Long-Term Capital, which followed the unexpected repudiation of debt by the Russian government in 1998. The real answer will come only after something unexpected happens and we all bear the burden of allowing secret, offshore, unregulated investment pools to operate with oceans of borrowed money from lenders that mix retail banking with investment banking. So far, with the collapse of Long-Term Capital and a few other funds that placed risky bets that did not work out, the failures have been small enough for the market, sometimes with help from the government, to ride out. That gives comfort, but not much.

The world is complex; even geniuses like Myron Scholes can make colossal errors in judgment, and all the new financial devices aimed at limiting risk may themselves meld into some disaster we cannot imagine. If the day comes when the disaster is so big that the market, the Federal Reserve, the Treasury, and all the king's men cannot put the financial Humpty Dumpty back together again, we could have the kind of world-wide financial collapse that Long-Term Capital nearly caused. That is the risk we are running under current government policies that favor the wealthy few, who take huge risks with the bank deposits of the many.

Another way to get rich is by rigging pay. The rank and file cannot do that, but senior executives can—and thousands of them did in ways that cheated investors. Our government knew about this, but did nothing until one brave bureaucrat took a stand.

Chapter 25

NONE DARE CALL IT STEALING

REMY WELLING IS A SMALL, NERVOUS WOMAN IN HER FIFTIES WITH light brown hair and a nose as slender as her athletic figure, which is supported by a backbone of extraordinary strength. Her lonely acts of heroism ought to earn her a statue on Wall Street as a champion of investors and another statute in Washington as a guardian of the public treasury. Instead, Welling was threatened with prison, forced to resign her career with the government after 22 years, and then barred by our government from working in her chosen field.

What Welling discovered was a corporate plot taken straight from *The Sting*, the 1973 movie starring Paul Newman and Robert Redford as two very creative con men. In the movie, they come up with a scheme to place horse-racing bets that are guaranteed to win. How? They place their bets after the races are run. And how do they do that? They trick the bookies into thinking the races have yet to start.

Many corporate executives also figured out a way to do something like that, only one that is far more lucrative and doesn't carry the risk of getting a belly full of lead if caught. Welling figured out what they were up to.

Her story shows how thoroughly our government looks out for the interests of the rich and powerful and how willing it is to savage those who reveal inconvenient facts. It shows how government secrecy shields corporate misconduct, letting executives steal from investors with little risk. And it underscores how a pervasive executive pay practice that enriched the few by cheating the many was not stopped when Welling brought it to the government's attention.

Welling's story begins in December 2002. It was a typical weekday in Silicon Valley, where the crush of morning traffic congeals into an awful traffic jam. Welling had to go to the office in San Jose that day, although she usually worked from her home, an airy little condominium.

By nature, Welling is a ferret. At the IRS, she specialized in assembling subtle clues into a map leading to well-hidden pots of untaxed riches. She honed these skills by putting together jigsaw puzzles, some with 1,500 pieces.

Welling had just finished a case in which she had uncovered $14 million of additional taxes owed by an entrepreneur. Later Welling learned that she had wasted her time. Her bosses let the man slip away without paying. To her, it was pretty much par for the course. It was a little like fly fishing. She would catch the tax cheats and, too often in her view, her bosses would release them. This taxpayer got away because he did the smart thing. He hired a fixer.

No one in America calls himself a fixer. Instead their business cards display titles like partner or vice president. The big accounting firms, and the specialty tax boutiques, are stocked with former IRS managers and executives who know how to go to bat for clients inside their former agency. They know from experience who is a team player and who, like Welling, is decidedly not. And they know who will be retiring and looking for a job soon. Like generals and colonels who approve inflated bills from military contractors and then retire into lucrative new careers, the tax world also has its public-private revolving door.

Fixing a case is easy under government rules, because secrecy is the overarching principle. Congress gives the IRS broad discretion to overrule what its auditors recommend. It can settle for pennies on the dollar. All a supervisor has to do is show that the case is so complicated or costly that litigation would tie up too much in resources to make it worth the fight. So long as the audit did not find blatant fraud, like a smoking gun memo about cheating the government, reasons to justify settlement are not that hard to develop. And if a taxpayer can show that an auditor made an error, however minor, the chances of getting the matter settled rise even further.

The only risk of doing a well-documented favor as a professional courtesy is that someone in the quality review squad might ask inconvenient questions. However, no one on that squad has ever been fired for *not* asking such a question.

The case that ended Welling's career began when her boss, Ron Yokoo, called her into his office. He gave her a thin file on the Micrel Corporation, a small semiconductor maker.

When Welling opened the file she was surprised to find not the usual paperwork, but a two-page document. It was titled "Department of the Treasury–Internal Revenue Service Closing Agreement on Final Determination Covering Specific Issues." The agreement required the IRS to cooperate with the company in not telling shareholders what was going on.

Welling refused to sign off on it. "An auditor cannot sign off on an agreement closing an audit before the audit. That's just not legal, not proper," Welling would say later.

Since Welling was known as a stickler in the extreme, it seems bizarre that Yokoo gave her this particular case. A team player might well have just signed the record and been done with it. Perhaps Yokoo never looked inside the file before he handed it over. Because of secrecy rules he won't say.

Outraged, and now determined to pursue the audit, Welling ordered copies of Micrel's tax returns. She tried to turn the jigsaw puzzle of all the numbers on all the forms into a coherent picture of what had happened. Before long she started focusing on the stock options Micrel had given to its executives and employees. Something did not add up. Welling started adding up the tax liabilities. The numbers were in the tens of millions of dollars.

Soon Welling discovered that earlier that year the IRS was approached by a former high-level IRS official named James Casimir, who had since joined the accounting firm PricewaterhouseCoopers. Without disclosing initially whom he represented, Casimir said he wanted the IRS's help in avoiding a big tax bill for his client. He said that his client had not been following the rules on stock options, the form of compensation most sought after in Silicon Valley.

An option is the right to buy a share of stock in the future at a price that is set today. For little companies anticipating a big future, options are a way to get rich fast if everything pans out, even briefly. The rules say that the option price, called the strike price, must be equal to or higher than the share price on the day the employee is given the option. This created a problem in the volatile market for high tech stocks. Shares at many Silicon Valley companies rose and fell as wildly as the wooden roller coaster in nearby Santa Cruz. Say all newly hired managers were granted 10,000 options. Joe gets hired on Monday when shares sell for $10 and Jane gets hired a week later when the price is only $5. Jane's options are worth a lot more than Joe's. If they both sell their options when the stock price reaches $15 then Joe gets $50,000 and Jane gets $100,000.

On the advice of the Deloitte & Touche accounting firm, Micrel gave employees options at the lowest price its shares traded at during a 30-day time period. The rules do not allow this practice, but Deloitte said it had found a way around the rule and would bless the sales in return for a substantial extra fee. No one outside the company knew, however, because Micrel did not tell its shareholders.

Under rules in effect at the time a company could often wait months before having to disclose the dates and prices of options granted to top executives. That government rule created an opportunity to just pick a date, the one with the lowest stock price, to make the options as valuable as possible. There was no way for investors to figure this out, either, from the reports sent out by the company.

Unable to get Yokoo or anyone else in the auditing division to act, Welling started looking outside for help. She went to the Securities and Exchange Commission, the FBI, the IRS's own criminal investigation unit, and the inspector general, as well as the Senate Finance Committee staff. Some of them told her to get lost. No one helped. Ultimately she came to me and to Warren Rojas, then with the magazine *Tax Notes*.

When the news broke, the IRS acted swiftly. Welling was threatened with prosecution, a very real threat given the way the law is written. She did not blink. Next the IRS dangled a disability pension in front of her. Welling would not budge. So they fired her. And when she applied to become a kind of income tax preparer called an enrolled agent, Welling was rejected on moral grounds.

The IRS commissioner, Mark W. Everson, citied the secrecy law in saying he could not discuss her case. He did say, however, that the agency "has long-established standards and safeguards designed to ensure that there is no undue influence over decisions by our enforcement personnel." There is no way to check that because of the secrecy law.

The last time Congress took a serious, rather than overtly political, look at the nation's tax police was back in 1952. It found rampant corruption, with bribes routine in some offices of what was then the Bureau of Internal Revenue. Hundreds of IRS agents, lawyers, specialists, and others have told me that a serious look today would show hardly anyone taking cash bribes as in days of old, but that favorable treatment is rampant for sophisticated taxpayers who hire former IRS executives and high-level managers.

What Welling had stumbled into was something far bigger than one small company listening to advice it wanted to hear about how to ignore the crystal-clear rules on stock options. Indeed, documents from Casimir showed that he represented other firms that had engaged in the same practice. So did papers in a lawsuit Micrel filed against Deloitte & Touche over its advice, as costly as it was bad, on backdating options.

In the months after Welling's story broke, a small number of companies reported that they had mispriced their stock options and were making adjustments to their financial statements. In a very few cases, executives left the companies.

The traffic in options was so huge that several professors of finance had been studying them. David Yermack of New York University wrote papers on curious patterns he detected. So did Erik Lie of the University of Iowa. It was Lie, together with Randall Heron of the University of Indiana, who finally put together solid evidence of the wrongdoing that the IRS, the SEC, and the FBI were told about, but had no interest in pursuing. Lie cited as his inspiration both my report in *The New York Times* and the more detailed article in *Tax Notes*.

Lie and Heron fed into a computer almost 39,000 stock-option grants made to executives at more than 7,700 companies between 1996 and 2005. Then they compared this to the ups and downs in the stock price of each company. The executives had an uncanny ability to have options granted to them on the days when the stock price was at its low point during each period. The timing was too perfect to be possible were the rules being followed.

The professors concluded that 14 percent of all stock options granted to top executives during those 10 years were backdated or otherwise manipulated. And for special stock-option grants, the kind a board might make to keep an executive from leaving, a quarter were on dates chosen after the fact.

Much later the serious disclosures came out, like the fabricated Apple board meeting that was worth an extra $70 million to Steve Jobs. The company blamed it on mistakes by a low-level employee.

Lie noted that backdating options was not only illegal, it cheated both investors and the government. Companies reported larger profits than they actually earned, which tends to push up their stock price, which tends to make options worth more. The companies also paid fewer taxes. And the whole scheme required filing false reports with the Securities and Exchange Commission. Manipulating stock option dates was "pervasive," Lie concluded.

Lax government rules, like the long delays in reporting when executives were given options, enabled these thefts. Equally lax enforcement is allowing the few who stole from the many to keep most of their ill-gotten gains. Only a relative handful of executives are being prosecuted.

Six of the most prominent tax lawyers in Washington wrote to the IRS in 2006 asking that they just allow all the companies that backdated their options to settle up with no penalties and put the matter behind them. The lead name on the letter was Pamela Olson of the Skadden, Arps law firm. In the early part of the decade, Olson had been the Bush administration's chief tax policy official at the Treasury Department.

In thinking about the executives who got away with their crimes, keeping their riches, and about Olson's letter asking that it all be treated as just a little mistake of no consequence, keep in mind the name Leandro Andrade. Andrade is a petty criminal, a thief. His last crime was stealing nine videotapes of children's shows from a California KMart. They were worth $150 retail. Andrade claimed he was going to give the tapes away. For this theft he was sentenced to 50 years in prison with no possibility of parole. The United States Supreme Court upheld that punishment in 2003. The high court ruled that it did not violate the Eighth Amendment prohibition against punishment that is cruel and unusual.

Stock-option thievery has decreased dramatically since Welling came across it and scholars like Lie documented how widespread it was. The reason is the Sarbanes-Oxley Act. It was passed in the wake of the Wall Street scandals at the turn of the millennium with the stated purpose of making executives responsible for what they do. One provision requires both chief executives and chief financial officers to certify the company's books. Ken Lay of Enron and even more so Bernie Ebbers of World-Com both claimed that they just did not understand the financial reports of the companies they ran.

Sarbanes-Oxley also requires companies to report grants of stock options within two days, not months. That eliminated most of the ability to pick days after the fact. Gutting that law is now one of the major goals of business lobbyists in Washington. Turn on any of the cable television programs that tout stocks and guests will denounce it as excessive regulation that is stifling business.

A few chapters back we examined the health care industry and how government policy has made a few very rich at the expense of the many. One of the biggest players in the stock-option scandals was William McGuire of UnitedHealth Group, the firm that manages to get around a Minnesota law that prohibits for-profit companies from providing health care. He made $125 million in 2004 and even more the next year.

McGuire held options valued at almost $1.8 billion in 2006. That was the result of his demand that company directors give him shares equal to 2 percent of the company. To approve the grant the directors, at least in theory, had to conclude that paying him this much was less costly to shareholders than his possible departure for being denied a raise.

It turns out that McGuire's stock options were exquisitely timed. His 1997, 1999, and 2000 options were given on the days when the company's shares hit their low points for those years. His 2001 stock grant just missed the bottom. *The Wall Street Journal* reported that the odds of this happening by chance were at best 1 in 200 million.

Before he resigned in late 2006, McGuire and his board agreed to reprice the options he had yet to exercise. The new strike price was the highest price at which the company's shares had traded in each year. How differently those on the top floor are treated from those on the shop floor. Steal a few videos and the Supreme Court says you can rot in prison until you die. Cheat your shareholders on a grand scale and you just sign a new contract with your employer.

In retirement, McGuire will collect a pension of more than $5 million annually for life. His employment contract also obligates United-Health to provide him and his wife with all the health care they need for life at no cost to the couple.

UnitedHealth provides health care as a fringe benefit to both its 55,000 workers and to retirees. But under both federal and Minnesota law, if UnitedHealth decides to cut off this benefit the retirees are out of luck. Not so McGuire. His employment contract requires the company to reimburse him for the full cost of replacement coverage.

Think about that in the context of what President Bush said in 2002 at a national summit on retirement savings. "What's fair on the top floor should be fair on the shop floor," he said.

Fair or not, five years after the president spoke those words government rules continue to favor the top floor over the shop floor. The administration is proposing to limit the tax break for health care plans offered by employers. In effect, it would raise taxes on some workers because they have quality health insurance.

Nothing in the proposal, however, would prevent companies from giving complete coverage to executives and even paying them the taxes on the value of the coverage if part of it becomes taxable. Anyone who doubts that companies would do this to get around the limit when it comes to those on the top floor need only read McGuire's employment contract. He had unlimited personal use of the company jet—and the company paid the taxes he incurred for these free flights.

Companies in the options backdating scandal reported more than $5 billion in charges to correct their financial reports, yet hardly any money was recovered from executives. The 2002 Sarbanes-Oxley law had a provision to recoup improper payments to executives, but the courts say only the federal securities regulators may invoke it, not shareholders. As of late 2007 the government had not brought charges in a single case.

There is yet another way that government rules favor executives over the rank and file. The rules allow troubled companies to cheat workers out of their full pensions despite a 1974 law intended to guarantee retirement income. The economics of funding pensions are simple, but corporations have persuaded Congress to make them complicated because they gain from complexity that subtly shifts risks onto workers.

Traditional pensions provide a monthly payment for life based on earnings and years on the job. The law requires that money be set aside each year to fund these pensions in advance. The safe and sound way to fund pensions is by investing in a portfolio of bonds that will pay interest on money set aside for the pensions. That is what insurance companies do when they sell private annuities, which are individual pensions.

Congress has authorized numerous seemingly minor changes to the pension-funding rules since 1974 that have had the effect of making it likely that too little money will be put aside. These rules limit pension fund contributions in years when pension assets are high relative to the obligation to pay, which are also the years when companies are likely to enjoy their best profits. These rules generally require companies to make larger contributions in years when the economy is weak and can least afford to make contributions. Companies short on cash can ask for permission to delay making contributions. Thus, both the good years and the bad create opportunities for "contribution holidays" in which little or no money is added to a pension plan, even as an additional year of work adds to the total eventually due to the workers.

Congress also allows a large portion of pension fund assets to be invested in risky stocks rather than secure bonds. While over the long haul stocks will return more, the up-and-down nature of stock values conflicts with the requirement of a pension plan to make monthly payments to each retiree. The risk is that many workers will enter retirement during a stock market slowdown, or even during the kind of severe drop in stock prices experienced in 2000, from which the market by 2007 had not fully recovered. Three or four years of lower stock prices while pension payments continue are a prescription for trouble.

Worse, Congress lets companies assume they will earn a specific return on their pension plan assets and to record it whether they do or not. This last technique is called "smoothing," and its real effect is to let companies put in less money than is needed to properly fund pensions.

Finally, Congress places artificial limits on pensions. Salaries of more than $225,000 at age 65 were not eligible for pensions guaranteed by the government in 2007. The result of this rule is to disconnect the interests of executives from the rank and file, since many executives make far more than that. An executive who makes ten times that amount, for example, gets a pension that is 10 percent in the system guaranteed by the government and 90 percent outside that system.

In theory, the government-guaranteed pension should be safer, more likely to actually produce income in old age. But executives outside the guarantees often are at far less risk than the rank and file. First, the government guarantee was $49,500 for someone who worked to age 65 and qualified for a pension plan that ultimately failed and had to be taken over by the government. Those who retired early, or were in pension plans that failed before they reached retirement age, typically get far less than they anticipated.

Executives are at less risk. Often when they leave they are allowed to take their benefit as a lump sum, especially the part above the government guarantee. John Snow did this at CSX, for example.

If the company files for bankruptcy protection, the portion of executive pensions not guaranteed by the government can be wiped out. That rarely happens. Instead, the executives demand that the creditors trying to rehabilitate the company guarantee their pensions as a condition of their staying on to keep the company going. In a few cases executives have gotten their executive pensions doubled in bankruptcy proceedings. The rank and file, and executives who have already retired, get no such benefits. Thus do government rules favor executives over Everyman.

Two decades of economic churning in the airline industry also demonstrate how government rules can enrich executives while devastating the retirement incomes of rank-and-file workers. Many pilots lost all of their pensions above the government guarantee. Because the guarantee applies at age 65, while by law pilots must retire at age 60, they cannot collect even the full, supposedly guaranteed amount of their pensions. Some pilots who had expected to collect $10,000 a month in their old age now get a third or less.

But the airline executives got rich. When Northwest emerged from bankruptcy in 2007, its chief executive, Douglas Steenland, was given $26.6 million in restricted stock and stock options. Glenn Tilton of United got almost $40 million when its parent exited bankruptcy proceedings. Doug Parker at US Airways got $6 million.

Back in 1998, before its first of two trips to bankruptcy court, the parent of US Airways paid its two top executives, Stephen M. Wolf and Rakesh Gangwal, more than the combined pay of the 25 top executives at the corporate parents of American, Continental, Delta, Northwest, and United. Wolf was paid $34.2 million and Gangwal $36 million. That same year it put very little into its pension plans, because government rules allowed the executives to get rich even as the pension plans were being shortchanged.

That any American who forgoes wages today for the promise of a pension tomorrow is not paid in full is a scandal. He has been robbed as surely as if a burglar broke into his or her home.

One of the great lies being spread in our time is that at big companies like General Motors and Ford there are not enough workers on the job today to sustain the pension benefits of those already retired. Current workers are not supposed to benefit those who came before. Each worker forgoes part of his or her current pay for a benefit in the future. Federal law requires that a pension be funded in advance by setting aside money for that benefit. Thus, over the life cycle of a company, as it grows from a single worker to a giant enterprise, and then passes into history, the number of workers on the payroll at any moment is not relevant to whether each worker collects the benefits deferred until old age.

All Congress needs to do to correct this problem is require sound financing of these plans. That means setting aside enough money each year for the benefit each worker earned and then investing that money in high-quality bonds. The problem for representatives and senators is that the simplicity of sound financing would mean a loss of fees for investment advisers and others who get rich off the current system. In turn, that would mean a reduction in the flow of campaign contributions to members of Congress. To business owners and executives, the cost of campaign contributions is chump change compared to the benefits of shortchanging pension plans.

Government rules permit and encourage a vicious cycle. To the extent that pensions are not fully funded, that their true costs are not paid each year, it means that corporate profits are inflated. Inflated profits mean that share prices for company stock are inflated, because they should represent the profitability of companies. And inflated stock prices mean, in turn, that executives cash in their options for more than they should get.

Stock options are just one part of a bigger scandal about how executives of publicly traded companies are paid. Congress and the courts have made it harder and harder for unions to organize, which inherently reduces the bargaining power of workers to get more for their labor. But Congress and agencies like the SEC have allowed the compensation of executives to become a rigged game. Among other abuses, directors who sit on the committees that decide how much to pay a chief executive often have indirect interests. And, of course, they have a direct interest in keeping their seat on the board.

Because of lax rules, the very top executives at companies are now paid with little regard for their performance. Just look at the mediocre to disastrous performances put in by the top acolytes of Jack Welch, the retired chairman of General Electric, when they moved to other companies. The poster boy for being overpaid for negative performance is Bob Nardelli. He left GE for the Home Depot, which turned out to be the best thing that could have happened for its major competitor, Lowe's.

Nardelli, like many executives, paid attention to numbers, not people. For a while the numbers like total sales and profits improved, but that is not sustainable without good people. Those helpful Home Depot workers who can show you tricks, and warn you about do-it-yourself mistakes that can ruin your new fixture, felt no respect once Nardelli came. To make the bottom line look better, Nardelli cut many of them from full-time to part-time. The best of them migrated over to the competition. Nardelli felt no need to restrain his own pay. He made $38.1

million in 2005. And his contract guaranteed him a $3 million bonus no matter what.

The annual meeting for Home Depot shareholders in 2006 proved a turning point. It was held in Delaware, not Atlanta where the company is headquartered. No one from the board attended. Nardelli treated the owners brusquely. In less than a year he was out, but he left with a stunning package—$210 million.

What was stunning was not so much the amount, but how he got it. It was negotiated up front when he joined the company six years earlier. Basically, Nardelli stood to walk away richer than rich no matter how he managed the company. Government rules on the pay of chief executives are so lax that even mismanagement can be worth a fortune. On the other hand, Nardelli could have made much more. "If Nardelli had been successful, he would have made $800 million," said Ira T. Kay, a leading executive pay consultant.

Kay says that "the dirty little secret" of executive pay is how government rules on golden parachutes have allowed many so-so executives to earn far more money than the market would pay them.

A golden parachute is money an executive is guaranteed if he is forced out for almost any reason short of being unmasked as a serial rapist. In fact, under some executive contracts, even that might not be grounds for dismissal unless the victims had some connection to the company. The typical parachute guarantees three years of pay and perks, which would be tens of millions of dollars for many CEOs. The three years follows a rule set by Congress.

"Basically companies had to bribe their executives with higher levels of pay so they would not be motivated to just get their golden parachutes" and walk away, Kay said. In contrast, Kay remarked, rank-and-file employees "have much less power; they are not leaving very much. The baby boomers, you can basically treat them terribly and they don't quit."

At least one boomer who stood up and blew the whistle on what was really happening on the top floor was rewarded for this diligence not with a golden parachute, but by being fired. For almost three years Remy Welling stewed about what happened to her. During that time, she pored over every story she could find about the stock-options scandal that she had been fired for bringing to light.

Among the stories that seized her attention were extraordinary *Wall Street Journal* pieces on stock-options abuses, for which reporters James

Bandler, Charles Forelle, Mark Maremont, Gary Putka, and Steve Stecklow won the Pulitzer Prize for Public Service.

Welling received no honors. But she did score one small victory. Just about the time the *Journal* reporters were picking up their well-deserved Pulitzer, Welling finally received a letter in the mail from the IRS. Inside was her enrolled agent card, which will allow her to represent taxpayers being audited by the agency.

So what does this all mean? What is the net effect on you of all these government policies that benefit the few at the expense of the many? Read on.

Chapter 26

NOT SINCE HOOVER

The fact is that income inequality is real; it's been rising for more than 25 years.

—President George W. Bush, January 31, 2007

OR THE RICHEST AMERICANS, THE YEARS SINCE 1980 HAVE BEEN very good. There were the seven fat Reagan years, as the editorial page of *The Wall Street Journal* often reminds readers, and then the even fatter Clinton years, which those pages credit to anything but that administration. Since then, despite the collapse of the Internet bubble in 2000, which wiped out $7 trillion of stock market wealth, the trend at the top has continued.

Remember, in 2005 the best-off 300,000 Americans had almost as much income as the bottom 150 million. It was not always so. And if we take into account all the devices—perfectly legal, questionable, and illegal—that the rich use to minimize the incomes they report, it is likely that the small group at the top has far more income than the bottom half.

There are many ways to analyze incomes. One is to examine changes in the average income of groups. Think of a ladder, the income ladder. The poorest Americans are at the bottom, the richest on the top rung, and everyone else stands somewhere in between. Some individuals move up and down that ladder, but once they have been working for a few years, many find themselves settled into a section of the ladder where they remain. The other way to examine income is to look at shares, or how the national income pie is sliced. There is a slice for the bottom 90 percent, which we will call "the vast majority." The other slice goes to the top 10 percent, which in 2005 basically included everyone who made more than $100,000. The top group's slice will be cut again to separate out the top 5 percent, the top 1 percent, the top tenth of 1 percent, and finally the top 1/100 of a percent, the last group comprising 30,000 Americans whose income for a single year would make anyone independently wealthy.

Let's have dessert first.

The income pie grew a lot larger in the quarter century from 1980 to 2005. It was like replacing a medium-size pie with a big one. As measured by what people put down on their income tax returns, the pie grew by 79 percent, while the population increased by only a third. This means that there was more pie for everyone before slicing it up. That makes comparing the way the pie was sliced in 1980 and in 2005 particularly interesting.

The vast majority's slice of income pie was thinner in 2005 than it had been back in 1980. That bottom 90 percent had almost two-thirds of America's income pie in 1980, but only a little more than half in 2005.

The precise numbers were calculated from tax-return data by Thomas Piketty and Emmanuel Saez, two economists who have been studying income data around the world going back nearly a century. The vast majority received 65.3 percent of the pie in 1980, but only 51.5 percent in 2005. Not since 1928, when the vast majority received 51.7 percent of the pie, has its share been so small.

Piketty and Saez analyzed the tax-return data based on what are called "tax units." That is anyone who files, or could have filed, a tax return. They excluded income transfers that are not caused by the market economy. For example, 151 million workers paid Social Security taxes while more than 48 million had Social Security income, a transfer their calculations ignore. Piketty and Saez count almost 145.6 million tax units, including people who did not have to file a tax return because they were too poor or had income, such as a disability pension, not subject to tax. A single person and a family are each counted as one unit. For simplicity we will treat each unit as having an equal share of the population. My analysis shows that this makes for modest distortions (nitpickers, have fun), but does not alter the big picture.

The top 10 percent of Americans got more pie. A lot more. Their slice grew from more than a third to almost half (34.6 percent in 1980 to 48.5 percent in 2005). But when we cut their slice of the pie more finely we see that this gross figure is misleading, because the slice is not distributed at all evenly among the top 30 million Americans.

For the bottom half of the top 10 percent, the slice of pie was unchanged (11.5 percent in 1980 and 11.4 percent in 2005). For the next group, those standing between the ninety-fifth and ninety-ninth rungs on the income ladder, the slice of pie grew somewhat. It increased from 13.2 percent to 15.3 percent.

It is when we start looking closely at the top 1 percent that things get really interesting. Their share of the income pie more than doubled, from 10 percent to 21.8 percent. Numerically this group is three million Americans, but in terms of how much money they make it is hardly a cohesive group. To get into the top 1 percent required an income in 2005 of $348,400. At the very top, several people made more than a billion dollars. It would take someone at the threshold of the top 1 percent nearly 3,000 years to make a billion dollars. So, we will cut this slice of income pie even more finely.

First, there is the top tenth of 1 percent, or 300,000 Americans. People in this group lived alone or in families with an income of at least $1.7 million for 2005. Their slice of pie more than tripled in size. They earned 3.4 percent of the 1980 pie and 10.9 percent of the 2005 income pie.

Then, let's consider the very best off, the 30,000 Americans, or 14,588 tax units, who made at least $9.5 million in 2005. Their slice of income pie in 2005 was four times larger than in 1980. They went from almost 1.3 percent of the pie in 1980 to a tad more than 5 percent in 2005.

So the vast majority had less pie in 2005 than in 1980. And even among the top 10 percent with their larger slice, nearly all of the growth

The Rich Get a Bigger Slice

SHARE OF INCOME REPORTED ON TAX RETURNS

	THE VAST MAJORITY	THE RICH	THE SUPERRICH
PEOPLE IN 2005	270 million	3 million	30,000
1980	65.3%	10.0%	1.3%
2005	51.5%	21.8%	5.1%

Source: Piketty and Saez

went to the top 1 percent—especially those at the very top who were already very rich, yet whose slice of pie grew even fatter.

Put another way, the rich enjoyed their biggest slice of the national income pie since Herbert Hoover was president. Indeed, their income share was virtually the same as in 1928 and 1929, the last of the Roaring Twenties and just ahead of the Terrible Thirties.

President Kennedy famously said that a rising tide lifts all boats. If a rising tide of income makes everyone better off, then changes in the shares people get do not matter so much. But that is not what is happening. Instead, as the numbers for average incomes show, the yachts are becoming personal ocean liners while the runabouts and dinghies, tied to the dock, are being swamped.

The national economy, adjusted for inflation, more than doubled in size from 1980 to 2005. However, because the population grew by a third during those years, the growth per person was only about two-thirds. That is, for each dollar per person that the economy produced in 1980, by 2006 output had grown to about $1.67. So what happens when we look at the income ladder?

The average income of the vast majority dipped slightly, from $29,495 in 1980 to $29,143 in 2005. The decline is about a dollar a day. So while the overall economy did quite well, the vast majority did not share in that prosperity. Moreover, if we reach back a bit further we find that the decline in income for the vast majority is actually quite severe.

The average income for the bottom 90 percent of Americans peaked in 1973 at $33,001. That is nearly $4,000 more per year than this group's average income in 2005. So after a generation of economic growth, over 32 years, the vast majority has to get by on about $75 less per week.

The declines are even greater if we examine the bottom half of the income ladder, which in 2005 was 150 million Americans. Piketty and Saez did not prepare such a breakdown. But the Tax Foundation, a group that favors less taxation, did. Its data cover only 1980 through 2004, but not having data from 2005 does not change the big picture.

Adjusted for inflation, the bottom half had an average income of $15,464 in 1980. That fell to $14,149 in 2004. That meant making ends meet with $25 less per week than in 1980.

There have been some offsetting changes. The portion of income paid in federal income taxes by the bottom 150 million Americans has been cut in half, the Tax Foundation calculated. Back in 1980 their average tax rate was a bit more than 6 percent, while in 2004 it was just under 3 percent. That means the after-tax decline in income was only $15 a week, not $25.

Things were a little different at the top of the ladder. For starters, to reach the ninetieth rung required $100,714 in 2005, up from $84,080 in 1980, Piketty and Saez calculated. That meant someone who was at the ninetieth rung in 1980 had to get an annual raise, after adjusting for inflation, of only $665 each year just to stay in place.

The higher one stood on the ladder above that, the more it took to stay in place. The threshold to be in the top 1 percent rose in tandem with the economy. Gross National Product per capita grew 67 percent, compared with a 71 percent increase in the threshold for the ninety-ninth rung on the income ladder.

To reach the top tenth of a percent, however, required increasing income since 1980 by slightly more than a million dollars, to more than $1.7 million in 2005. And for the very top, the best-off 1/100 of 1 percent, the threshold rose from $2.5 million to $9.5 million. Looking at the average income of that top group provides an even more startling figure. Their average income was $5.2 million in 1980, but more than $25.7 million in 2005. Remember that increase in annual income, $20.5 million, is *after* adjusting for inflation.

The pattern here is clear. The rich are getting fabulously richer, the vast majority are somewhat worse off, and the bottom half—for all practical purposes, the poor—are being savaged by our current economic policies.

Incomes Rose Only at the Top
AVERAGE ANNUAL INCOME

	THE VAST MAJORITY	THE RICH	THE SUPERRICH
PEOPLE IN 2005	270 million	3 million	30,000
AVG. INCOME: 1975	$ 29,968	$ 359,501	$ 3,430,164
1985	$ 29,210	$ 533,401	$ 9,414,999
1995	$ 27,614	$ 654,057	$ 10,574,657
2005	$ 29,143	$ 1,111,560	$ 25,726,965
CHANGE AFTER 30 YEARS	(825)	$ 752,058	$ 22,296,801
PERCENT CHANGE	(3%)	209%	650%

Source: Piketty and Saez

That those at the top have been pulling away from everyone else in the past three decades is now so long established, so visible across many different measures of income, and so well analyzed that it is accepted by everyone who has examined the data, save for a few ideological crackpots at some of the ideology-marketing organizations that pose as think tanks. Even President Bush, a man who has joked about how closely he is identified with what he called "the haves and have mores," sees this growing divide as a problem. "I know some of our citizens worry about the fact that our dynamic economy is leaving working people behind," he said early in 2007. "We have an obligation to help ensure that every citizen shares in this country's future."

To appreciate fully how much the fruits of economic growth are, under current government policies, being concentrated in the hands of the few, it is useful to perform another kind of analysis. We will examine the ratio of income growth between different groups over several long periods of time, starting with a comparison between the lower 90 percent, our "vast majority," and the top 1 percent.

Let's consider three eras. The first would be from 1950 to 1975, a quarter century when a rising tide did lift all boats and the nation was transformed into a land of broad prosperity. Setting the second era from 1960 to 1985 allows us to incorporate an early part of the era in which government began changing its policies in ways favored by many of the rich. Finally, it would be good to compare 1980 with 2005, but that will not work mathematically because the ratio would include negative numbers, since the income of the vast majority declined slightly. So instead we will use 1981, a recession year, to compare to 2005. The vast majority's average annual income was $114 higher at the end of those 24 years.

The measure is a ratio. For each additional dollar going to each person in the vast majority, how many went to each of those in the top 1 percent?

For 1950 to 1975, the ratio is four dollars more at the top for each dollar going to the vast majority. For 1960 through 1985, the ratio is $17. And for 1981 through 2005, it is almost $5,000.

Dramatic as those numbers are, they understate the concentration of income. Let's now compare income growth for the vast majority with the top 1/100 of 1 percent, those 30,000 Americans at the very top of the income ladder.

For 1950 to 1975, the ratio was $36 to one. For 1960 through 1985, it was $459. And for 1981 through 2005, it was $141,000 to the dollar.

Examining different periods produces the same basic result: since the market-based solutions came to dominate government policy, the winners have been the rich, the very rich and, most of all, the superrich "have mores."

A major component of the markets-are-the-solution policies has been the drive to lower tax rates on those with high incomes and on investors. When President Reagan was elected, the top income tax rate was 70 percent, meaning on the last dollar of income those at the top paid 70 cents in taxes. Those high rates fueled the sale of tax shelters, which advocates of lower rates said would be a much smaller problem if rates were cut. (Instead, tax shelters continue to proliferate among the rich.)

Today the top tax rate is 35 percent. President Bush said during the third election debate in 2004 that most of the tax cuts he sponsored went to low- and middle-income Americans. That was not even close to true.

In fact, most of the savings—53 percent—will go to people with incomes in the top 10 percent over the first 15 years of the cuts, which began in 2001 and would have to be reauthorized to keep them in effect through 2015. More than 15 percent of the tax cuts will go to the top tenth of 1 percent, a group that is now 300,000 people.

In addition, because of the Bush tax cuts, those earning more than $10 million a year pay a smaller share of their money in income, Social Security, and Medicare taxes than those making between $100,000 and $200,000.

The Tax Policy Center calculated these numbers at my request in 2005. Their help was sought because the computer models used by the government do not parse the top 1 percent, despite the enormous span of incomes it represents, and a model at the Heritage Foundation was not yet operating.

The center is a joint project of the Urban Institute and the Brookings Institution, two middle-of-the-road-to-liberal research organizations in Washington. The economists leading the Center—Len Burman, Bill Gale and, Gene Steuerle—served as tax policy advisers to President Reagan, the first President Bush, and President Clinton. Again and again over the years, officials at the Bush Treasury Department have gone out of their way to express respect for both the reliability of the Tax Policy Center model and the integrity with which the economists who created it have approached their work.

So when shown the center's analysis and asked for comment, it was not surprising that the Bush administration said it had no quarrel with any of the findings. A spokesman deemed the model used to generate the estimates "reliable."

The administration did press one point that it said was important. The tax cuts sponsored by President Bush have made the income tax system more progressive, shifting the burden slightly more to those with higher incomes. The administration emphasized that the president supports a progressive tax code in which the more you have, the greater the share of your gain is paid in taxes.

The idea of progressive taxation is central to democracy. Indeed, the idea that taxes should be based on ability to pay was intertwined with the birth of the first democracy, 2,500 years ago. Ancient Athens had been a tyranny in which each person paid the same tax—a hard burden for most, a trifle for the rich. Then a moral principle was developed: The more one gained economically from living in civilized society, the greater one's duty to maintain that society by paying taxes. Every classic worldly philosopher—Aristotle, Plato, Adam Smith, Karl Marx, David Ricardo, John Locke, and all the rest—endorsed this moral principle, arguably making it the most conservative principle in Western civilization.

However, the Bush administration claim that the recent tax cuts had made the income tax system more progressive seems to fly in the face of a recent Internal Revenue Service study. It found that the taxpayers in the top tenth of 1 percent also saw their share of taxes decline in 2001 and 2002. The Tax Policy Center computer model results also did not seem to support the Bush administration's claim. Then a Treasury spokesman, Taylor Griffin, explained. Griffin said that the income tax system is more progressive if the measurement is based on the share borne by the top 40 percent of Americans, rather than the top tenth of 1 percent.

The Bush administration is right that the share paid by the top 40 percent is higher now than it was in 2000. Those in the 39.9 percent immediately below the very top may find small comfort in that detail, however.

There was another point the Bush administration could have made, but did not. It concerns the 400 very-highest-income taxpayers, a truly thin slice of Americans. To get into that group in 2000 required an income of at least $88 million. They averaged almost $174 million each. Those 400 taxpayers, about 1,200 people, were so well off that they had more than 1 percent of all the reported income in America in 2000. The Bush administration continues to analyze the incomes and taxes of the top 400 taxpayers, but will not disclose the numbers for years after 2000, which would have shown the impact of the Bush tax cuts.

Here is what I found by analyzing the 2000 data as if the Bush tax cuts had applied. A separate analysis by Robert S. McIntyre of Citizens for Tax Justice, using more sophisticated techniques, produced almost identical figures.

Out of their average incomes of nearly $174 million, under the Bush tax cuts the top 400 taxpayers would have paid the government 17.5 percent in income, Social Security, and Medicare taxes. For people who make $100,000 to $200,000, the tax burden is much higher at 20.6 percent.

Even more interesting results arise from comparing the effects of the Bush tax cuts with the changes for investors that President Clinton signed into law in 1997. During Clinton's two terms, the effective income tax rate of the top 400 fell from almost 30 percent to 22.2 percent. Applying the Bush tax cuts yields a rate of 17.2 percent for income taxes only. That means Clinton gave the richest of the superrich a much bigger tax cut than Bush. Under Clinton, their effective tax rate fell by almost eight cents on the dollar; under Bush, it fell only five.

Societies in which the few deepen their pockets while the many see theirs grow lighter are not stable. America is so fabulously prosperous that we have seen only at the extreme edges the kind of political upheaval that can grow from a loss of hope and a lifetime of work for a shrinking paycheck. And when the growing income gap of America is compared to other countries, we look most like three nations whose societies most Americans would not find appealing—Brazil, Mexico, and Russia.

A young life is a terrible thing to waste. Most modern nations try to limit childhood poverty for reasons both moral and practical. Better than one in six American children live in poverty, about 12.3 million children in 2005, the Census Bureau calculated. Compared to other modern nations, many of them far less rich, the United States does poorly by its children. In terms of material well-being, the United Nations ranked the United States seventeenth on a list of 20 modern countries, right below Portugal.

Allowing so many children to grow up in poverty imposes huge costs, but is of little or no value in terms of soliciting campaign contributions. So just how much does it cost our society to have so many children grew up in poverty? What are the costs of reduced productivity, smaller incomes when they grow into adulthood, a greater propensity to commit crimes, and the costs of being less healthy? About $500 billion a year, according to a study commissioned by a liberal advocacy group, the Center for American Progress. But once Congress heard that report in early 2007, and the inevitable criticisms that the number was just an estimate, it quickly turned its attention back to matters more pressing to the party of money.

Even Alan Greenspan, the once-obscure economist whom President Reagan elevated onto the national stage and who then served as Federal Reserve chairman, warned Congress in 2004 about the widening gap between the rich and the poor. "For the democratic society, that is not a very desirable thing," Greenspan said.

We now have almost three decades of experience with the idea that markets will solve our problems. The promised results are not there and there is no reason to believe that they are over the next horizon, just a few more subsidies away. Electricity costs more and its delivery is less reliable. Many hundreds of billions of tax dollars have been diverted to the rich, leaving our schools, parks, and local government services starved for funds. Jobs and assets are going offshore, sometimes to the detriment of not just the economy, but national security.

We have layered subsidy upon giveaway upon legal absolution for reckless conduct in a chaotic attempt to protect jobs, and it has not worked. We pour billions into subsidies for sports teams and golf courses, a folly Adam Smith railed against in his day. Our health care system costs us far more than that of any other industrial country and yet we live shorter lives than the Canadians, Europeans, and the Japanese. We stand alone among modern societies in making tens of millions of our citizens go without health care, many of whom die or become disabled because of this nutty idea that medicine is a business, not a service. We have erected obstacles to the earnest but poor who seek to better themselves through library study and higher education.

And our politicians in both parties are hypocrites of the first water, nearly every one of them. They vote to make the poor sacrifice again and again so that the rich can have more, yet they run for office handing out photos showing that they regularly attend religious services. To those who do not get this last point, take a moment to ponder the inner thoughts of the Pharisees. Do you think they thought themselves evil? Of course not. In their own minds, they had justifications for what they did, assuring themselves that they were the most moral of men.

Except for our technology, our electricity and powerful motors, we are the same as the ancients. And like great societies that we can look back upon, which reached a high point and then headed down the road to oblivion, we too are taking from the many to give to the few. "He that oppresseth the poor to increase his riches, and he that giveth to the rich, shall surely come to want," it says in Proverbs 22. Wise words to memorize.

We have become a society in which this injunction, and many others like it, are ignored. Even when we seek to help people, as with the drug benefit for older Americans, the mechanism often is designed first and foremost to take care of the corporate rich. The net effect of our policies, the evidence for which is overwhelming, is that we are redistributing income up. Through subsidies and tax cuts and rules that depress the incomes of most workers, the immediate future looks very bright for the already rich. Indeed, to borrow from the song, their future's so bright they gotta wear shades.

So what, if anything, can we do? Here's the good part. After reading all of these blood-boiling stories, we actually can do something. The whole idea of America is that we can solve any problem we want to solve. We can form a more perfect union, establish justice, ensure domestic tranquillity, provide for the common defense, promote the general welfare, and secure the blessings of liberty to ourselves and our posterity. For some thoughts on what we can do, please read on.

Conclusion

WHAT TO DO?

This disposition to admire, and almost to worship, the rich and the powerful is the great and most universal cause of the corruption of our moral sentiments.

—**Adam Smith**

Woe unto him that buildeth his house by unrighteousness, and his chambers by wrong; that useth his neighbour's service without wages, and giveth him not for his work.

—**Jeremiah 22:13**

RONALD REAGAN SET THE NATION ON A NEW COURSE IN 1980 with his simple question, "Are you better off now than you were four years ago?" We now have a quarter century of experience and data that allows us to judge whether to stay the course or change direction.

In real terms, America today is more than twice as wealthy as in 1980 and the economy is putting out two-thirds more per person. Those are tremendous accomplishments. So where are the benefits of all this increased wealth and economic output?

Incomes for the vast majority have stagnated, not grown. The share of workers earning poverty-level or lower wages declined only slightly, from a little more than 27 percent of all workers in 1979 to a little under 25 percent in 2005. For private production and nonsupervisory workers, which covers four out of five wage-paying jobs, pay increased in real terms, but just barely. The increase was the equivalent of getting a raise each January of about a penny an hour. This average wage increased from $15.78 to $16.11, or just 33 more cents per hour after 26 years.

Family incomes are up slightly, but that is because more people hold two jobs and a growing share of women with children earn wages. Having less time for child rearing imposes its own social costs.

The percentage of American children living in poverty in 2004 had barely changed since 1980, with growing poverty among whites and Hispanics more than offsetting a one-third decline in the poverty rate among young African Americans.

Year after year, we are told there is less money for the basics that sustain society. Hospitals close. Libraries reduce hours, buy far fewer books, and in some places are shuttered. Schools eliminate classes in music and art and, in some places, reduce the teaching of arithmetic because of federal mandates to test in only one subject, reading. Maintenance of the infrastructure is deferred for lack of funds, a malign neglect of public assets that results in the collapse of bridges and dams, in sinkholes that appear out of nowhere, and explosions of steam pipes and other unseen urban support systems.

This is not for lack of government spending. Despite all the rhetoric about cutting taxes, combined federal, state, and local spending as a share of the economy is basically the same now as in 1980.

The official figures understate reality, however. Government keeps borrowing as well as taxing. Borrowing is a kind of tax on the future that crowds out other spending. Interest on the federal debt in 2006 totaled more than $405 billion, an amount equal to all the individual income taxes paid from early August through year-end. The government did not have the cash to make all of these interest payments, however, since so much of it was paid by taking on more debt.

Our state and local governments also cut spending on basics, while taking on ever more debt. Under Governor Jeb Bush, for example, Florida cut state taxes by $19 billion while borrowing $22 billion on which its citizens now must pay interest.

This has happened when the overwhelming focus of policy in Washington, and to a lesser extent the state capitals, has been on the economy. Both parties have bought into the Reagan policy of speaking about government in economic terms, mostly in how it takes from you in taxes and costs business through regulation. Ask not what you can do for your country; listen instead to what government should do for your bottom line.

At the same time, those at the top have done fabulously well. Chief executive officers, who in 1980 made about 40 times what workers did, now make hundreds of times more than their workers. The hedge-fund managers make astonishing sums, the top 25 each averaging $11 million *per week* in 2006, while paying taxes at lower rates than middle-class workers. The share of national income going to the top 1 percent, the top tenth of 1 percent, and the top 1/100 of 1 percent are at levels not seen since Herbert Hoover was president. The share of stocks, bonds, and other corporate wealth owned by those at the top keeps rising despite all the individual retirement plans government has promoted to replace the traditional defined-benefit pension. The number of people with savings accounts at the bank or credit union dwindles, while the supply of tax-free bonds sold to the highest-income Americans proliferates.

These results should not surprise. For a generation the policy of the federal government has been to make the rich richer, even when those riches come at the expense of everyone else. There are many elements to this policy. Giveaways of money and seizures of property to avoid market forces, for example, impoverish everyone but the recipients of this largesse. Rules that make it easy to rig markets, break unions, and short-change workers all benefit the rapacious among the rich. Then there are trade policies that allow capital to move freely across borders, combined with a determined effort to make less government information available on the grounds that it will interfere with the privacy of businesses. For the already rich the least risky, most profitable way to grow even richer is through government favors, be it cash, property, favorable rules, or law enforcement that either lacks the resources to act or looks the other way.

We have gone astray.

The founders did not create America to make us rich. Washington, Jefferson, Franklin, and the others were among the wealthiest men in the colonies. They were not seeking to enhance their own wealth when they stuck their necks out. They risked their lives and property for the principle of self-determination, for the idea that whatever our problems, we can solve them ourselves better than King George, a parliament we did not elect, or any power not accountable to the people.

The founders risked their lives so that the human spirit might flourish and make the world a better place. They created America so that we could be free to live our lives as we choose without regard to religion or creed, to which we have since added race and gender.

At first, they failed. The original American government collapsed because the Articles of Confederation bore little relationship to the self-evident truths articulated by Jefferson and the common sense of Thomas Paine. That failure should remind us that the government we have, and the freedoms it protects, are perishable.

The second American republic has endured for more than two centuries because, under the Constitution, we devised elegant and principled solutions to problems that have vexed man since the first organized society. One was the need for a government with the revenue and authority to act, but that derived its powers from the consent of the governed, working for their benefit, not as a power unto itself. Another was creating a structure of three separate and equal branches to make, administer, and interpret laws. This structure limits the use of power, the great corrupter.

Under the Constitution, we enumerated the rights of the people, including the right to speak our minds, worship or not as we choose, and be free from predation by the state, which historically dealt with the inconvenient individual by having him killed or thrown in the dungeon. All of our other rights ultimately stand on that one, habeas corpus, the right to have our case for freedom heard by an independent judiciary. Since then, we have expanded the franchise beyond white men with property to everyone who reaches adulthood.

In this way we created a nation of laws, not of men. We set forth the principles for this bold experiment in 52 words whose eloquent wisdom we too often forget:

> We the People of the United States, in Order to form a more perfect Union, establish Justice, insure domestic Tranquility, provide for the common defence, promote the general Welfare, and secure the Blessings of Liberty to ourselves and our Posterity, do ordain and establish this Constitution for the United States of America.

Those concepts inform our guideposts: Society. Justice. Peace. Security. Commonwealth. Freedom. What did not make the list as a purpose of our nation? Individual riches. That we may each become rich, if we choose and luck is with us, is a by-product rather than a purpose of our system of government.

Yet for more than a quarter century, we have acted as if economic gain is the great purpose of government. Our Supreme Court has equated with free speech the dollars given to politicians in the form of campaign contributions, concentrating the corrosive effect of money on sound policy by giving greater voice to those with both the means and the reason to influence who wins elections. Our policies have resulted in concentrations of wealth and income at the very top that make us more like Brazil, Mexico, and Russia than Canada, Europe, Japan, and Australia. And we have seen that the fear Reagan spoke of—that the rabble would drain the government's treasury—has come true, but with a twist. It is the rich who are gorging themselves on the government with giveaways, favors, contracts, rules that rig the economy, tax breaks, and secret deals.

No society can endure if it ignores the problems of a growing share of its people. Adam Smith told us this when he wrote, "What improves the circumstances of the greater part can never be regarded as an inconveniency to the whole. No society can surely be flourishing and happy, of which the far greater part of the members are poor and miserable."

We are not merely 300 million individuals who share the same geography, but a society—and a great one provided we remain true to the precepts of liberty and justice for all.

Three principles can help guide us to make wise decisions about our economic policies. They epitomize the fact that rules define a civilization:

- A society that does not embrace a common purpose for its existence has no standard against which to judge itself, making it vulnerable to the corruptions of men who chafe at the limits of law.
- A society that does not address the needs of its members, especially the vulnerable, weakens itself from within while wasting its most valuable resource, the minds and talents of all its citizens.
- A society that takes from the many to give to the few undermines its moral basis and must in the end collapse.

How many of your family, friends, and neighbors are you willing to see bankrupted by medical bills or condemned to awful disabilities or early death because they cannot afford proper health care? How much should you, your family, and people like you sacrifice so that corporations, including insurance companies, can maximize their profits by providing only the minimum care necessary?

What does it profit us if we remove from our land the jobs of the many who work with their hands? How do we benefit as a society when government rules tell the owners of factories, patents, and copyrights to go offshore?

Why do we allow less and less competition—there are only four major accounting firms, for example—when there is clear evidence that this results in higher prices and worse service? Do we want to become a society mostly of service workers, when for many that means being a servant? Will it all fall apart, as Scott Cook, the one-armed Oregon entrepreneur, warns, because we pursue short-term profit, focus on service jobs, and subsidize the rich while diminishing the bounty nature provides us?

Do we really want to tax ourselves so that rich men can spend less flying in luxury to play golf? Must we be forced by the coercive power of government to give part of our sustenance to the mass opiate of our age, commercial sports? How much are you willing to give up from your paycheck so that Dick Cabela and Johnny Morris can sell fishing tackle and guns from stores that you bought for them with your taxes? How many hours are you willing to work each year so that Tyco and General Electric and Honeywell can get free labor to check out burglar alarms?

How much more are you willing to pay each month for electricity on the theory that competitive markets are superior to regulation, when the evidence shows that regulated utilities and municipally owned systems provide reliable power at lower cost? Do you want more markets that are easily manipulated?

Do you want a government that allows trillions of dollars of borrowed money, wrapped in veils of secrecy by unregulated hedge funds, to influence the markets in which government says you must keep your 401(k) nest egg? Are you willing to give the government a much larger share of your income than do the hedge fund managers who every few days make more than you will in a lifetime?

The gifts, favors, and tax breaks we bestow on the rich would shock the conscience of Andrew Mellon, the oil man and banker whose words are often invoked in support of current policies favoring the rich. As with Adam Smith, Mellon's words are often quoted selectively by those who shill for the rich. Consider what Mellon wrote in his 1924 book *Taxation: The People's Business*:

> The fairness of taxing more lightly income from wages, salaries or from investments is beyond question. In the first case, the income is uncertain and limited in duration; sickness or death destroys it and old age diminishes

it; in the other, the source of income continues; the income may be disposed of during a man's life and it descends to his heirs.

Surely we can afford to make a distinction between the people whose only capital is their mental and physical energy and the people whose income is derived from investments. Such a distinction would mean much to millions of American workers and would be an added inspiration to the man who must provide a competence during his few productive years to care for himself and his family when his earnings capacity is at an end.

"People." "A man's life." Mellon shows empathy when he employs those words—a moral sensitivity missing from the acts of our elected officials who embrace the policies of taking from the many to benefit the few. As our government has focused increasingly on riches, its leaders have lost sight of our people.

The problem of taking from the many to further enrich the few will change only when we begin to address it. We must start by acknowledging our failures, just as the founders did when the Articles of Confederation proved unworkable.

For starters, look at what we have done to health care. America spends more and gets back less from its system than any other industrial country. We rank by various measures down with Cuba, of all places. That alone should scream at us that our policy of corporate health insurance does not work. That one in seven of us has no health coverage at all should shame us. Even apart from shame, on a practical level having so many people without health care coverage is a drag on our economy through lost productivity—from injuries and illnesses not properly treated, lives shortened, and financial devastation caused to families who played by the rules, but were not winners in a system that makes caring for people a profit-driven business.

Just as counterproductive is our policy of driving up the cost of housing through government policies. The result is making us poorer, not richer, by adding enormously to debt burdens. The official data show that for every additional dollar of home equity people added since 1980 they took on two more dollars of debt. We have replaced the ideal of home ownership with a hamster wheel, with most citizens working harder and harder to pay mortgage interest and saving ever less for retirement. This is folly.

And all of the welfare we shower on the rich, from Warren Buffett to George Steinbrenner to Dick Cabela? The market cannot work its magic when Buffett gets a freebie. Competition cannot set the price when an industry is exempted from the laws of competition. Honest businesses like Gander Mountain cannot succeed when the government slips money to the competition. Bad money drives out good.

Regulation by detailed rules has not worked. A century ago the reformers of the Gilded Age believed that if we just got the rules right, a just society would follow. Instead, the rules became ever more finely diced, creating unintended opportunities for mischief and often creating loopholes and favors for those whose conduct the rules were supposed to constrain.

Those rules work best which are self-enforcing, rules that by their nature reward proper conduct and punish misconduct. A good example can be found in the rules that for many decades governed lawyers and accountants. Under the old partnership rules, each partner was fully responsible for the deeds of every other partner. This created an incentive for lawyers and accountants to police their partners, to stick in their noses at any hint of misconduct, out of pure self-interest. The rule created a simple reality: look the other way, lose your house.

But at the start of the current era of government for the rich, those rules were changed. Now we have "limited liability partnerships." The LLP structure rewards those who look the other way. Under these new rules, you may lose your investment in the firm itself, but that is all your liability. Given the brazen misbehavior by the major accounting firms, and by more than a few law firms, it is time to go back to the old rules.

The fundamental policy for those on whom we confer power as lawyers, accountants, executives, and stewards of other people's money should be rules that make the costs of misconduct so high that no rational person would violate them. As *New York Times* columnist Gretchen Morgenson says, if you add up all the fines imposed on Wall Street and compare them to the profits these firms earn, the penalties get lost in the rounding. Fines, whether imposed on railroads for safety violations or on Wall Street for cheating investors, are meaningless unless they are so large that they take back all of the ill-gotten gains and then take even more to make the price of misconduct too dear to risk.

We should not allow the fact that many issues today challenge normal human understanding and as a result create opportunities for cheats. We need to strengthen law enforcement to thwart thievery by contract or computerized calculation. We need to vote out officials, even ones we like for some emotional reason, when they work against our interests. When it comes to handouts to the rich, we need to just say no.

So what to do?

The solution lies not in changing this rule or that, but in altering our attitude about our power to shape our democracy. We are not powerless to address any of these problems or the many others that confront us. It may seem that the problems are so large, and individually we are so insignificant, that we must just accept things as they are. We are encouraged in this belief—that we lack the power to change the course of history—by those who profit from our meekness. But the notion that we cannot shape our own destiny is nonsense. It is also profoundly un-American.

It is also morally reprehensible for the rich to take from those with less. If our hearts do not tell us this is so, the Bible does again and again and again. So do all of the other great religious and moral texts that have come down to us through the ages. In this the ministers, rabbis, imams, and other moral leaders can exert great influence by preaching from the religious texts, citing the myriad references to how it is wrong to give to the rich, wrong to take from the poor, wrong to build up great wealth by taking even from the merely prosperous to add to the fortunes of the rich.

To fail to do this is to push us back to the time when property was theft, when the rich were so only because of what they took from others by force or threat. The creation of wealth through the concepts of ownership, trade, insurance, the time value of money, and the rise of mass manufacturing and now digital design has been an enormous benefit to mankind. So have the advances from our knowledge of how to manipulate the physical and conceptual worlds, from vaccines and clean water to algorithms. No good can come from undermining the legitimacy of property, but much damage can be done by abusing the coercive power of government to take from those who have less to benefit those who have more.

As part of this, we need to restore the ethos that cheating is wrong. Period. If we honor athletes who take steroids to pump up their performance, how can we complain when business owners pocket subsidies? Cheating, like pregnancy, is not a halfway condition.

Taking a stand will no doubt be difficult for those organizations that purport to favor free markets, because so many of their donors are on the dole. They should ask themselves how much they are willing to sully their reputations, where they will draw the line. Would they take money from a drug lord? An embezzler? From those who solicit subsidies? Better to fold with integrity than press on with dishonest money.

What of those who assert, as many business owners interviewed for this book did, that if the rules allow them to take subsidies then there is nothing wrong with doing so? Indeed, one billionaire argued that failing to take a subsidy could be seen as a wrong in itself, a failure to maximize profit for shareholders. Must one take money left on the counter by a merchant? Just because you *can* do something does not mean you must, or even should. Their attitude serves to reinforce the importance of rules in shaping behavior.

There is one major reform that could speed the return of a government that cares more about its people than the bottom lines of a few. It goes to the corrupting influence of money in selecting who rises to elective office, gaining the power to make the laws, administer and interpret them. Our Supreme Court has sanctioned this legalized bribery, saying we can do little to reduce the influence of money on elections. In that case, let's forget about campaign finance reform and focus instead on politician finance reform.

Americans seek a free lunch when they do not pay the real costs of government, but instead expect elected officials generally, and members of Congress in particular, to rely on the kindness of strangers. Free rides in the company jet, golf outings, dinners, and a host of other emoluments naturally exert a tug on the system, pulling it toward those who do the giving. In recent years, we have seen politicians hire their spouses as fund-raisers and pay them a portion of the donations they raised. Others see their family members hired by the very groups who lobby them.

We cannot stop all of these abuses. But we can stop many of them by taking a principle in our Constitution and expanding on it. We allow every representative and senator to send out all the mail they want for free. It's called the *franking privilege*. Let's extend that concept to their expenses.

Let each member of Congress spend however much he or she deems necessary to do his or her job. If we can imbue representatives and senators with the power to make laws, surely we can give them the authority to manage their own expense accounts.

This would come at a price: No more free trips, no more free meals, and no more gifts. Senator, if you need to inspect the cleanliness of the sink behind the bar at a resort in Tahiti, go right ahead, just give us the receipts with an explanation of the costs. We will collect the receipts from every elected representative monthly and post it all on the Internet in a format that makes for easy analysis.

Every dollar, and every meeting, must be disclosed. And we will pay for it all, subject only to the usual penalties for embezzling, the punishments accorded by the full House or Senate because of their exclusive right to judge the fitness of members, or the decision by voters to oust a spendthrift.

In this we can move politics back toward the people and away from monied interests. The penalties for taking anything—even a free shot of whiskey—should be swift, certain, and severe. Take a gift, go to jail. Call it zero tolerance for lawmakers.

Let us also pay the real costs of maintaining two households, one back home and one in Washington, as well as going back and forth as often as the lawmaker chooses. Sure, the Congresswoman from Hawaii will spend more on travel than the one from Northern Virginia, but people are smart enough to figure that out.

This approach will cost us more in terms of the budget for Congress. But it would save us far more by reducing the giveaways, the rigged rules, and the favors for the rich. Think about all the lawmakers who for a few thousand dollars cost the taxpayers millions, even billions. Surely paying the real costs of Congress has to be cheaper than the dishonest system we have now. A free lunch always costs more than an honest one.

Just debating the idea that we should pay the full costs of Congress would have value, opening our eyes to the subtle ways that we systematically corrupt our political system. A debate on making members of Congress into public servants, instead of beggars for favors, would get us thinking as a nation about how every single free lunch cheats us all.

In the end, we must be the ones who make our government work, fulfilling the promise of the preamble to our Constitution. No one else is going to do it for us. Reform begins with *you*.

Acknowledgments

Although my name appears as the author, this book represents the contributions of many people. Since the reporting in this book extends back more than thirty years, I will surely overlook some of the people to whom I am indebted. To those I neglect to properly acknowledge, my apologies.

Unnamed sources, on whom I rarely rely in print, are invaluable for tips about the golden nuggets of fact buried in the mountains of bureaucratic paperwork created by government and business. To those of you who will go unnamed here, but who will surely recognize your contributions, my deepest thanks. Sources are the mother's milk of reporting and the most treasured are sources who possess the integrity to argue the other side, making the case for those with whom they disagree, the better to communicate the significance of the issues.

The reporters for *Free Lunch* did marvelous work. Alicia Mundy, the Washington correspondent for the *Seattle Times*, showed why she has long been one of the very best journalists in the nation's capital. David Wethe of the Fort Worth *Star-Telegram* went to great lengths to document the story of the Texas electricity legislation, listening to official tape recordings to ascertain precisely how many times the word *no* was spoken in one exchange recounted in the chapter "Trojan Horse."

I also hired three young journalists who have the right stuff to carry on the important work of investigating our society into the second half of this century. Anna Lenzer, who studied science at the University of British Columbia, exhaustively reviewed the record on conversions of nonprofit health care enterprises to for-profit businesses. Cindy Santos, who studied journalism at the University of Southern California and created the news Web site ocsource.net about Orange County, California, endured long days in a subbasement reading official records to find a single elusive document and did superb follow-up interviews. Rachel Monahan, who studied at Columbia University before reporting for the New York *Daily News*, produced valuable economic charts with remarkable efficiency. Editors should read these words as recommendations.

Friends found these young reporters. I owe thanks to the author and investigative reporter Wayne Barrett; my former editor Ed Guthman; and my colleague Louise Story for introducing me to, respectively, Lenzer, Santos, and Monahan.

Danelle Morton, that rare writer who can be deadly serious or delightfully hilarious, polished some of my thoughts. Kate Berry of *American Banker*, a student of mine long ago at the University of Southern California, contributed some additional reporting on health maintenance organizations and reviewed chapters. Angela Spalding set up my files. Evan Lowenstein hunted down obscure facts using his knowledge of social sciences.

My friend David Crook, the creator and founding editor of *The Wall Street Journal Sunday* (the nation's largest-circulation business publication) provided crucial focus when I found myself gasping for coherence in a miasma of facts. My pal Dennis McDougal also offered wry advice.

Many colleagues at *The New York Times* graciously gave of their time, opened their files, and connected me to sources. In a world where so much stenography and hype passes for journalism, it is an honor to be associated with these men and women. Among those who dug into their records to share material were Charles V. Bagli, Walt Bogdanich, Joseph Nocera, and Mary Williams Walsh.

Thanks also go to my colleagues Edmund L. Andrews, Kassie Bracken, Eric L. Dash, Claudia Deutsch, Stuart Elliott, Milt Freudenheim, Mark Getzfred, Linda Greenhouse, Steven Greenhouse, Diana B. Henriques, Larry Ingrassia, Glenn Kramon, David Leonhardt, Gretchen Morgenson, Dan Niemi, Floyd Norris, Eduardo Porter, Tom Redburn, Joseph B. Treaster, Louis Uchitelle, and Margot Williams.

The cooperation of reporters from other news organizations was superb. I am especially thankful for the help provided by Nigel Jaquiss of *Willamette Week* in Oregon, Steve Duin and Jeff Manning of the *Oregonian*, Lee Sheppard of *Tax Notes*, Jim Neff and members of his investigative team at *The Seattle Times*, and Tim Redmond of the *San Francisco*

Bay Guardian. For many reasons I am indebted to these superb journalists: Don Barlett and Jim Steele, Laurie Becklund, Gene Roberts, Bob Sipchen, Henry Weinstein, and the extraordinarily shrewd Wallace Turner.

Volunteers who read chapters and offered criticism included Jeff Brown, the financial columnist; Nelson Blish, a patent lawyer and novelist; Ryan J. Donmoyer of Bloomberg News; Michael Graham, a superb investigative reporter turned screenwriter; Betty Lukas, a retired but never retiring *Los Angeles Times* editor; Michael Ravnitzky, a genius at finding important but obscure government documents; and Robin Palley, an excellent reporter for the *Philadelphia Daily News* who became an excellent executive.

At home in Rochester, New York, many people provided valuable insights, including Allen Blair, Joe and Nancy Briggs, Mark Goldgeier, Nancy Yanes-Hoffman and Dr. Marvin Hoffman, Bob Leahy, Dan Meyers, Geoffrey Rosenberger, Richard Sands, and John "Dutch" Summers. At monthly lunches, Mike Millard, a Russian and classical history buff, helped me refine the torrent of raw facts into sensible thoughts.

I am also indebted to many professors, including Fred Brock at Kansas State University; Dorothy A. Brown of Washington and Lee University; Jack Coffee at Columbia University; Susan Pace Hamill at the University of Alabama; William D. Henderson at Indiana University; Bruce H. Mann at Harvard Law School; Tim Smeeding at Syracuse University and Ed Wolff at New York University; Judge Richard D. Cudahy of the Seventh Circuit Court of Appeals; Dick Armey with his thoughts on subsidies and the self-interest of politicians; and Edward Luttwak on how government rules affect economic outcomes, often in unexpected ways.

Also, Dean Baker, Bruce Bartlett, Bill Beach, David Bean, Brenda Breslauser, Nancy Brown, Lynnley Browning, Sheldon Cohen, Bettina Damiani, Jason Eisdorfer, Chris Edwards, Martin Feldstein, Ann Fisher, Brian Foley, Serge Kovaleski, Paul Krugman, Iris Lav, Greg LeRoy, Trudy Lieberman, Paul C. Light, Lauren Lipton, Bob McIntyre, Morton Mintz, Jeff Rohaly, Noah Rosenberg, Russell Sadler, Max Sawicky, Syl Schieber, Chuck Sheketoff, Allan Sloan, Tyson Slocum, Howard Spinner, Dan Steinberg, Paul Turk, Bud Vos, Jack B. White, Jody Wiser, and Eric Woychik.

My publisher, Adrian Zackheim, shared my vision and was then exceptionally patient, which says it all. My agent of many years, Alice Fried Martell, more than delivered, as always, and at key points was a source of encouragement.

Some of my thoughts about society have been influenced by my relationship with Kevin Ranger, as fine a young man as I have met, but who, like some of my own children, attended schools that did not provide him with the quality of education that serves as a springboard for success.

As always I involved some of my eight children, the better for each generation to learn about the world and each other. My fourth child, Amy E. Boyle Johnston, took time from her own research into the works of Rod Serling to check and recheck fine details. My youngest, Molly and Kate (to whom we gave their mother's last name) applied their skills to initial copyediting. Their youthful eyes also spotted cultural references and concepts that might have eluded younger readers but for the elaborations they suggested. Molly, who graduated magna cum laude with a degree in classics from Bryn Mawr College on her way to study law at the University of Toronto, enhanced my knowledge of Greek mythology.

Most of all I am indebted to my wife, Jennifer Leonard, who despite all her hard work to improve our adopted hometown through her leadership of Rochester Area Community Foundation, always found (or made) time to generously support me in this endeavor.

Notes

This book is based largely on my reporting for *The New York Times*, that of other reporters, and extensive reporting for *Free Lunch* by me and those retained as reporters for this book. The primary sources for official data are the statistical reports posted on the Internet by the Bureau of Labor Statistics, the Census Bureau, the Commerce Department, the Congressional Budget Office, the Federal Reserve, the Internal Revenue Service, and the White House Office of Management and Budget.

I have taken one liberty for clarity. In the few places where people's thoughts are recounted in italics, their recollections are presented with more formal structure than had they been quoted directly as they recalled their thoughts and feelings.

Copies of some documents are posted at www.freelunchbook.com and www.freelunchthebook.com.

Chapter 2. MR. REAGAN'S QUESTION

9 **On the surface:** Computed from Bureau of Labor Statistics and Census Bureau data.

10 **Even at $3 a gallon:** McMahon, Timothy. "Gasoline Prices 1918–2006 Adjusted for Inflation." Financial Trend Forecaster, fintrend.com/inflation/images/charts/Oil/Gasoline_inflation_chart.htm.

10 **For the bottom 90 percent:** Picketty, Thomas, and Emmanuel Saez. "Income Equality in the United States, 1913–1998." *Quaterly Journal of Economics* 118 (2003), 1–39, updated Table A6 at elsa.berkeley.edu/~saez/TabFig 2005prel.xls.

11 **How government encourages:** Data on 150 million Americans from

Prante, Gerald. "Summary of Latest Federal Individual Income Tax Data: Fiscal Fact No. 66," Tax Foundation, September 25, 2006, at taxfoundation .org/taxdata/show/250.html.

11 **In ways that most Americans:** Organization for Economic Co-operation and Development *Factbook 2007* at sourceoecd.org/factbook.

16 **Steve Jobs, a founder:** Dash, Eric. "No Charges for Apple in Options," *The New York Times*, April 25, 2007, and Apple filings at sec.gov.

18 **Consider one example:** 99.25 percent interest at www.cashcall.com/ General/Rates.aspx.

22 **The evidence of a growing:** Transcript of Bush remarks at the Waldorf-Astoria on October 20, 2000, from "A Pause for Humor," *The NewsHour with Jim Lehrer*, at www.pbs.org/newshour/bb/politics/july-dec00/alsmith_ 10-20.html.

24 **There is a reason that 35,000 people:** From Hamilton, Lee. "We Pay a High Price for Special-interest Lobbying," The Center on Congress at Indiana University, www.centeroncongress.org/radio_commentaries/we_pay_a_ high_price_for_special-interest_lobbying.php, and reports at opensecrets.org.

25 **"A democracy cannot exist":** "Roar Approval for Barry," *Manchester Union Leader*, March 6, 1964, front page.

Chapter 3. TRUST AND CONSEQUENCES

26 **Half an hour before daybreak:** "Railroad Accident Report: Derailment and Subsequent Collision of Amtrak Train 82 with Rail Cars on DuPont Siding of CSX Transportation Inc. at Lugoff, South Carolina, on July 31. 1991," National Transportation Safety Board RAR-93-02; "National Transportation Safety Board Safety Recommendation, R-93-18 through -22," November 30, 1993; Bogdanich, Walt, "Death on the Tracks: Amtrak Pays Millions for Others' Fatal Errors," *The New York Times*, October 15, 2004; Needle, Jodie, "Angel Rises," South Florida *Sun-Sentinel*, October 9, 1997; Claybrook, Joan, letter to Rodney Slater, Secretary of Transportation, October 27, 1997; President, Public Citizen; "A Close Look at Lugoff," Camden, South Carolina *Chronicle-Independent*, March 1, 2007.

34 **Measure deaths by the distance traveled:** author e-mail interview with Tom White, Association of American Railroads, April 18, 2007; hazmat.dot .gov/riskmgmt/riskcompare.htm (adjusted for different measures, one million miles for trains and 100 million for trucks and airliners).

Chapter 4. CHINESE MAGNESTISM

37 **So much capital:** Barboza, David, "China Builds Its Dreams, and Some Fear a Bubble," *The New York Times*, October 18, 2005.

38 **About 260 people:** Christian, Nichole M. "GM President's Council Okays Plan to Sell Magnequench," Dow Jones, March 21, 1995; "GM Is Quietly Completing Pact to Sell Indiana Magnet Plant to Chinese Group," *The Wall Street Journal*, March 22, 1995; U.S. Congress, House of Representatives, "Report of the Select Committee on U.S. National Security and Military/ Commercial Concerns with the People's Republic of China," House Report 105-851, Government Printing Office, 1999; "Production Halted, Doors Closing at Magnequench Plant," Erler, Susan, Munster, Indiana, *Northwest Indiana Times*, September 30, 2003; "Bayh Calls for Increased Oversight of Foreign Takeovers with National Security Concerns," Office of Senator Evan Bayh, October 6, 2005; Lague, David, "China Corners Market in a High-Tech Necessity," *International Herald Tribune*, January 22, 2006.

38 **At the time of the sale:** Butterfield, Fox, "Under Deng, Running China Has Become a Family Affair," *The New York Times*, July 2, 1989; Tyler, Patrick E., "China's First Family Comes Under Growing Scrutiny," *The New York Times*, June 2, 1995.

40 **When foreign governments or firms:** Sanger, David E., "Dubai Deal Will Undergo Deeper Inquiry into Security," *The New York Times*, February 26, 2006.

40 **Like the Chinese income tax:** Yergin, Daniel, *The Prize*, New York: Free Press, 1993.

43 **As recently as 1985:** From tables at census.gov/foreign-trade/balance/c5700.html.

45 **Dave Cummings specializes:** Lucchetti, Aaron, "Firms Seek Edge through Speed as Computer Trading Expands," *The Wall Street Journal*, Dec. 15, 2006.

47 **In 1990, foreign-owned companies employed:** Scott, Robert E., "Economic Snapshots," Economic Policy Institute, April 5, 2006, http://www.epi.org/content.cfm/webfeatures_snapshots_20060405.

49 **In the next decade or two:** Wessel, David, and Bob Davis, "Pain from Free Trade Spurs Second Thoughts," *The Wall Street Journal*, March 30, 2007; Blinder, Alan S., "Offshoring: The Next Industrial Revolution?" *Foreign Affairs*, March–April 2006.

Chapter 5. SEIZING THE COMMONS

54 **Mullaly was a reporter:** "John Mullaly, Park Founder, to Be Honored," *New York Herald Tribune*, Oct. 20, 1929; Mullaly life timeline at nynjctbotany .org/lgtofc/mullalypark.html; Mullaly, John, *New Parks beyond the Harlem with Thirty Illustrations and Map*, Record and Guide, 1887 (portions online at Google Books).

55 **The beneficiary of this exercise:** newyork.yankees.mlb.com; Good Jobs New York, "Loot, Loot, Loot for the Home Team," February 2006, and other reports at goodjobsny.org.

57 **With passage of Proposition 13:** Johnston, David [Cay], "The Dead Parks: Insufficient Funding, Drugs and Violence Drive Many Away from City Recreation Areas," *Los Angeles Times*, September 3, 1987.

60 **Milton Friedman, the intellectual:** Friedman, Milton, *Capitalism and Freedom*, University of Chicago Press, 1962; Parker, Richard, "The Pragmatist and the Utopian," *The Boston Globe*, February 6, 2005; Sanera, Michael, "Sanford should end golf subsidy," February 27, 2006, at johnlocke.org; Sowell, Thomas, "Priceless Politics," Townhall.com, February 20, 2007.

Chapter 6. PRIDE AND PROFITS

62 **From St. Petersburg:** U.S. Congress, House of Representatives, Committee on Oversight and Government Reform Subcommittee on Domestic Policy, "Public Financing for Construction and Operation of Sports Stadiums and Economic Revitalization and Development in Urban America," March 29, 2007.

64 **To see how that observation:** Sandomir, Richard, "Nationals Have New Owner, and Baseball Turns Big Profit," *The New York Times*, May 4, 2006.

64 **Even before they moved the team:** Heath, Thomas, and Lori Montgomery, "MLB Officials Sign Lease for D.C. Stadium," *The Washington Post*, March 6, 2006.

67 **"The pride and the presence":** Moynihan, Daniel Patrick, citing *Cleveland* magazine, September 1996, *Congressional Record*, Vol. 143, No. 4, Page S501, January 21, 1997.

68 **In Seattle, Howard Schultz:** Brunner, Jim, and Ralph Thomas, "'Little Hope' for Sonics Now," *The Seattle Times*, April 17, 2007; Brunner, Jim, "Tale of Two Arenas, Here and in Denver, Is Revealing," *The Seattle Times*, May 29, 2006; and other coverage in *The Seattle Times*, the *Seattle Post-Intelligencer*, and *Seattle Weekly*.

73 **That Steinbrenner would eagerly stuff:** Nocera, Joseph, "George Steinbrenner, Welfare Case," *Esquire*, July 1990; Hackworth, David H., "Defending America," *Newsweek*, August 8, 1995.

73 **Two other oilers:** Navy T-AO 187 Kaiser Class Oiler Contracts, hearings of the U.S. Congress, Senate Permanent Investigations subcommittee, May 2 and 4, 1995, Government Printing Office, 1995.

74 **Klein thought:** Interview by Alicia Mundy, Jan. 31, 2007.

75 **Prickly as a cactus pear:** U.S. Congress, House of Representatives, Committee on Oversight and Government Reform Subcommittee on Domestic Policy, "Public Financing for Construction and Operation of Sports Stadiums and Economic Revitalization and Development in Urban America," March 29, 2007.

Chapter 7. YOUR LAND IS MY LAND

79 **The Mathes family:** Records of Sports Facilities Development Authority, Inc. and *City of Arlington v. Clairwood, N.V., Ramshire, N.V.*, Cause # 91-47154-1, Tarrant County, Texas, numerous news accounts, and interviews with attorneys Glenn Sodd and Ray Hutchison.

Chapter 8. BOUNTY HUNTERS

86 **Blankenship was not alone:** *Wilkins et al. v. Cuno et al.*, Supreme Court case 04-1724 and related state litigation.

89 **Professor Thomas concluded:** Thomas, Kenneth P., "The Sources and Processes of Tax and Subsidy Competition," hhh.umn.edu/img/assets/6158/Thomas_paper.pdf.

Chapter 9. GOIN' FISHIN'

96 **Cabela's began:** From history at cabelas.com.

104 **Relative to the size:** Ewald Consulting, "Example of Subsidies Received by Cabela's"; "What Gander Mountain and Ewald Consulting Don't Want You to Know," and "Despite Competitor's Claims, Cabela's Brings True Economic Development Opportunities to the Table," position papers from Cabela's.

105 **In the three years:** Cabela's 10-K.

Chapter 10. JUST SAY NO

110 **Lobbying pays fabulously well:** Shenon, Philip, "Lobbyist Sought $9 Million to Set Bush Meeting," *The New York Times*, November 10, 2005.

111 **None of the politicians:** Justice, Glen, et al., "For Lobbyists, a Seat of Power Came with a Plate," *The New York Times*, July 6, 2005.

113 **The White House said in 2006:** Philip, Shenon, "Report Finds 82 Contacts Between Abramoff and Rove," *The New York Times*, September 28, 2006.

113 **Gerald S. J. Cassidy:** Cassidy & Co. Form S-1 at sec.gov.

114 **Jefferson would be appalled:** Letter at Library of Congress, *Information Bulletin*, June 1998, Vol. 57, No. 6; nobeliefs.com/jefferson.htm.

119 **One idea was to question:** Kennedy, Sam, "Have Cabela's Tax Breaks Paid Off?" Allentown *Morning Call*, October 17, 2004.

122 **Bass Pro even talked:** Pre-development Agreement, Erie Canal Harbor District, Buffalo, New York, posted May 26, 2007, at greaterbuffalo.blogs .com.

Chapter 11. BEAUTY AND THE BOUNTY

124 **Mike Keiser acted on his own:** Author interviews May 2007; *Dream Golf: The Making of Bandon Dunes* by Stephen Goodwin, Algonquin Books.

124 **Even so, without asking:** Johnston, David Cay, "Assisting the Good Life," *The New York Times*, June 15, 2007.

126 **For thousands of years the Coo:** Robbins, William G., *Hard Times in Paradise: Coos Bay, Oregon*, Seattle: University of Washington Press, 1988; files of Western World, Bandon, Oregon.

127 **Like Keiser, Bandon area native:** Johnston, David Cay, "A Man Would Lose His Land While Another Would Benefit," *The New York Times*, June 15, 2007; and "Who Pays to Play," a video by David Cay Johnston and Kassie Bracken at video.on.nytimes.com under Business/Business News.

Chapter 12. FALSE ALARM

133 **Three dozen terrified children ran:** Johnston, David [Cay], "The Dead Parks: Insufficient Funding, Drugs and Violence Drive Many Away From City Recreation Areas," *Los Angeles Times*, Sept. 3, 1987.

135 **The commercials are effective:** Johnston, David [Cay], "Burglar Alarms: False Reports Drain Police Resources," *Los Angeles Times*, Aug. 9, 1982.

135 **Of the $29 average monthly fee:** "The U.S. Burglar Alarm Market," by Stat Resources, 2004; additional industry statistics at alarm.org/stats-industry. html.

136 **Worse, almost three decades:** Justice Department Bureau of Justice Statistics, Tables 106 and 107; Blackstone, Erwin A., Simon Hakim, and Uriel Spiegel, "Not Calling the Police (First)," *Regulation*, Spring 2002.

137 **In the sixties and seventies:** Johnston, David [Cay], "Many Require Security Devices in Buildings," *Los Angeles Times*, Aug. 30, 1976.

Chapter 13. HOME ROBBERY

141 **A title proves ownership:** Saranow, Jennifer, "Title Insurance for Used Cars: Is It Worth It?" *The Wall Street Journal*, September 18, 2006.

143 **Erin Toll:** U.S. Congress, House of Representatives, Committee on Financial Services, "Problems and Concerns Regarding the Marketing and Sales of Title Insurance and LandAmerica Financial Group Inc.'s Conduct Regarding Federal and State Examinations of Title Insurance," April 26, 2006.

145 **Even though kickbacks:** "An Investigation into the Use of Incentives and Inducements by Title Insurance Companies," Office of the Insurance Commissioner, Washington State, October 2006.

148 **In 2005 the industry paid:** "Title Insurance Statistical Analysis by Family," American Land Title Association, alta.org.

Chapter 16. SUFFER THE LITTLE CHILDREN

162 **The story begins:** *William Barron Hilton v. Conrad N. Hilton Foundation et al.*, Los Angeles County Superior Court case #P644 729 and related litigation; interviews with lawyers by author or Cindy Santos in 1986 and 2007; Johnston, David [Cay] and Al Delugach, "Fight Over Conrad Hilton Estate Gets Increasingly Bitter," *Los Angeles Times*, March 4, 1986.

166 **And what of the stated purpose:** Story, Louise, "Blackstone to Acquire Hilton Hotels," *The New York Times*, July 4, 2007.

Chapter 17. TROJAN HORSE

169 **"Oft the clashing sound":** Translation by John Dryden, poet laureate of England, 1697.

Chapter 18. SIGHTLESS SHERIFFS

181 **At their April 17 meeting:** Lazarus, David, "Memo details Cheney-Enron links," *San Francisco Chronicle*, January 30, 2002.

Chapter 19. PAYING TWICE

187 **Talukdar created an ideal market:** Talukdar, Sarosh and Kong-Wei Lye, "Symmetry and Verification: Critical Parts of Market Design," Carnegie Mellon University, June 2005.

190 **Consider what happened:** Johnston, David Cay, "Paying the Highest Price for Power," *The New York Times*, November 21, 2006.

193 **Some of these plants were then resold:** Johnston, David Cay, "In Deregulation, Plants Turn into Blue Chips," *The New York Times*, October 23, 2006.

Chapter 20. RISING SNOW

202 **This work to reduce regulation:** Cover story, *IndustryWeek*, October 18, 1982.

204 **The executive who ran Conrail:** Labich, Kenneth, "The Great Conrail Sweepstakes," *Fortune*, February 18, 1985.

204 **CSX also regarded:** Bogdanich, Walt, "For Railroads and the Safety Overseer, Close Ties," *The New York Times*, November 7, 2004.

205 **The falling stock price did not align:** Deutsch, Claudia H., "A Career as a Window to the Future," *The New York Times*, December 25, 2002.

206 **Snow also benefited:** Johnston, David Cay, "Executive Pensions Eclipse Years on the Job," *The New York Times*, December 17, 2002.

Chapter 21. UNHEALTHY ECONOMICS

208 **When Linda Peeno became:** "Managed Care Ethics," testimony before U.S. Congress, House of Representatives, Commerce Subcommittee on Health and the Environment, May 30, 1996.

209 **At its core:** Schlesinger, Mark, and Bradford H. Gray, "How Nonprofits Matter in American Medicine, and What to Do About It," Urban Institute, Oct. 13, 2006; Lieberman, Trudy, "The Medicare Privatization Scam," *The Nation*, July 16, 2007.

211 **The uniquely American system:** *The World Factbook 2007*, Central Intelligence Agency and *OECD Health Data 2006* at oecd.org.

Chapter 22. LESS FOR MORE

218 **Wasserman and Anderson offered:** Maxicare SEC filings and author interviews with Wasserman.

219 **The money paid to buy FHP:** Johnston, David [Cay], "State to Enter Legal Battle of 2 HMOs," *Los Angeles Times*, October 3, 1985; and Johnston, David [Cay], "Judge Blocks Buy-Out Plan for FHP, Inc.," *Los Angeles Times*, October 4, 1985, and numerous other articles.

221 **Gumbiner won:** *John K. Van de Kamp v. Robert Gumbiner*, Los Angeles County Superior Court Case C-56507.

Chapter 24. "I'M BEING TRAPPED"

251 **Simons charged even higher fees:** Nocera, Joseph, "$100 Billion in the Hands of a Computer," *The New York Times*, November 19, 2005.

Chapter 25. NONE DARE CALL IT STEALING

264 **In thinking about:** Bill Lockyear, *Atty. Gen. v. Leandro Andrade*, Supreme Court case 01-1127, decided Nov. 5, 2002.

Chapter 26. NOT SINCE HOOVER

272 **For the richest Americans:** From the Piketty and Saez tables cited in the chapter; computations by the author.

278 **In fact, most of the savings:** "The Wealthiest Benefit More from the Recent Tax Cuts," *The New York Times*, June 5, 2005.

280 **Allowing so many children:** Holzer, Harry, Diane Whitmore Schanzenbach, Greg J. Duncan, and Jens Ludwig, "The Economic Costs of Poverty," Center for American Progress, January 24, 2007.

Index